*The Campus History Series*

# PHILADELPHIA FRIENDS SCHOOLS

*On the cover*: Please see page 37. (Courtesy of Greene Street Friends School.)

*The Campus History Series*

# PHILADELPHIA FRIENDS SCHOOLS

FRIENDS COUNCIL ON EDUCATION
WITH JANET CHANCE AND MARK FRANEK

ARCADIA
PUBLISHING

ISBN 978-0-7385-6242-1

Published by Arcadia Publishing
Charleston SC, Chicago IL, Portsmouth NH, San Francisco CA

Printed in the United States of America

Library of Congress Control Number: 2008934222

For all general information contact Arcadia Publishing at:
Telephone 843-853-2070
Fax 843-853-0044
E-mail sales@arcadiapublishing.com
For customer service and orders:
Toll-Free 1-888-313-2665

Visit us on the Internet at www.arcadiapublishing.com

# CONTENTS

# Acknowledgments

This collection is made possible by the inspired industry of archivists, historians, and volunteers from these Philadelphia-area Friends schools (listed alphabetically): Judy Hill, director of communications, Jenny Hammond, director of alumni affairs, and Jocelyn Faulkner Casey, development intern, at Abington Friends School; Margaret Trickey, business manager, and J. Terrence Farley, principal from 1969 to 2005, at Frankford Friends School; Robyn Richmond, archivist, Denise Koehler Morris, archivist, Paula Williams, parent volunteer, and Clayton L. Farraday '32 (deceased), former archivist, at Friends' Central School; Dick Hoffman, archivist, Colleen Puckett, director of marketing, and Tina Dougherty, art director (marketing office), at Friends Select School; Betty Bakley Craighead, library assistant, Jane Dunlap, Latin teacher, Odie LeFever, director of advancement, Juliana Rosati, public relations and special events coordinator, and Marion Wells, instruction librarian, at George School; Michael Boorse, director of publications and public information, Sid Cook, archivist, and Stacey Minyard, director of development operations, at Germantown Friends School; Emily F. Harmar, director of development, and Denise Larrabee, volunteer archivist, at Greene Street Friends School; Madelyn Ladner, admission and development assistant, and Nancy Corson and Suzanne Marinell, Plymouth Meeting Historical Society, at Plymouth Meeting Friends School; Mary Uhl Brooks, archivist, and Kevin A. Gallagher, archives assistant and faculty member, at Westtown School; Allan Brown, director of archives, Sharon Sexton, director of marketing communications, and John Burkhart, Penn Charter '72 and social studies teacher, at the William Penn Charter School.

A hearty thanks goes to the Friends Council on Education, an organization that has preserved and strengthened Friends schools across the nation over eight decades. Executive director Irene E. McHenry and associate director Sarah Sweeney-Denham provided strong, steady guidance from the conceptual genesis of this book, through the writing stages, to the final editing of page proofs. April Diop, Friends Council on Education staff, and Mary Hanisch, volunteer, made valuable contributions, as did Liz Jarvis and Edith Willoughby. Finally, Arcadia editor Erin Vosgien deserves recognition for invaluable guidance throughout the process.

# FOREWORD

This book exemplifies a basic tenet in Friends education—the valuing of the cooperative search for knowledge. Precious photographic imagery, gathered by archivists in 10 historic Philadelphia-area Friends schools, illustrates the calling of Friends education, which in the words of Quaker educator Earl Harrison is "to sustain joyful, efficacious schools in which children are cherished and learning is exciting."

Janet Chance and Mark Franek thoughtfully selected and arranged images to tell the compelling, thematic story of what Friends education has offered for more than 300 years. What does a Friends school have to offer? In the words of a 1994 graduate, "Students who graduate from a Quaker school walk away with a strong sense of social understanding, skills to deal with adversity, tolerance and respect for others, and a strong sense of self-worth so that they have the power needed to succeed." Through a picturesque lens, the story of an enduring educational pedagogy that emerged from the political and religious turbulence of 17th-century England is told. The philosophy and practice of Quaker education has dynamically flourished through the centuries, growing from a "bedrock of love and humanity."

The Friends Council on Education celebrates this publication, honoring the core purpose of its member schools that create deliberate learning communities centered in the Quaker principles of respect for human dignity and diversity, peaceful resolution of conflict, and constant search for truth through challenging the mind and nourishing the spirit. As you reflect on these pages, may your mind be challenged with fresh insight and your spirit quickened with hope for ways of being in the world that strengthens us all.

Irene E. McHenry, Executive Director, Friends Council on Education
Sarah Sweeney-Denham, Associate Director, Friends Council on Education

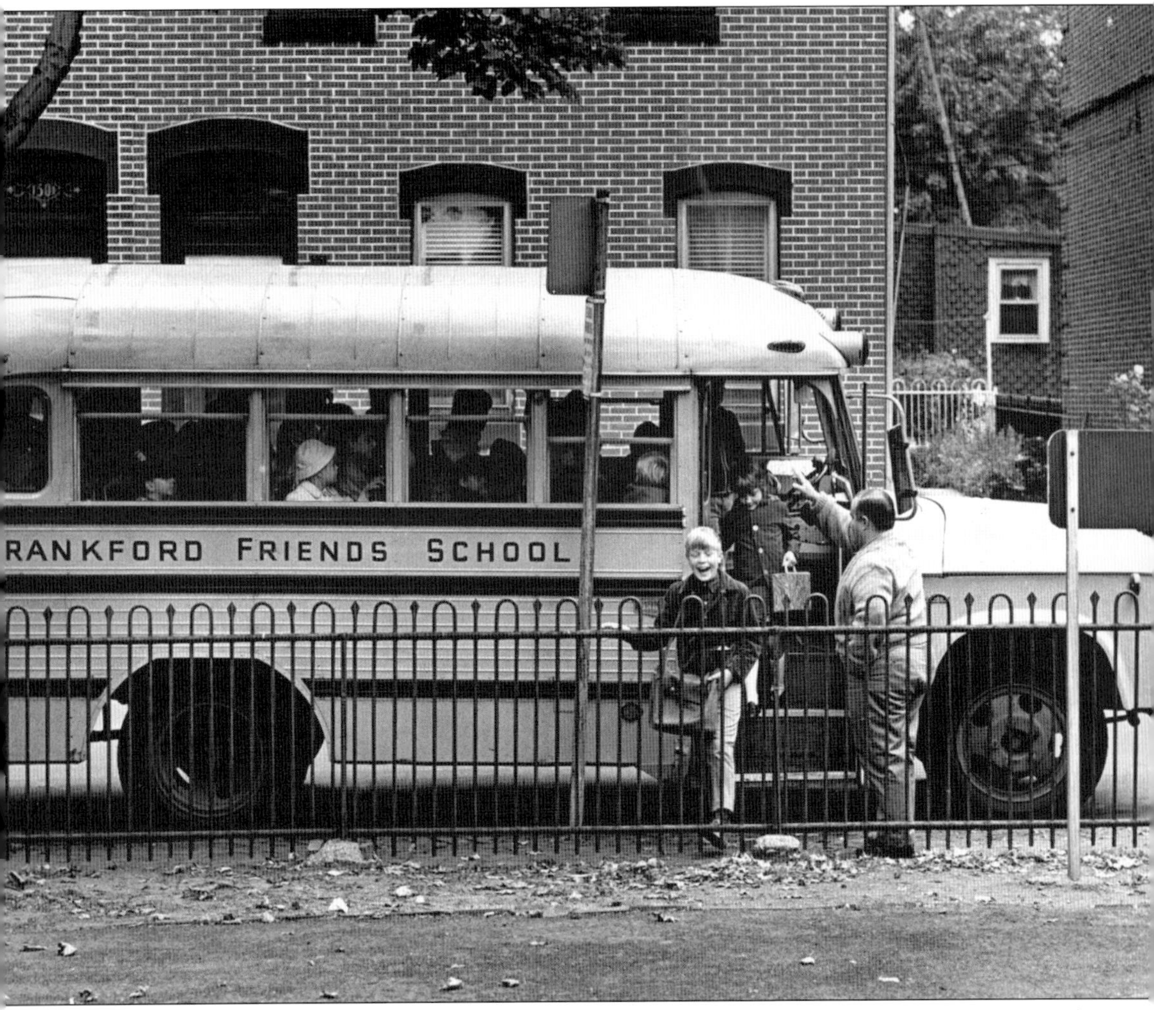


**New Beginnings.** Students arrive ready to begin their school day at Frankford Friends School, around the 1970s. (Courtesy of Frankford Friends School.)

# INTRODUCTION

*Let your life speak.*

—Quaker adage

Quaker education in the United States began in the late 17th century with the arrival of William Penn and continues to this day with the rich diversity of Friends schools in and around Philadelphia. The historical thread can be traced to 1681, when King Charles II gave William Penn territory in the New World, which removed a debt to Penn's father, an admiral in the Royal Navy, and provided a clear path across the Atlantic Ocean for a despised religious group, the Quakers. Penn, a young idealist, named the large tract of land Pennsylvania, or Penn's Woods, and transported the principles and values of the Religious Society of Friends to the New World. Philadelphia became the center of his "holy experiment." Penn realized that a society built on religious freedom and participatory government, and concerned with the practical applications of love and justice, needed schools rooted in the same philosophy. In 1689, with Pennsylvania's provincial government and the Philadelphia Friends Meeting, Penn established the Friends Public School in the heart of Philadelphia, making the City of Brotherly Love the birthplace of Quaker education in America.

This book contains a unique series of photographs from the archives of the Philadelphia-area Friends schools that were founded before the 20th century: Friends Select School and the William Penn Charter School, both of which trace their roots to 1689; Abington Friends School, 1697; Plymouth Meeting Friends School, 1780; Westtown School, 1799; Frankford Friends School, 1833; Friends' Central School, 1845; Germantown Friends School, 1845; Greene Street Friends School, 1855; and George School, 1893.

After a glimpse into the origins of each school (chapter 1), this book focuses on the unique pedagogy of the Philadelphia-area Friends schools during the 20th century. The chapters highlight distinctive features of Quaker education: meeting for worship (chapter 2), inquiry and innovation (chapter 3), community and collaboration (chapter 4), experiential learning (chapter 5), and peace and social justice (chapter 6). An introduction explains the importance of the each chapter's theme and its relevance to Quaker pedagogy. Concluding the collection is a chapter on the Friends Council on Education, the umbrella organization for Friends schools in the United States.

In creating this book, the archivists and publicists of the 10 Philadelphia-area Friends schools founded before the 20th century helped construct the book's themes by finding photographs that illuminated the unique qualities of Quaker education. The editors pored over the images to see what themes organically emerged. The archivists provided caption information for the final photographs, which the editors then used to create the narrative told by the themes. Every person involved in this project generously volunteered time and expertise to gather and organize information amid the hurly-burly of the school day.

Curiously, many of the images and captions in this book would not surprise Quaker schoolchildren in a bygone era of modest schoolhouses and meeting rooms, of cobbled streets and dirt roads, nor would this book seem quaint or mysterious to current students. Friends schools have always had a distinct philosophy of education. Friends believe that each person has the capacity for goodness, and the school takes responsibility to nurture that goodness. Friends schools believe that education is preparation for the whole of life: the lively development of intellectual, physical, and social-emotional capacities, as well as the development of the spirit. Friends schools are spiritual communities based on the belief that there is that of God in everyone, yet Friends schools do not proselytize or seek to convert students or faculty.

The curricular approach in Friends education is committed to the rich exploration of multiple perspectives. Friends schools develop peace studies and practices for creative problem-solving and nonviolent conflict resolution and teach each subject in a way that enhances student understanding of justice and human dignity. Friends schools encourage students to become informed and compassionate people who use analysis and reflection to take action. The values learned and lived by students and faculty in Friends schools influence their communities, and those communities influence the world. Modern Friends schools operate in complex environments and have opened their doors to increasingly diverse communities while continuing to attract students from Quaker backgrounds. These realities have not fundamentally altered their mission.

In the pamphlet *The Peculiar Mission of a Friends School*, Quaker educator Douglas Heath suggests that Friends schools are moral communities concerned with empowering members to "seek the Truth," specifically by helping students grow in the areas of honesty, compassion, integrity, commitment, and individual courage. Over the centuries, Friends schools have heralded new ways of teaching and learning. Such practices as collaborative learning, experiential learning, service learning, and learning communities have antecedents in Friends schools' values, which have remained remarkably consistent over 300 years and inspire students today to live up to what is best and brightest about the human spirit.

This volume presents images from the archives of the oldest Philadelphia-area Friends schools that provide glimpses into the universal heart and spirit of all Friends schools. Let their lives speak.

Mark Franek and Janet Chance, Editors

# *One*

# ORIGINS

*The school is grounded in the Quaker belief that there is "that of God" within us all, a Divine Spark, which when nurtured can illumine our lives.*
—From a 17th-century Friends school statement of philosophy

In 1668 in England, George Fox, the founder of the Religious Society of Friends (Quakers), advised Friends to set up schools where children could be taught to be useful members of society. Shortly thereafter, in the New World of the colonies in 1689, William Penn implemented this advice in Pennsylvania by establishing the Friends Public School in Philadelphia to provide a moral education based on Quaker principles. Three Friends schools currently operating in the Philadelphia area come from this early period. Friends Select School and the William Penn Charter School date their beginnings to 1689. Abington Friends School started in 1697.

In the 18th century, 13 more Friends schools were founded in Pennsylvania. By 1779, there were five Friends schools in Philadelphia under the overseers of the Friends Public School, a Quaker committee set up by Penn's charter. Six other schools were founded by Quakers in Philadelphia. One of these, the Negro School, was founded by a convinced Quaker, Anthony Benezet, who also set up the first public girls' school in America and started the first antislavery society.

The history of Quaker education in the United States began with elementary schools during the 17th and 18th centuries, then boarding schools and colleges during the second half of the 19th century. This chapter provides a glimpse into the origins of Philadelphia-area Friends schools in the 17th, 18th, and 19th centuries.

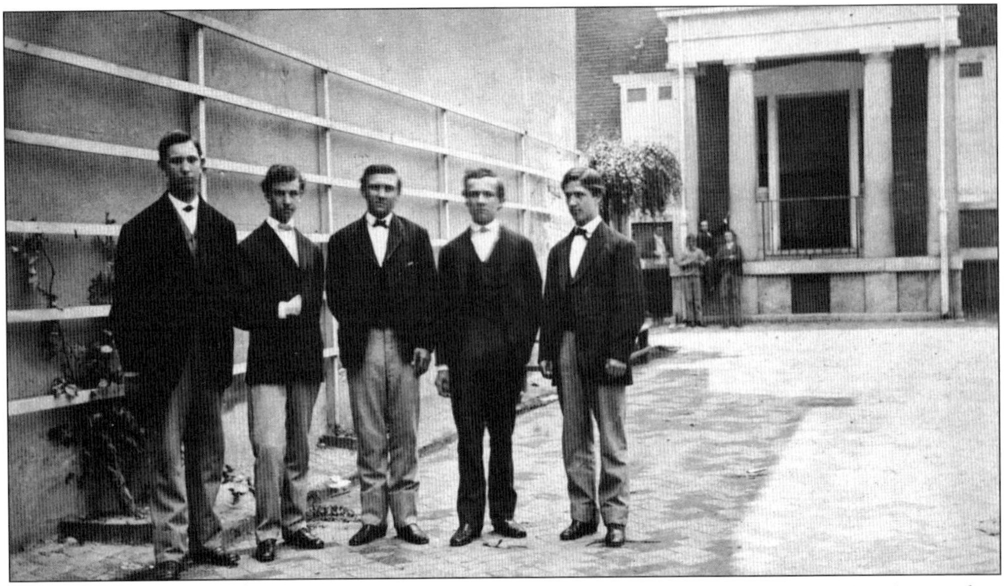

**Friends Select School.** Friends Select School traces a line of evolution back to 1689 through the Monthly Meeting of Friends of Philadelphia, one of the two Friends meetings that oversee the school today. During the school's history, a Select School for Boys and a separate Select School for Girls opened in 1833 in Philadelphia. The boys' school was located at 820 Cherry Street; the girls' school was on Seventh Street, near Race Street. The schools combined in 1890 to become Friends Select School. The word *select* in the school name dates back to 1827, when Orthodox Quakers created schools to "select" and educate only Orthodox Quaker children. Friends Select School abandoned this practice by 1877 and today welcomes children from all religions, nationalities and ethnicities. Of the many historically select schools, Friends Select School is the only school that retains the word *select* in its name. (Courtesy of Friends Select School.)

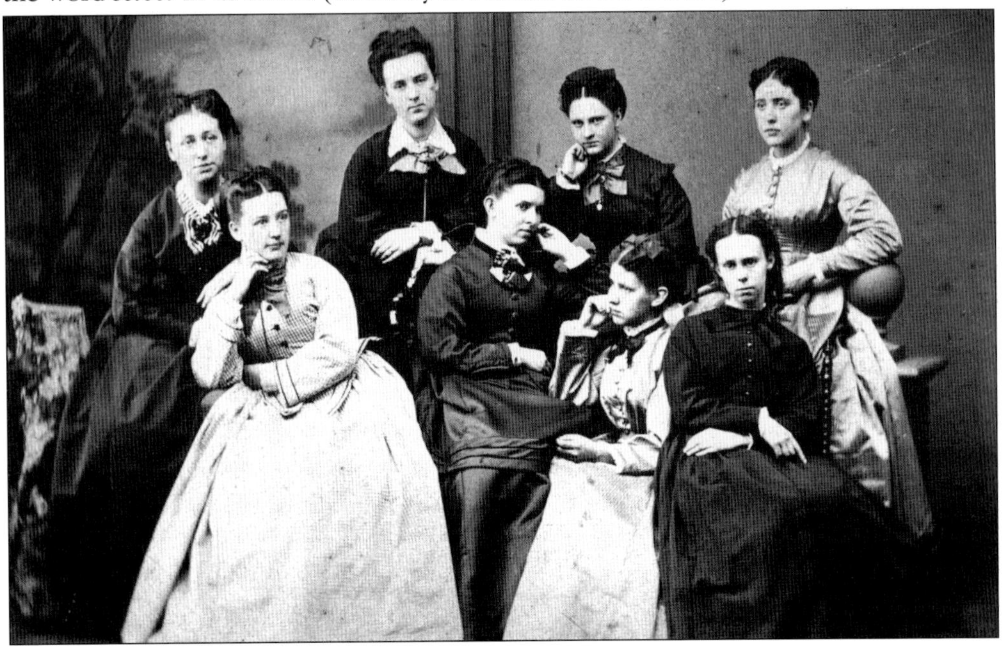

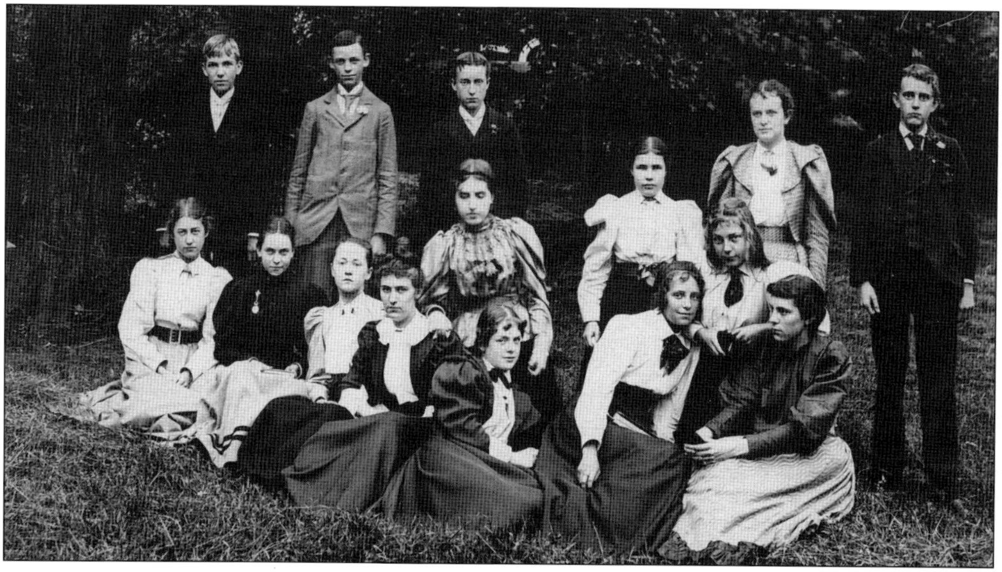

**Coed Classes.** From the beginning, Quakers have been committed to universal education and equal education for men and women. Paradoxically Quakers pioneered both coeducation and separate boys' and girls' education, creating opportunities for young women to learn and develop leadership skills. Shown here is one of the first coed classes at Friends Select School. The Select School for Boys and Select School for Girls moved to one building (with separate entrances) at 140 North Sixteenth Street in 1886, but the two schools did not fully merge until 1890. Friends Select School still sits on this same city block. (Courtesy of Friends Select School.)

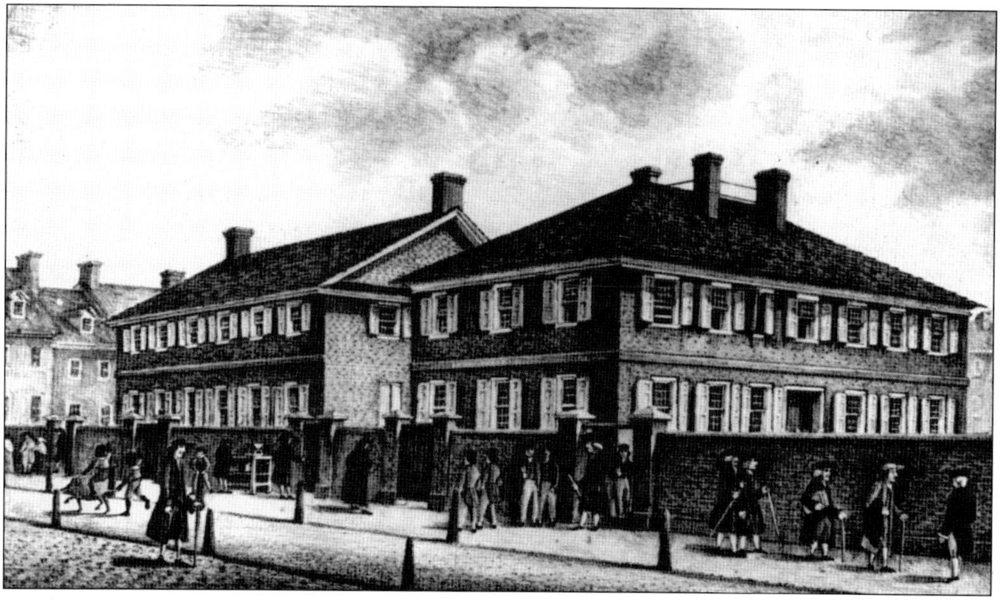

**William Penn Charter School.** The William Penn Charter School moved from its original location on High Street (present-day Market Street) near Second Street to this location on Fourth Street around 1700, which is where it remained until the mid-19th century. It has been said that William Penn often presided at school meetings during his second stay in Pennsylvania, 1700 to 1702. (Courtesy of the William Penn Charter School.)

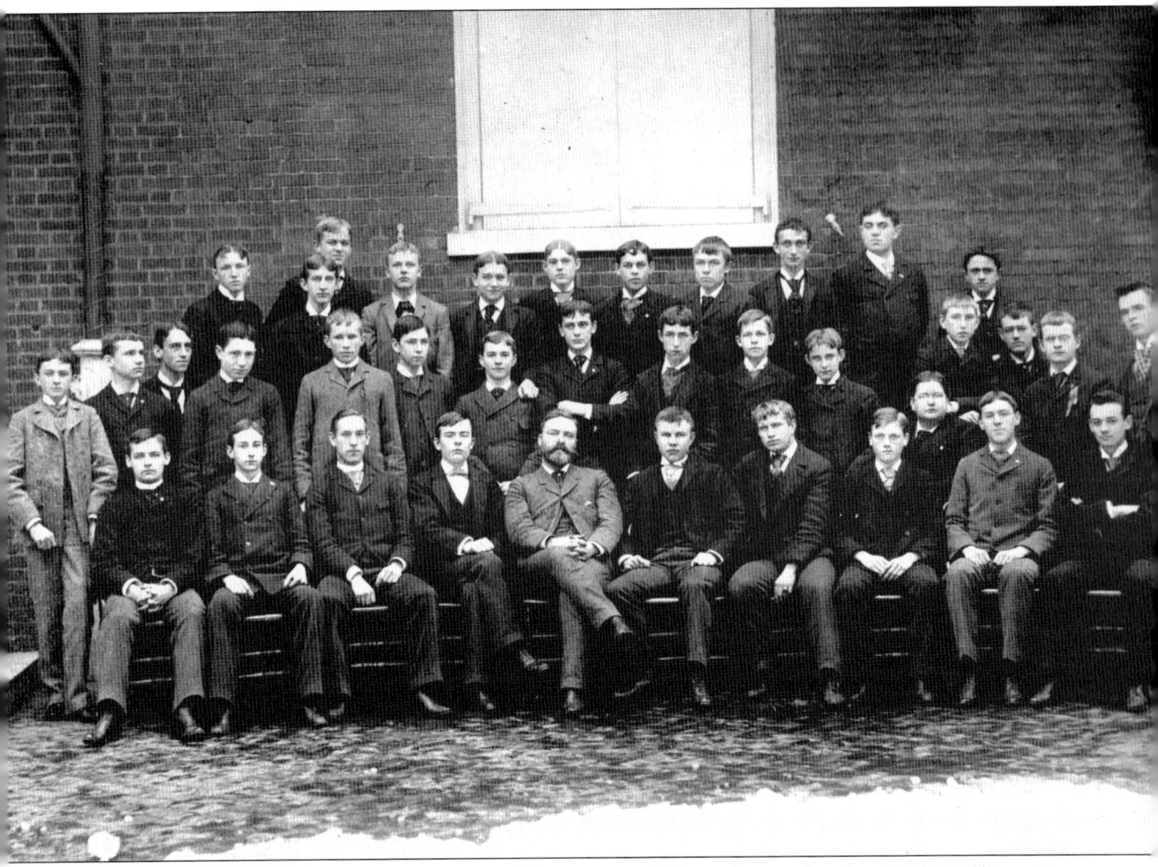

**Classical and Modern Curriculum.** There were 29 graduates in the 1892 William Penn Charter School graduating class, who went on to Harvard University, the Massachusetts Institute of Technology, Lehigh University, the Wharton School of the University of Pennsylvania, Drexel University, and Haverford College. The school's classical curriculum consisted of Latin and Greek language and history, with the modern curriculum including French, German, history, chemistry, physics, algebra, and plane geometry as well as English literature, composition, and grammar. Electives included elocution, debate, and parliamentary rules. (Courtesy of the William Penn Charter School.)

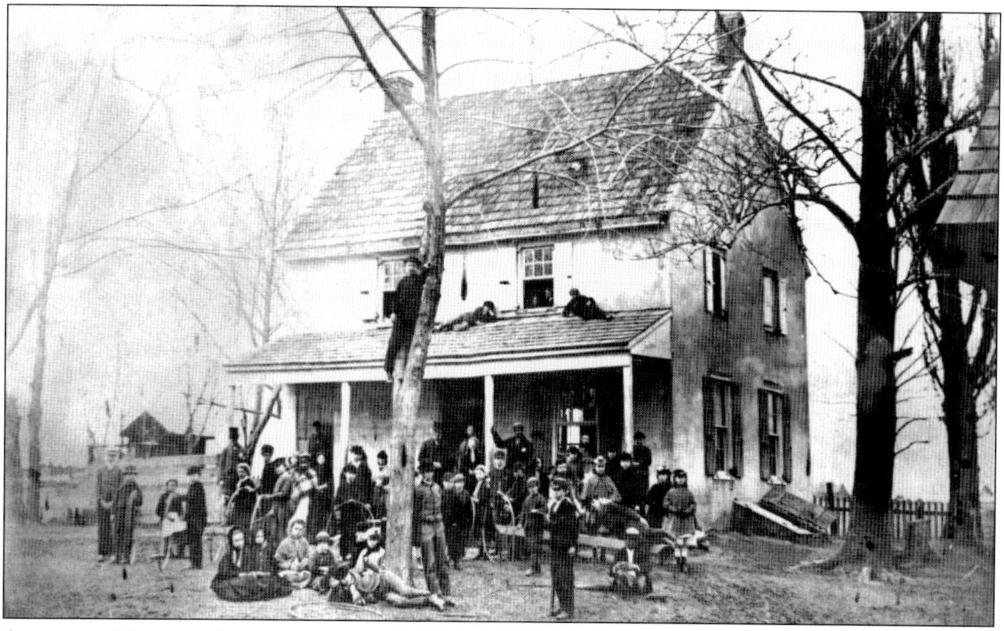

**Abington Friends School.** This oldest-known photograph of Abington Friends School, 1869, depicts the original building. Abington Friends School traces its origins to 1697, when John Barnes, a Philadelphia Quaker, donated 120 acres of his estate and £105 for a meetinghouse and school. Oxford Monthly Meeting, the parent body of Abington Friends Meeting, wished to establish a school with a comprehensive religious education. (Courtesy of Abington Friends School.)

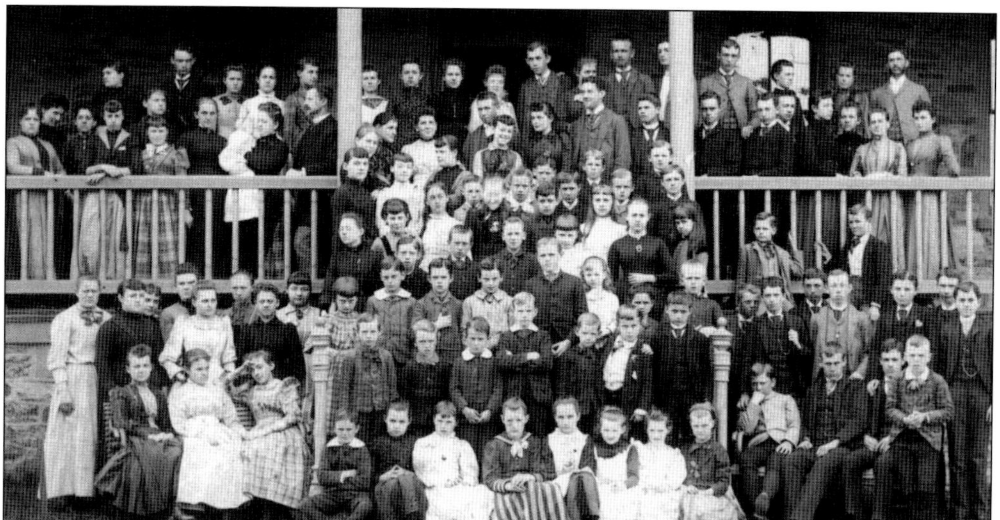

**Abington Friends School, Late 1800s.** Abington Friends was a boarding school from 1887 to 1914 with more than 150 students, nearly a third of whom boarded. The eight faculty members, all Quakers, were devoted to "furthering a thorough religiously guarded education at a modest cost." The original school building was located at the intersection of Greenwood Avenue, Meetinghouse Road, and Jenkintown Road. (Courtesy of Abington Friends School.)

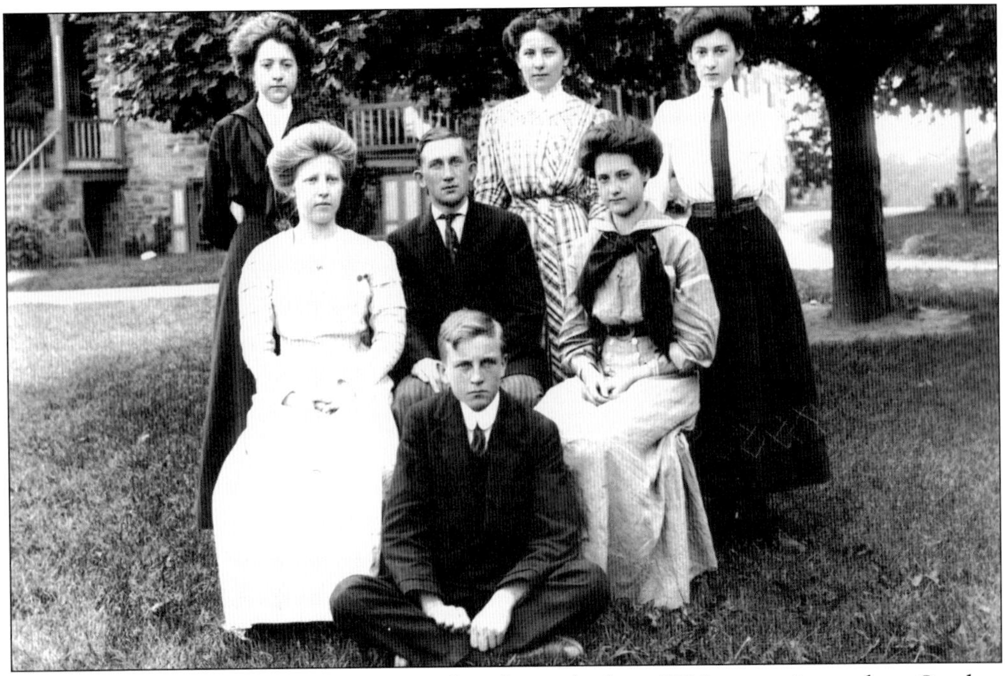

**Transformation.** This class photograph is from the late 1800s, at a time when Quaker minister Edith Atlee almost single-handedly expanded Abington Friends School's program to one that served kindergarten through grade 12. All grades studied scripture as well as the journals of Quakers George Fox and John Woolman. (Courtesy of Abington Friends School.)

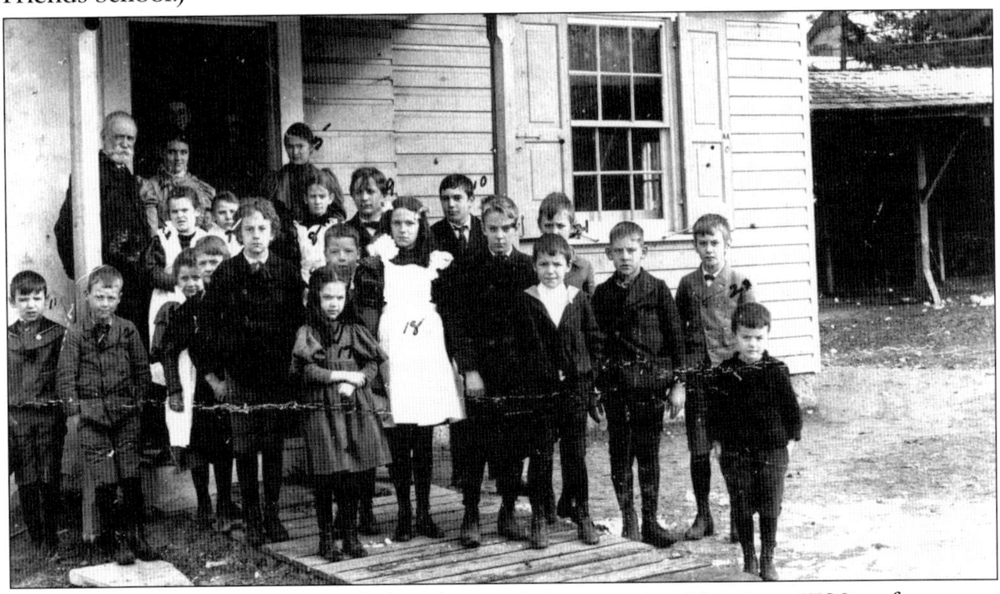

**Plymouth Meeting.** Minutes of the Plymouth Preparative Meeting, 1780, reference a committee that supervised building a meetinghouse addition for use as a school. A member of the Williams family left £100 for this purpose. A log stable was built for the horses of pupils who rode from neighboring towns. Pictured here are principal Benjamin Smith and pupils around 1897. (Courtesy of Plymouth Meeting Friends School.)

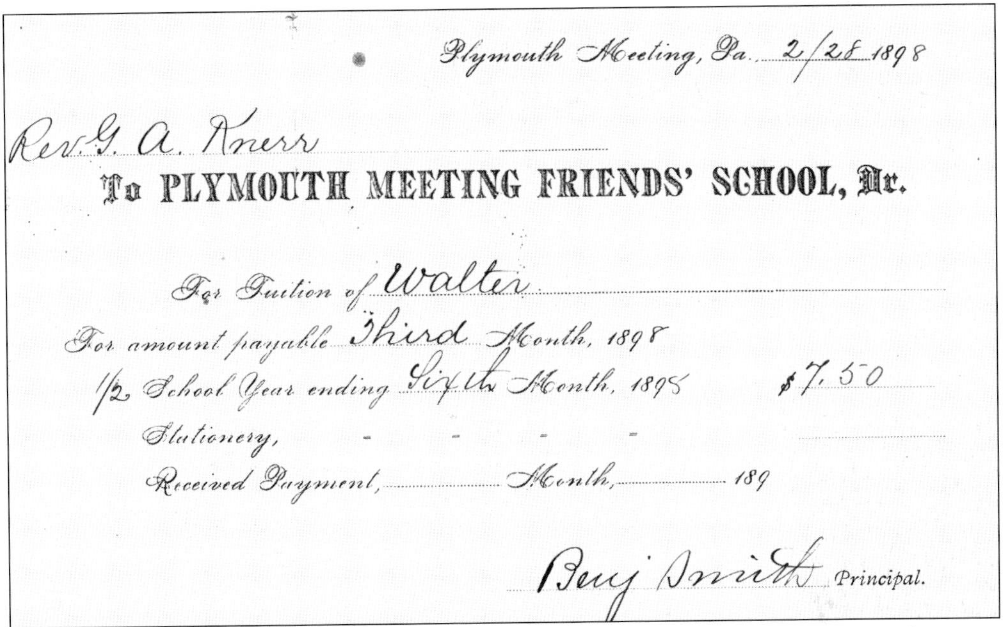

Plymouth Meeting, Pa. 2/28 1898

Rev. G. A. Knerr

To PLYMOUTH MEETING FRIENDS' SCHOOL, Dr.

For Tuition of Walter

For amount payable Third Month, 1898

1/2 School Year ending Sixth Month, 1898 $7.50

Stationery, - - - -

Received Payment, Month, 189

Benj Smith Principal.

**TUITION RECEIPT.** In 1891, the Philadelphia Yearly Meeting Committee on Education became interested in Plymouth Meeting Friends School and recommended making a graded school with primary, intermediate, and high school departments. This change was made and the building enlarged, and Benjamin Smith became principal in 1895. The photograph shows an 1898 receipt for tuition. (Courtesy of Plymouth Meeting Historical Society.)

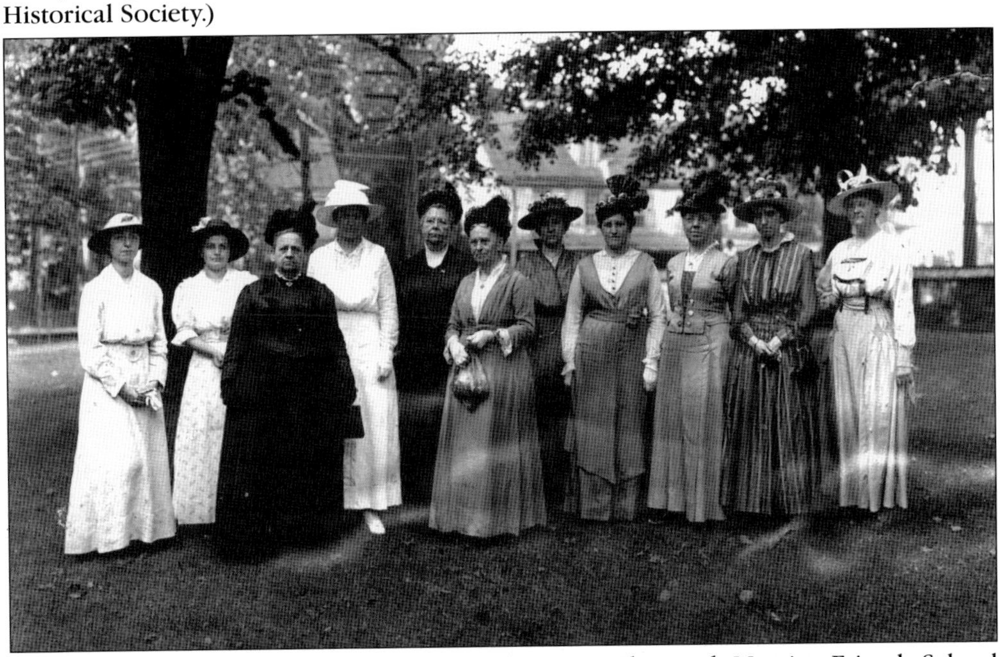

**ANNIVERSARY CELEBRATION.** In 1912, past and present Plymouth Meeting Friends School teachers gathered for the 200th celebration of Plymouth Monthly Meeting of Friends. The school and the meeting continue their mutual care relationship to this day. (Courtesy of Plymouth Meeting Friends School.)

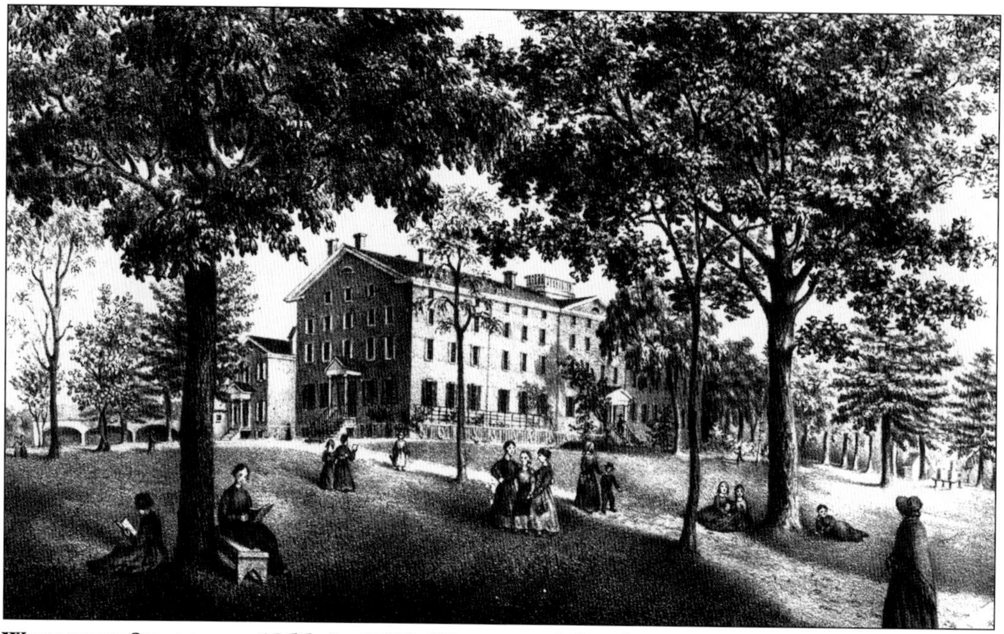

**WESTTOWN SCHOOL, *C.* 1855.** In 1799, Westtown School, under the care of Philadelphia Yearly Meeting, opened its doors to boys and girls from Quaker families. The all-boarding school was founded to provide an academic education in an environment wholly dedicated to the students' spiritual formation. Westtown School was built on 600 acres of land in Chester County, a full day's stage ride from Philadelphia. (Courtesy of Westtown School, artist John Collins, lithographer T. Sinclair.)

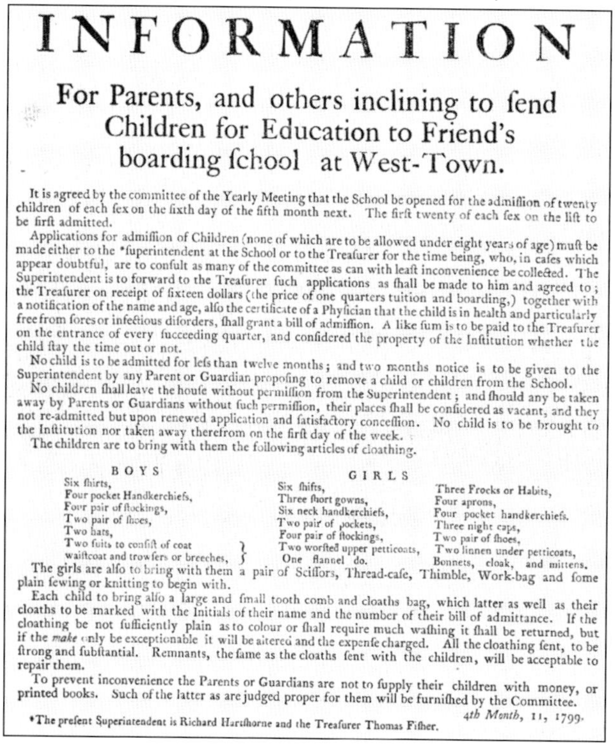

# INFORMATION

## For Parents, and others inclining to ſend Children for Education to Friend's boarding ſchool at West-Town.

It is agreed by the committee of the Yearly Meeting that the School be opened for the admiſſion of twenty children of each ſex on the ſixth day of the fifth month next. The firſt twenty of each ſex on the liſt to be firſt admitted.

Applications for admiſſion of Children (none of which are to be allowed under eight years of age) muſt be made either to the *ſuperintendent at the School or to the Treaſurer for the time being, who, in caſes which appear doubtful, are to conſult as many of the committee as can with leaſt inconvenience be collected. The Superintendent is to forward to the Treaſurer ſuch applications as ſhall be made to him and agreed to; the Treaſurer on receipt of ſixteen dollars (the price of one quarters tuition and boarding,) together with a notification of the name and age, alſo the certificate of a Phyſician that the child is in health and particularly free from ſores or infectious diſorders, ſhall grant a bill of admiſſion. A like ſum is to be paid to the Treaſurer on the entrance of every ſucceeding quarter, and conſidered the property of the Inſtitution whether the child ſtay the time out or not.

No child is to be admitted for leſs than twelve months; and two months notice is to be given to the Superintendent by any Parent or Guardian propoſing to remove a child or children from the School.

No children ſhall leave the houſe without permiſſion from the Superintendent; and ſhould any be taken away by Parents or Guardians without ſuch permiſſion, their places ſhall be conſidered as vacant, and they not re-admitted but upon renewed application and ſatisfactory conceſſion. No child is to be brought to the Inſtitution nor taken away therefrom on the firſt day of the week.

The children are to bring with them the following articles of cloathing.

| BOYS | GIRLS | |
|---|---|---|
| Six ſhirts, | Six ſhifts, | Three Frocks or Habits, |
| Four pocket Handkerchiefs, | Three ſhort gowns, | Four aprons, |
| Four pair of ſtockings, | Six neck handkerchiefs, | Four pocket handkerchiefs. |
| Two pair of ſhoes, | Two pair of pockets, | Three night caps, |
| Two hats, | Four pair of ſtockings, | Two pair of ſhoes, |
| Two ſuits to conſiſt of coat waiſtcoat and trowſers or breeches, | Two worſted upper petticoats, | Two linnen under petticoats, |
| | One flannel do. | Bonnets, cloak, and mittens. |

The girls are alſo to bring with them a pair of Sciſſors, Thread-caſe, Thimble, Work-bag and ſome plain ſewing or knitting to begin with.

Each child to bring alſo a large and ſmall tooth comb and cloaths bag, which latter as well as their cloaths to be marked with the Initials of their name and the number of their bill of admittance. If the cloathing be not ſufficiently plain as to colour or ſhall require much waſhing it ſhall be returned, but if the *make* only be exceptionable it will be altered and the expenſe charged. All the cloathing ſent, to be ſtrong and ſubſtantial. Remnants, the ſame as the cloaths ſent with the children, will be acceptable to repair them.

To prevent inconvenience the Parents or Guardians are not to ſupply their children with money, or printed books. Such of the latter as are judged proper for them will be furniſhed by the Committee.

*4th Month*, 11, 1799.

*The preſent Superintendent is Richard Hartſhorne and the Treaſurer Thomas Fiſher.

**QUAKER GUIDELINES.** This circular was printed one month before Westtown opened its doors for the first time. These guidelines depict the intentions of Philadelphia Yearly Meeting of Friends, which founded the school so that students would be immersed in a worshipful daily atmosphere of uniformly simple dress, food, and furnishings and live in community as a family with plain Quakers for teachers and staff. (Courtesy of Westtown School.)

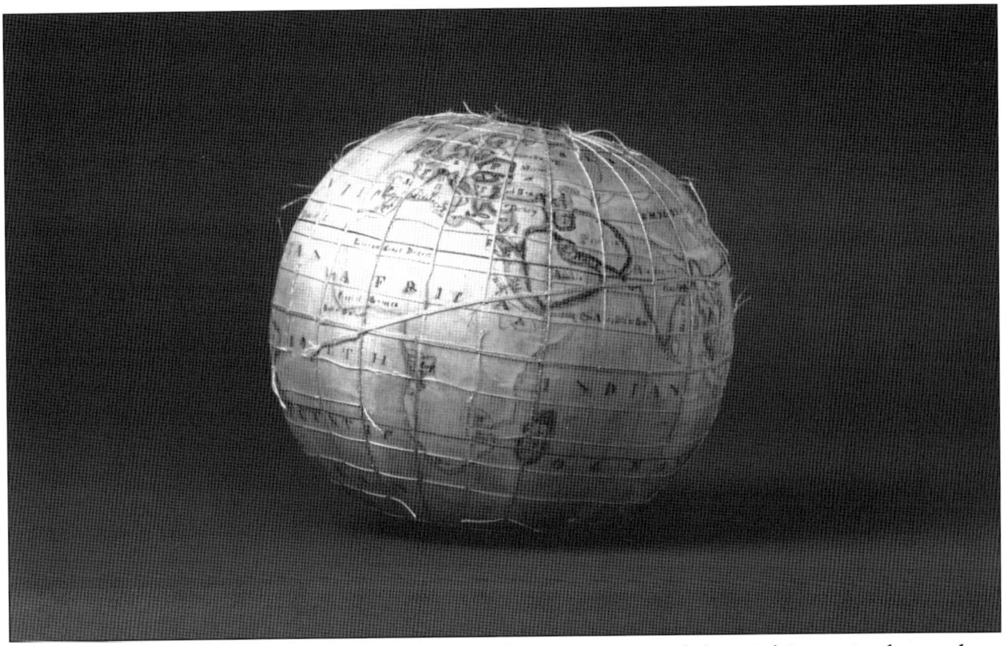

**Silk Needlework Globe, *c.* 1817.** Sewing class was part of the girls' curriculum when Westtown opened in 1799, along with classes in reading, penmanship, bookkeeping, geography, mathematics, and the natural sciences. This globe is attributed to Hannah B. Gibbons, who entered Westtown at age 12. Productive work with one's hands has always been a central component of Quaker education. (Courtesy of Westtown School.)

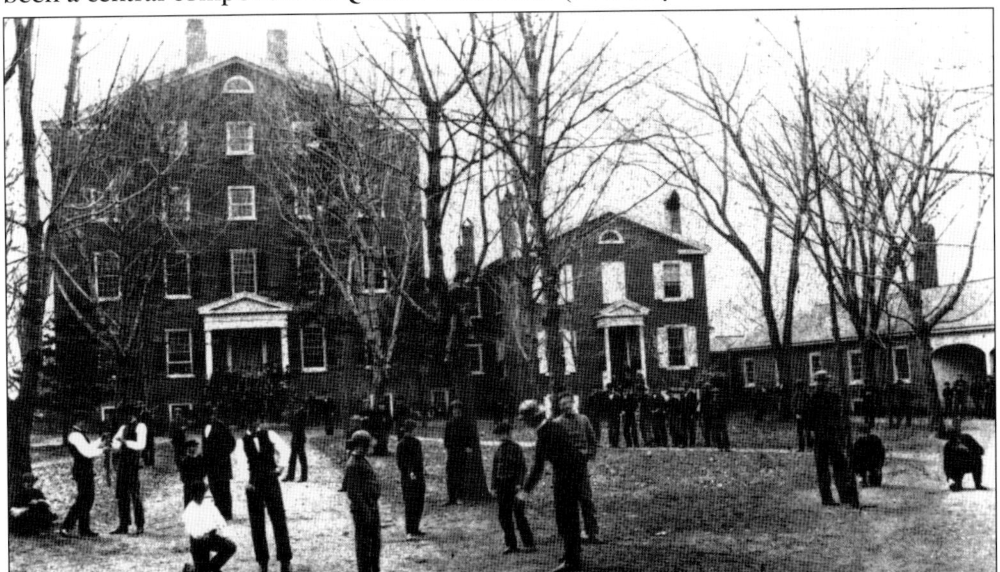

**Boys' Play Yard, 1864.** Outdoor recreation was an important part of 18th-century life at Westtown, as evidenced by these students—dressed in their school clothes—playing outside. Activities included yard games, hiking, collecting nuts from trees, and even catching squirrels. A recreation area for girls was located on the other end of the school building. (Courtesy of Westtown School.)

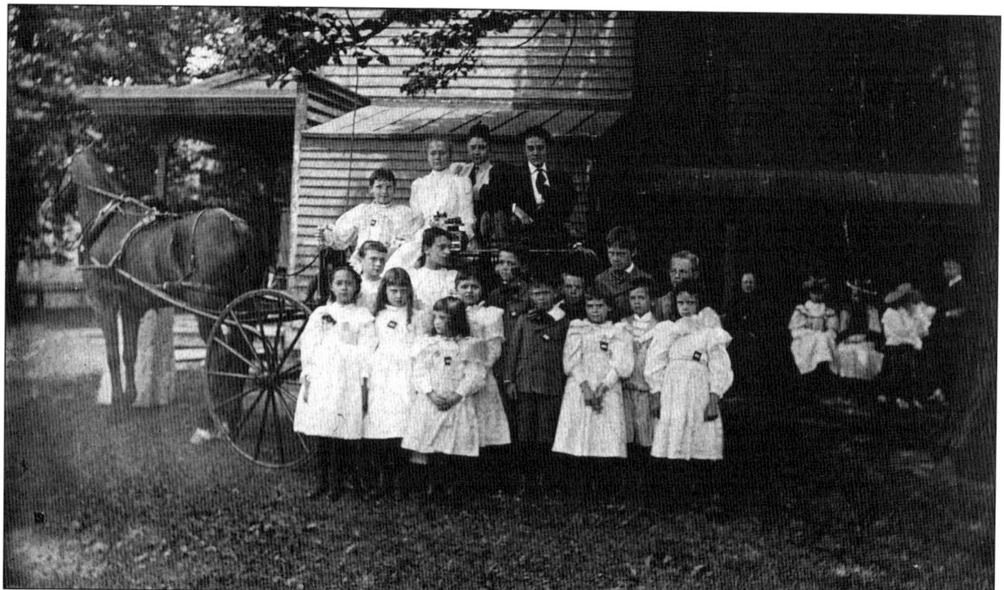

**Frankford Friends School.** Frankford Friends School originated in 1833, when Orthodox Friends purchased a piece of ground for a new meetinghouse. Later that year, 20 children moved into a new schoolroom on the second floor of the Frankford Friends Meetinghouse. This 1897 photograph shows the student body at the annual closing exercises. (Courtesy of Frankford Friends School.)

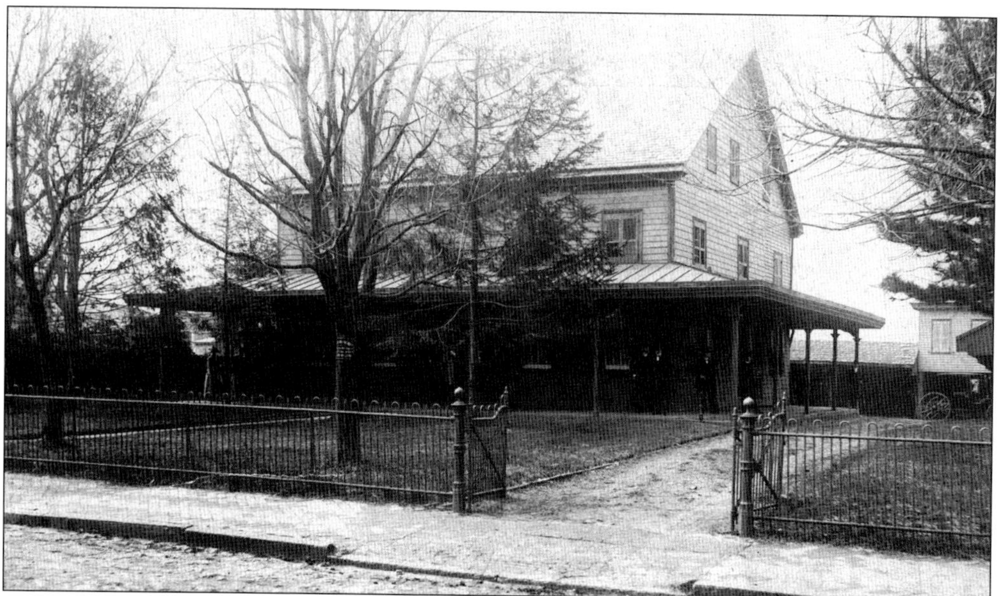

**The 1891 Meetinghouse.** Pictured here are Frankford Friends Meetinghouse and School with horse carriage sheds in the rear. The horse sheds were later removed, and the school building is now entirely brick. The iron hairpin fence along Orthodox Street still exists. (Courtesy of Frankford Friends School, photograph by Gilbert Cope.)

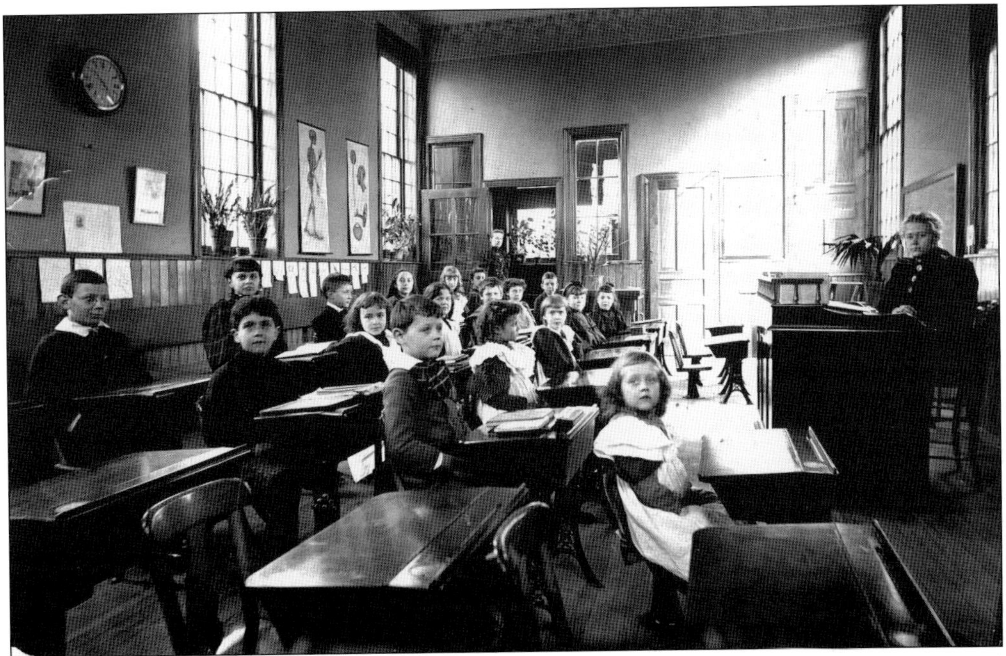

**ONE-ROOM CLASSROOM.** In this photograph from the close of the 19th century, head of Frankford Friends School Caroline Smedley poses behind her solid wooden desk. During this time, students were organized roughly by age. The classroom, with many adaptations, is still in use today. (Courtesy of Frankford Friends School.)

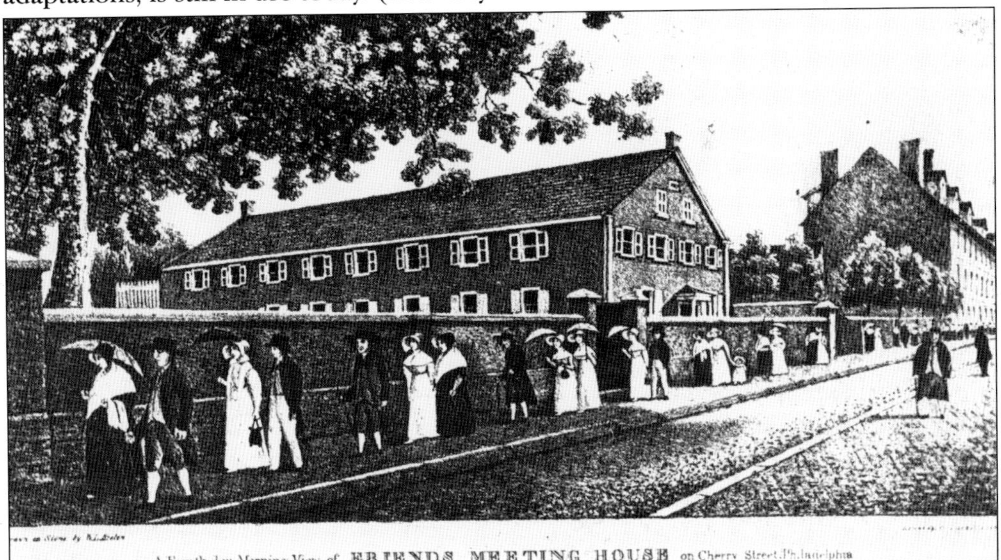


**A CENTRAL SCHOOL.** Formed by the Joint Committee on Education of the Cherry Street, Green Street, and Spruce Street Quaker Meetings, Friends' Central School opened in 1845 with approximately 200 students. Affiliated with the school were three elementary Friends schools. After completing sixth grade, the students came to the "central" school for their secondary education, hence the school's name. Pictured here are the school, the Race Street Meetinghouse, and the Race Street Friends Meeting. (Courtesy of Friends' Central School.)

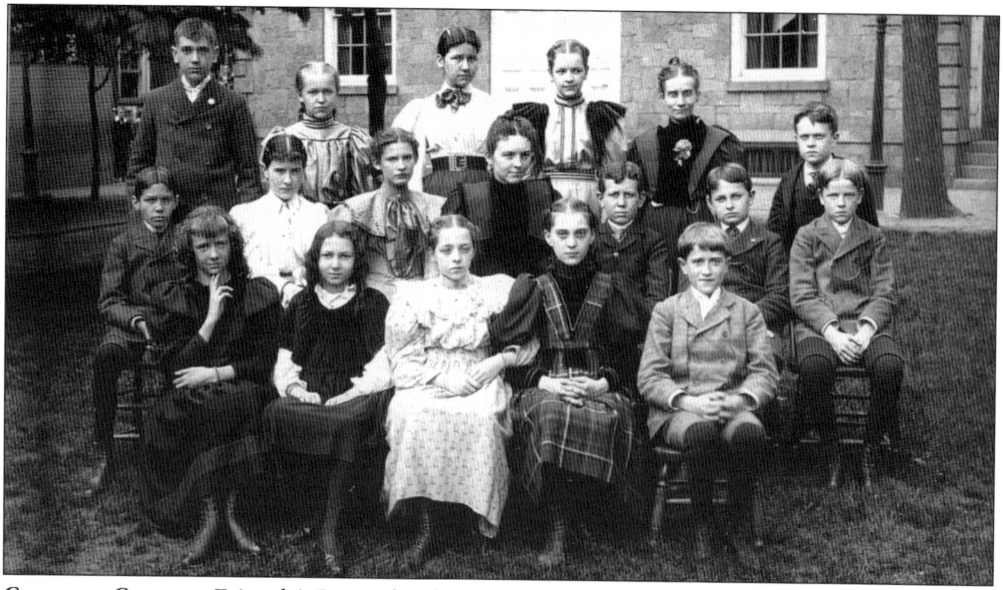

**Growing Classes.** Friends' Central School functioned in its original location at Fourth and Cherry Streets until 1857, when a new building was erected adjacent to the new meetinghouse at Fifteenth and Race Streets. As enrollment increased during the 1870s, classroom space became limited. In an effort to ease the crowding, the school took sixth grade out of Friends' Central School, so students stayed on an extra year at their elementary schools. Shown here is the seventh-grade class in 1897. (Courtesy of Friends' Central School.)

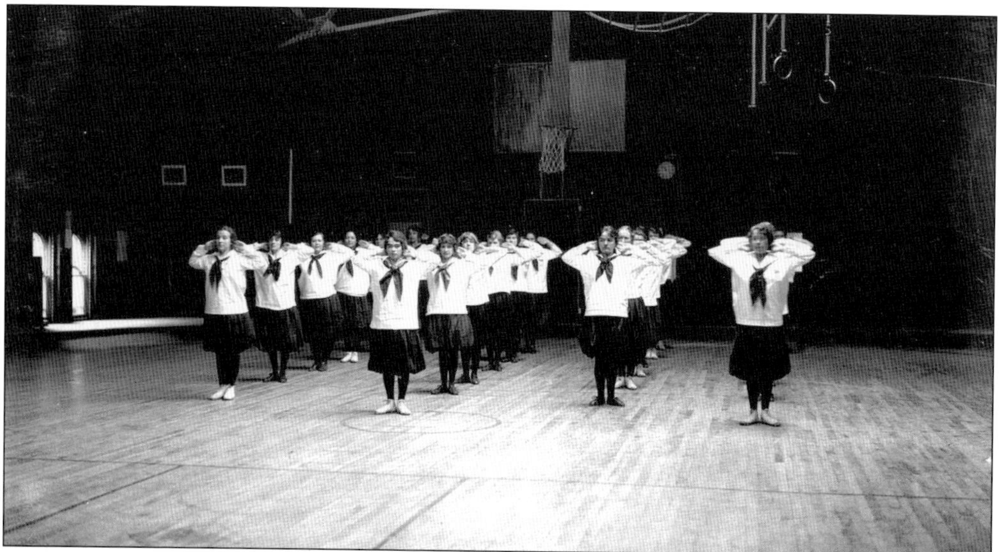

**Together Yet Apart.** When Friends' Central School moved to Fifteenth and Race Streets in 1857, the boys' and girls' departments were strictly separated, each with its own principal. The boys' classrooms occupied the third floor and the girls' were on the second floor. In 1905, teachers were asked to work in both schools, and in 1906, the tradition of separate principals ended. Separate homerooms for boys and girls continued until the 1960s, even after the school relocated to Overbrook in 1925. (Courtesy of Friends' Central School.)

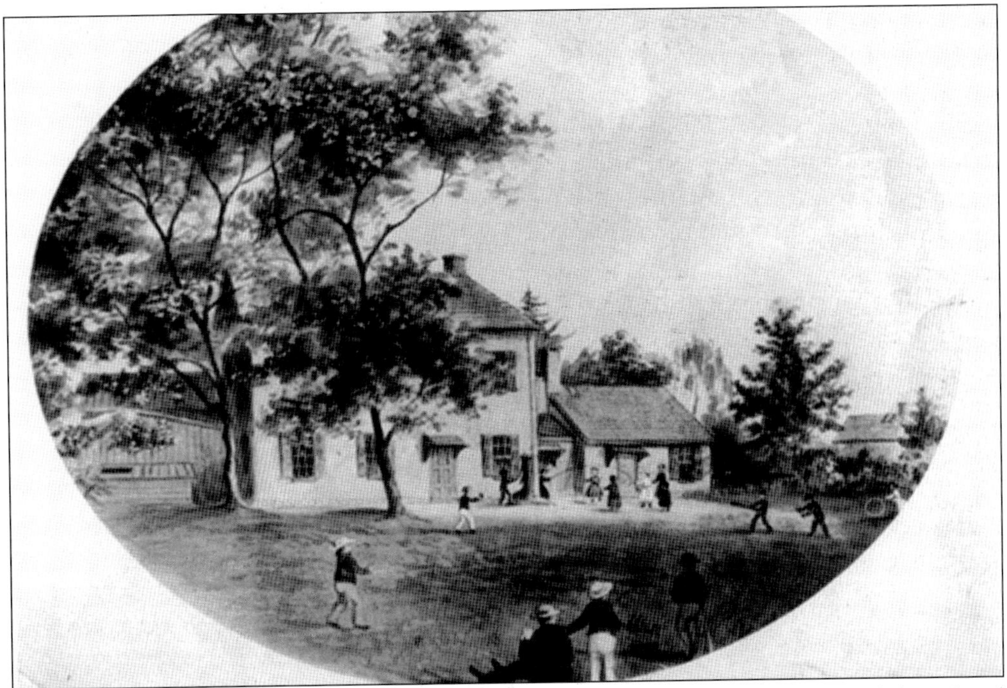

**Germantown Friends School.** The Friends of Germantown Meeting founded the school in 1845 "for the purpose of giving to the children of Friends a good academic education under the guardian care of the meeting, and in conformity with the Christian principles and practices of their religious society." While originally open only to Friends, the school later changed its policy, admitting non-Quakers beginning in 1885. The first Jewish student was admitted in 1928, and the first African American student was admitted in 1946. In 1957, after a conscious and intentional decision-making process, Germantown Meeting declined an offer to move the school to the suburbs. This decision reinvigorated the school's commitment to its community of Germantown. Seen in the 1860 image above is the original school building. In the image below, the main school building is seen in 1910. (Courtesy of Germantown Friends School.)

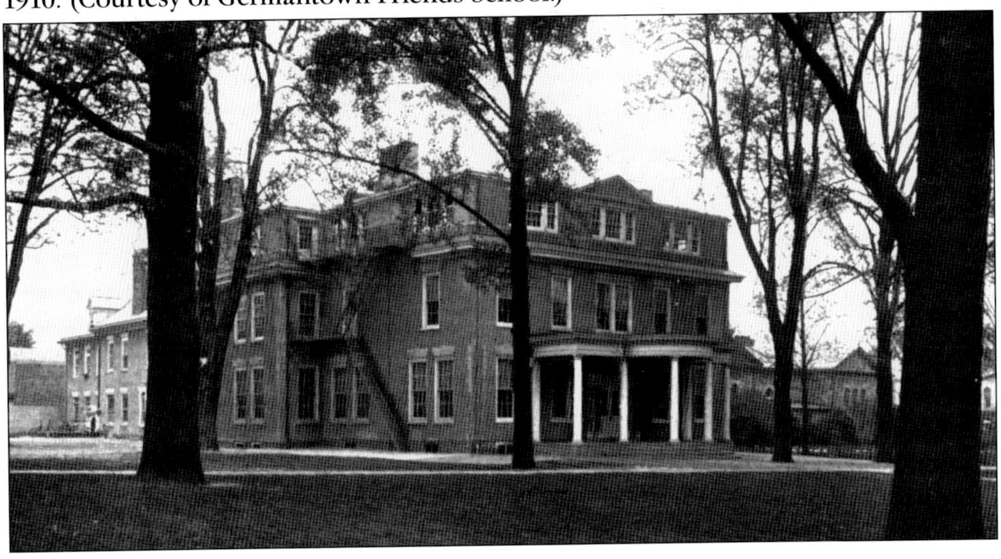

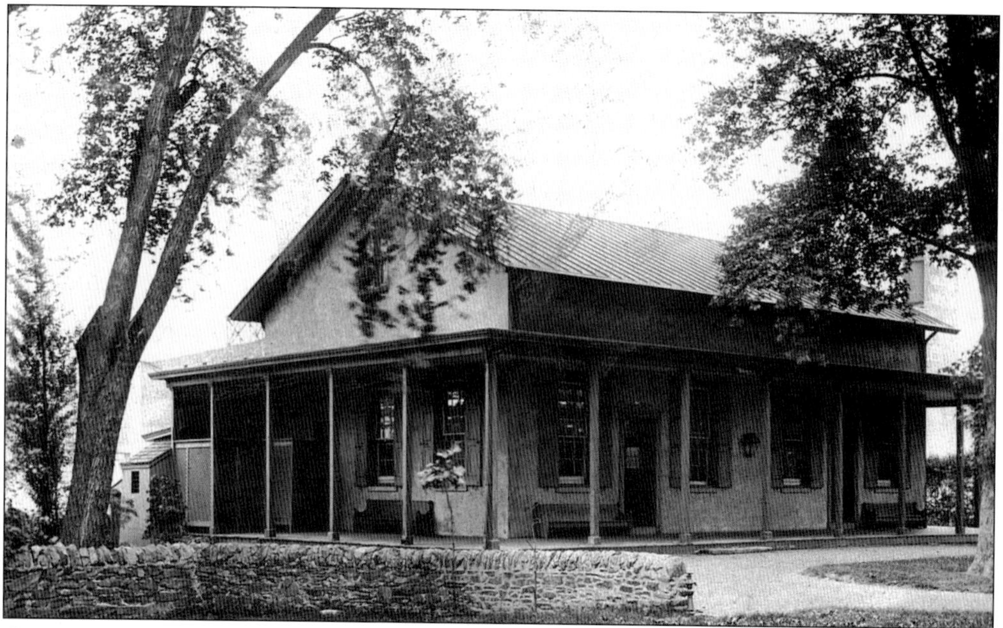

**Greene Street Friends School.** Greene Street Friends School was founded in 1855 with the twin purposes of educating children in the Green Street Meeting and from the Germantown community. The first Green Street Meetinghouse was built in 1828 on the front portion of the present property on School House Lane at a cost of $210. The photograph above shows the second Green Street Meetinghouse, built in 1854, when the first became too small. Once the second meetinghouse was completed, the original served as the school's first home. The photograph below, around 1896, demonstrates the school's growth in enrollment. In 1864–1865, there were 16 pupils and one teacher; by 1868, enrollment had reached 47. In 1876, there was sufficient interest to warrant building the present stone schoolhouse on Greene Street, which now houses the lower school. (Courtesy of Greene Street Friends School.)

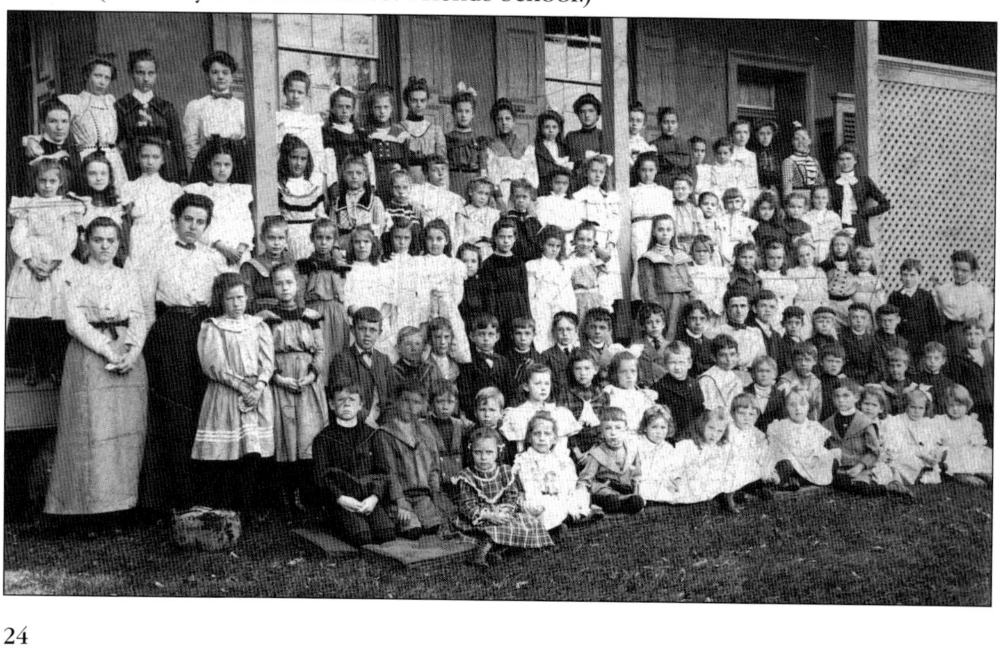

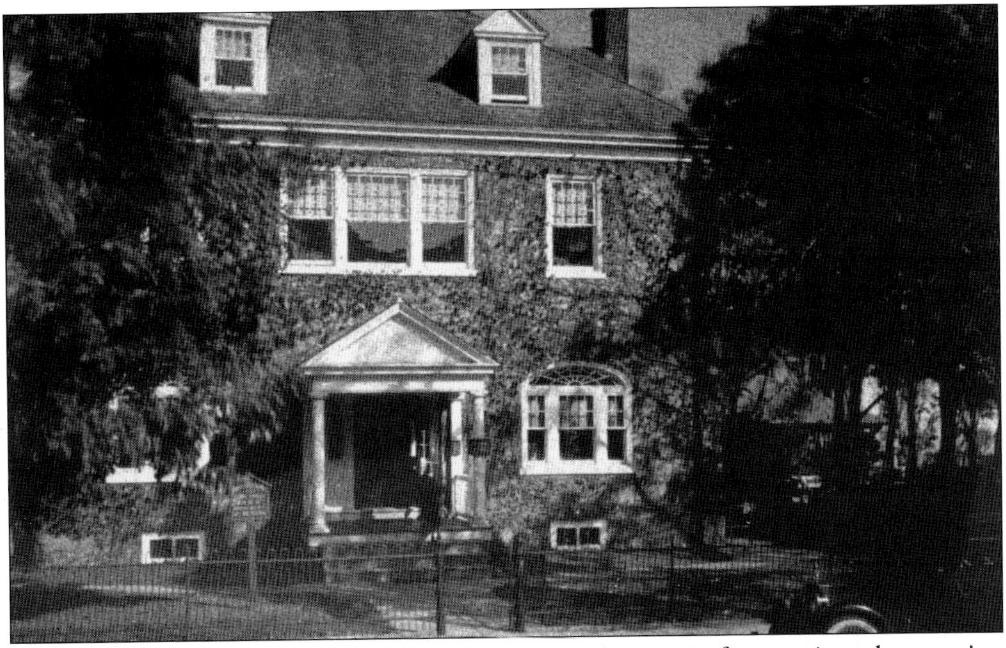

**The Care Relationship.** When a school is "under the care" of a meeting, the meeting takes a direct role in shepherding the school's Quaker character. Minutes from the 1870s Hicksite Friends Yearly Meeting underscored this important relationship. Current Friends schools and meetings describe this relationship as one of mutual care. Digitized from a broken lantern slide, this image from the early 20th century captures the front of what is now known as the lower school. (Courtesy of Greene Street Friends School.)

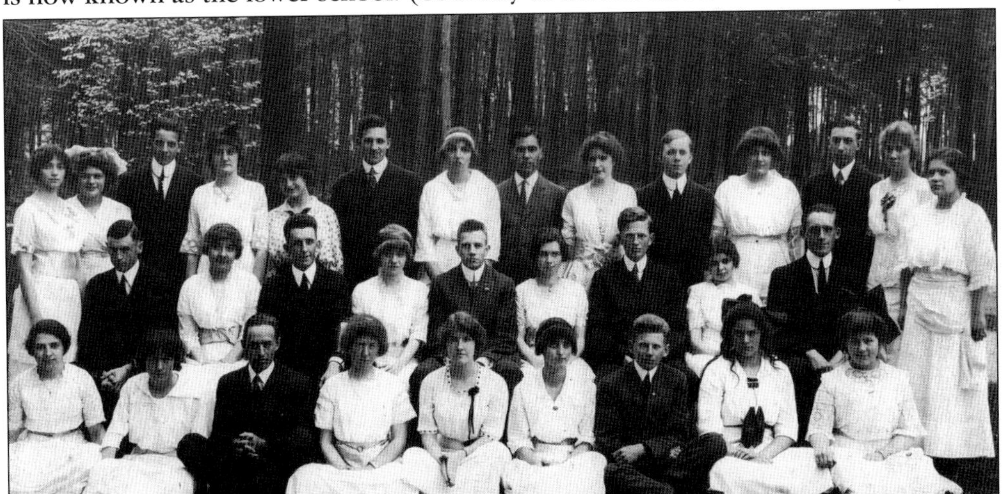

**Founding of George School.** Using a grant from the will of John M. George "for the purpose of erecting a boarding school," the founders purchased Worth Farm in Bucks County. In 1893, George School opened its doors to 155 boys and girls, embracing coeducation as part of its mission. Pictured here is the class of 1910. At that time, tuition was $300. George School is under the spiritual care of Philadelphia Yearly Meeting. (Courtesy of George School.)

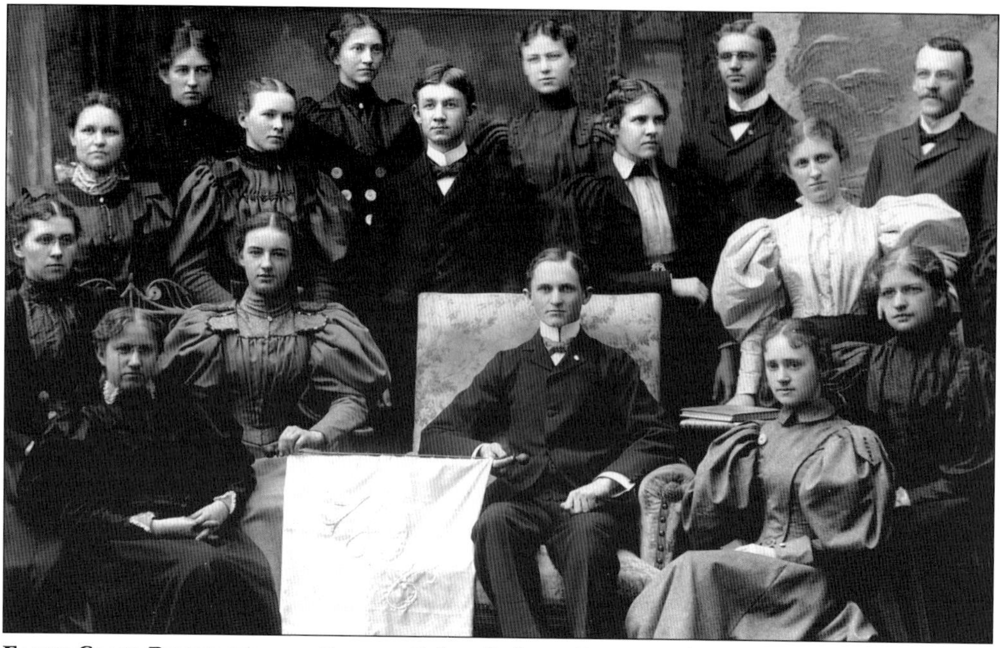

**Early Class Photographs.** George School's founding was due in part to the 1827 rift between Orthodox and Hicksite Quakers. Since Orthodox Friends maintained a dominant position on the governing committee of Westtown, Hicksites felt the need for a boarding school reflecting their approach to Quakerism. School policy stated that "p1lainness and simplicity should be the rules. Pupils and teachers should regularly attend religious Meetings of Friends. The charter of the instruction should be useful and thorough. Some form of elementary hand training and industrial training should be made a feature." These images show some of the earliest George School students. Pictured above is the 1896 graduating class, and seen below is a 1902 all-school photograph. (Courtesy of George School.)

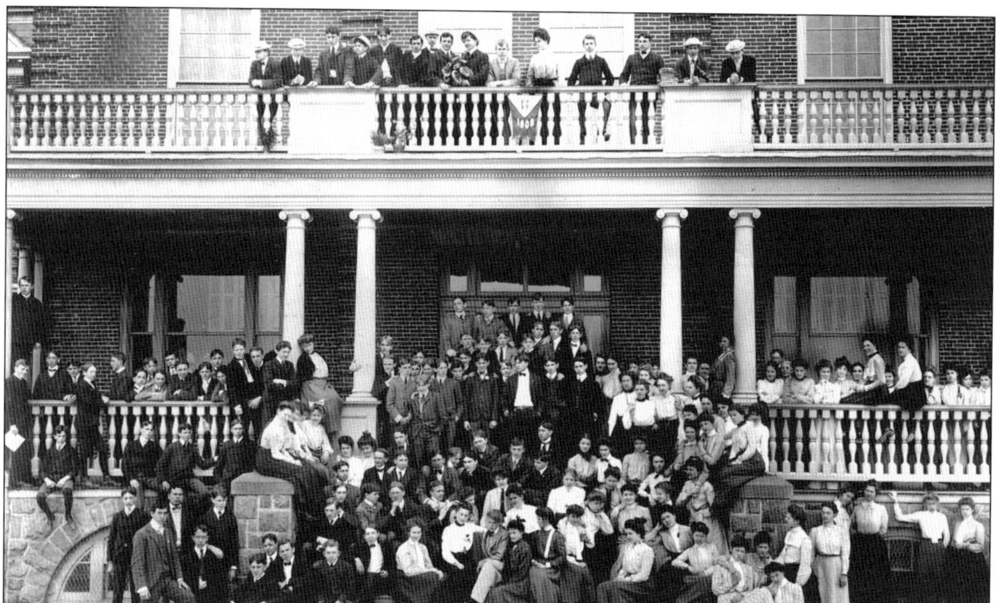

# *Two*

# Meeting for Worship

*Simple in design, minimally comfortable and as broad as space allows, the Meeting bench has been a Friends school's most important learning tool for more than 300 years.*

—Robert Smith, Quaker educator

Meeting for worship—or simply, meeting—has played a central part in the curricula of all American Friends schools since their emergence in Philadelphia more than three centuries ago. Even though meeting does not appear anywhere on the transcript, it is the spiritual and educational center of the school. Not only do Friends schools discuss the importance of community, they also deliberatively protect and nourish their community. In perhaps no other sustained educational activity is the interconnection and possibilities of the individual and the group publicly under construction each week. Quaker educators and philosophers have variously described meeting as a budding flower, a waiting stream, and a night sky. While no two meetings for worship are exactly the same, the general idea is that members of the community assemble in the meeting room, settle into silence, and remain in silent reflection unless someone—from a kindergartner to the head of school—is moved by the spirit or an inner voice to stand up and speak. The messages are surrounded by long periods of silence. Occasionally a story is shared that is so powerful and memorable that it illuminates the room like a northern star. Other messages come and go like fireflies. At still other times, the message emerges from the communal silence and washes up on shore of the individual mind, like a true unexpected treasure. Genuine reflection and the notion that all lives are hopeful and intertwined are difficult concepts to model and teach week after week, yet that is what Friends schools are doing. This chapter contains images of meeting for worship from the archives of Philadelphia-area Friends schools. The photographs are not ordered by date; instead, they show how the meeting unfolds from the perspective of schoolchildren, who arrive at Friends schools with a wide variety of religious beliefs and practices, including some with solely secular backgrounds.

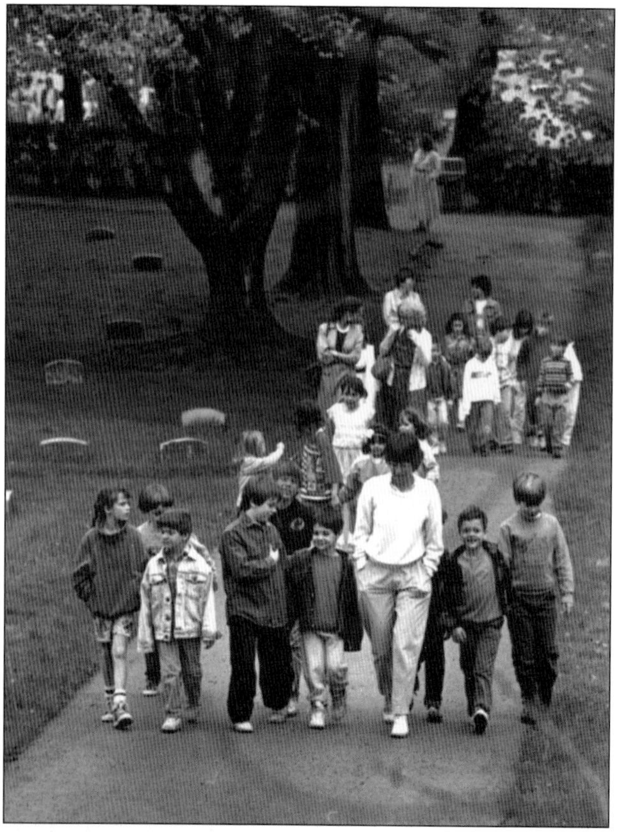

**Walking to Meeting for Worship.** The success of the meeting for worship experience often depends on the manner of preparation for it, and especially the time leading up to the meeting. Here children in the lower school at Abington Friends School in the 1980s meet their partners—first and fourth graders—and journey together across a cemetery toward the meetinghouse. Establishing a community based on trust and friendship is one of the central goals of Friends schools. (Courtesy of Abington Friends School.)

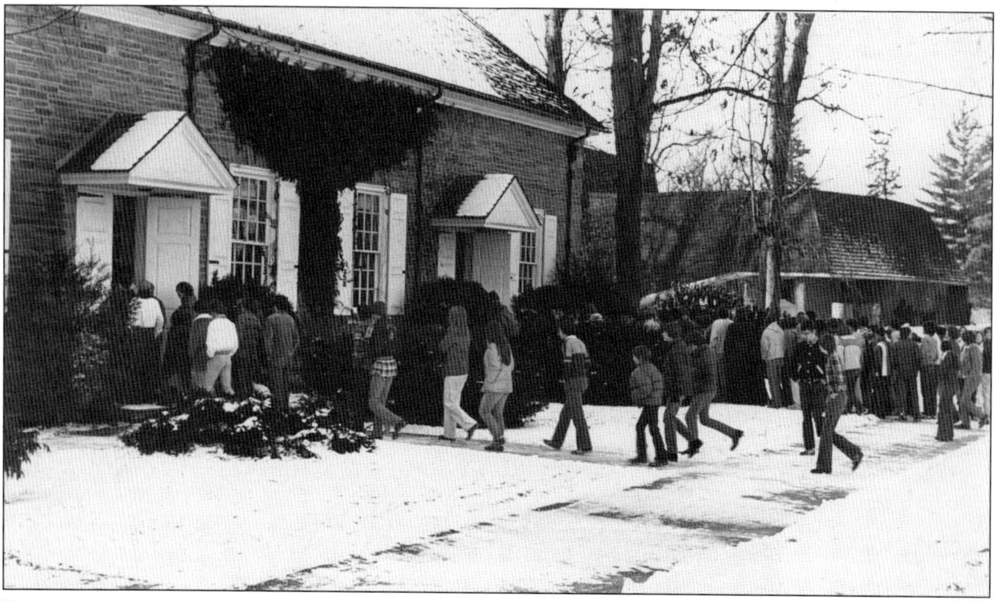

**Entering the Meeting Room.** The communal aspect of walking to meeting prepares students for the worship and fellowship that is to come. Here Westtown School students in the 1970s enter the meetinghouse, built in 1929. (Courtesy of Westtown School, photograph by Donald H. Byerly.)

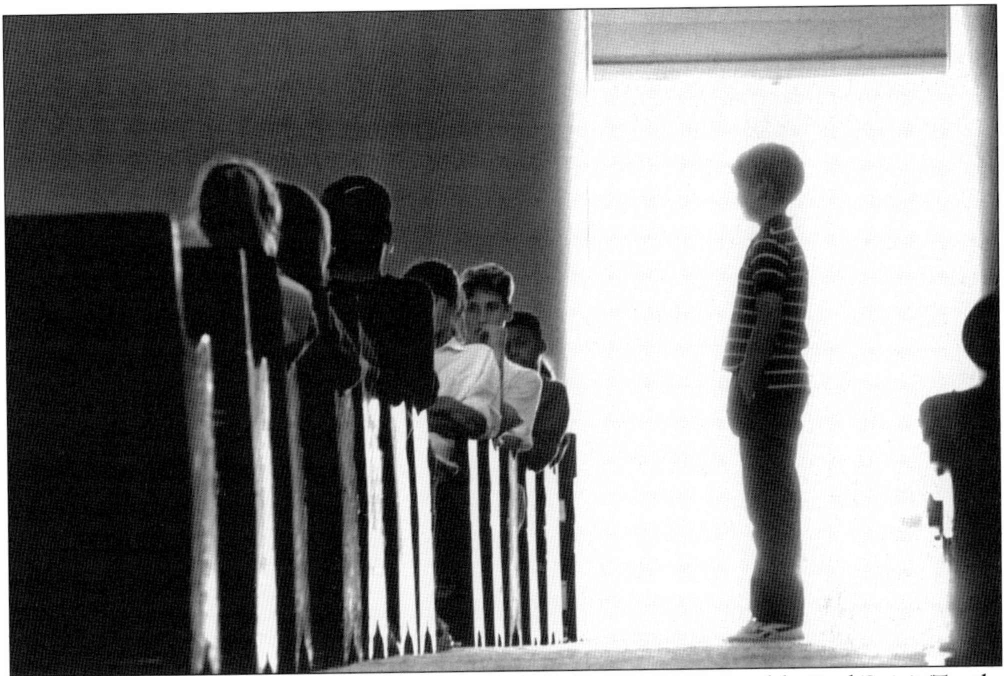

**Light Within.** What Quakers call the "Inner Light," or interchangeably God/Spirit/Truth, is equally available to all who are open to it. In Friends schools, as in Friends meetings, there is no proselytizing, no seeking to convert, and no prescriptions for how to worship during meeting. This photograph is from 1980. (Courtesy of Germantown Friends School.)

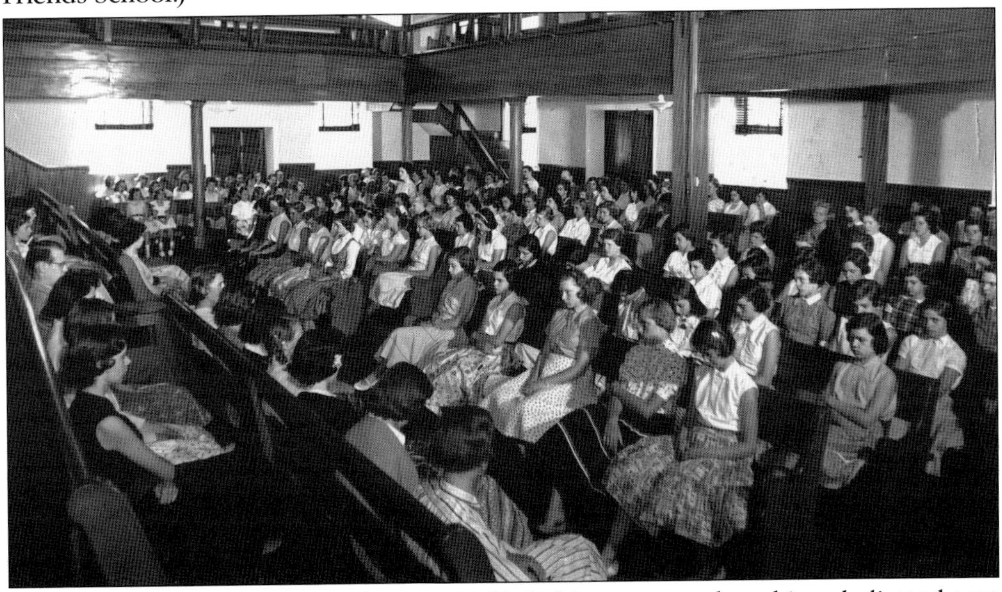

**Sacred Time.** Meeting for worship is usually held once a week and is a dedicated part of the school schedule for all students and teachers. Here Abington Friends School students and teachers settle into silent reflection during a 1960s meeting. Worship is protected space; no bookbags, no homework, and no distractions are allowed. (Courtesy of Abington Friends School.)

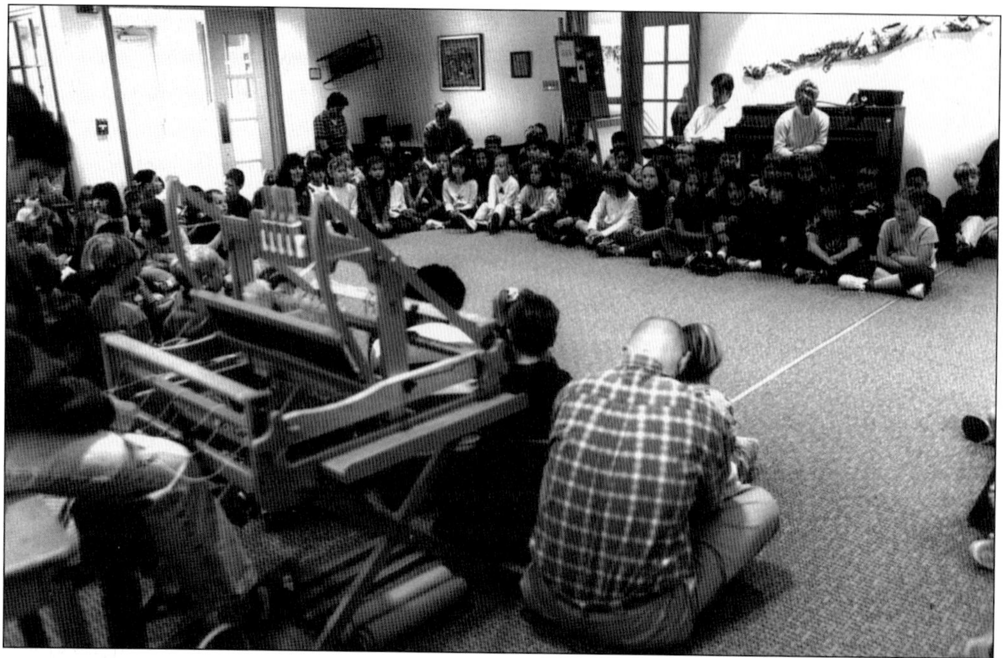

**Settling into Silence.** Worship gives children the opportunity to grow in the understanding and use of silence—a fundamental concept of Friends worship—and to speak as he or she is led. Occasionally there is a planned activity at the beginning of worship to help children center their thoughts. Lower school students and teachers at Westtown School in this 1990s picture gather for a shared weekly 30 minutes of worship. (Courtesy of Westtown School.)

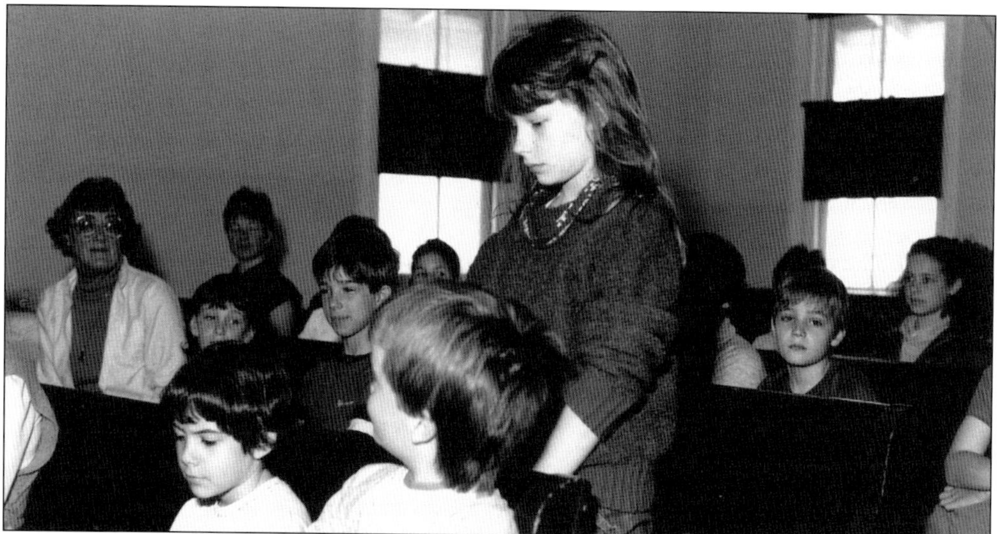

**Gathering in Expectant Waiting.** The fundamental practice of gathering in "expectant waiting for Divine guidance" can be traced to the origin of Quakerism and continues to this day in Quaker meetings and in Friends schools. Worship habituates students to silence, recollection, and reflection, valuable skills for learning and for life. Here Frankford Friends School student Molly Snyderman '87 shares a message. (Courtesy of Frankford Friends School.)

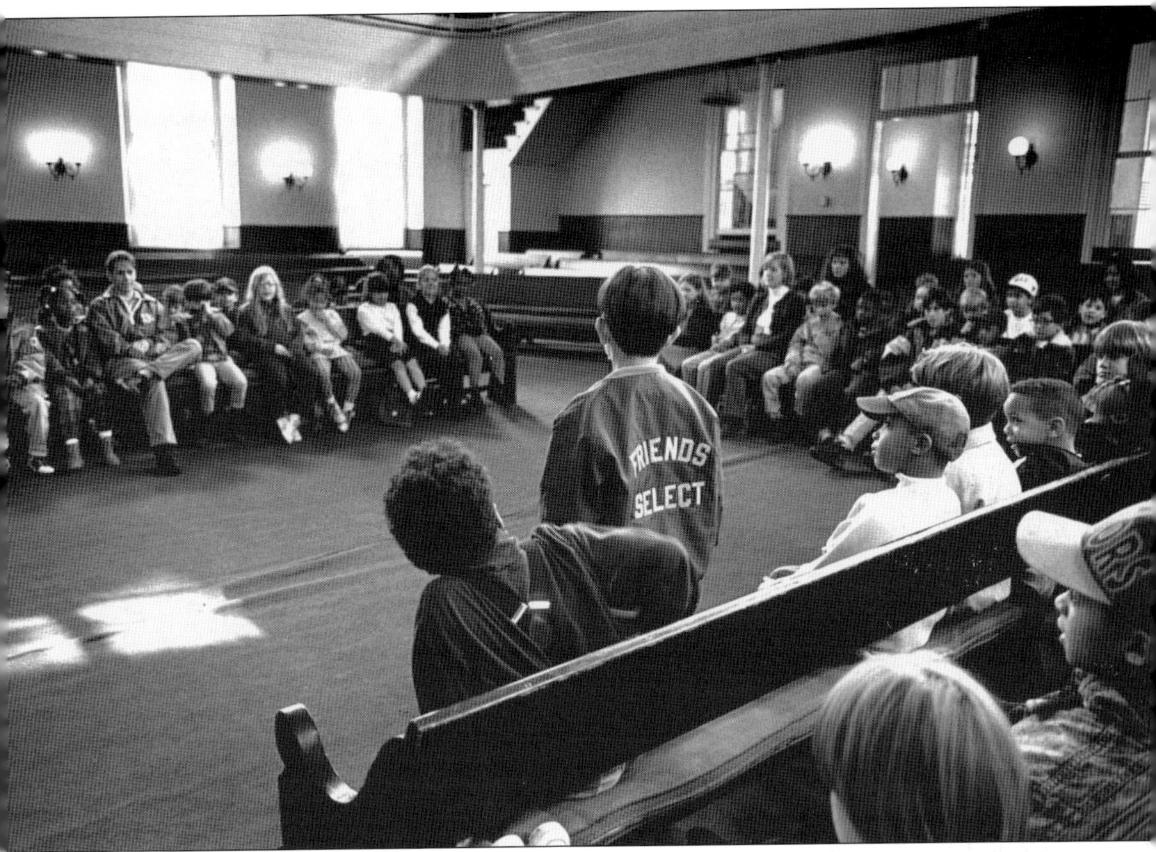


**Harmony and Humility.** When a message arises from the assembled group, it can come from any member, young or old, and from any bench. "My favorite memories of Meeting for Worship," offers a Friends school alumnus, "came from specific individuals who distinguished themselves over the years and became regular speakers in Meeting. Without realizing it, these people—both teachers and peers—had a tremendous impact on the way I view the world." Spoken messages emerge from the silence and harmonize with the spirit of the meeting. The spoken words are often humble, simple in language, spontaneous, compatible with other messages (though not in direct response to them), and brief. The meeting is especially powerful when messages fall within a theme, which is known as a "gathered meeting." In this image, lower school students from Friends Select School gather at meeting for worship at the Race Street Meetinghouse, around 1990. (Courtesy of Friends Select School.)

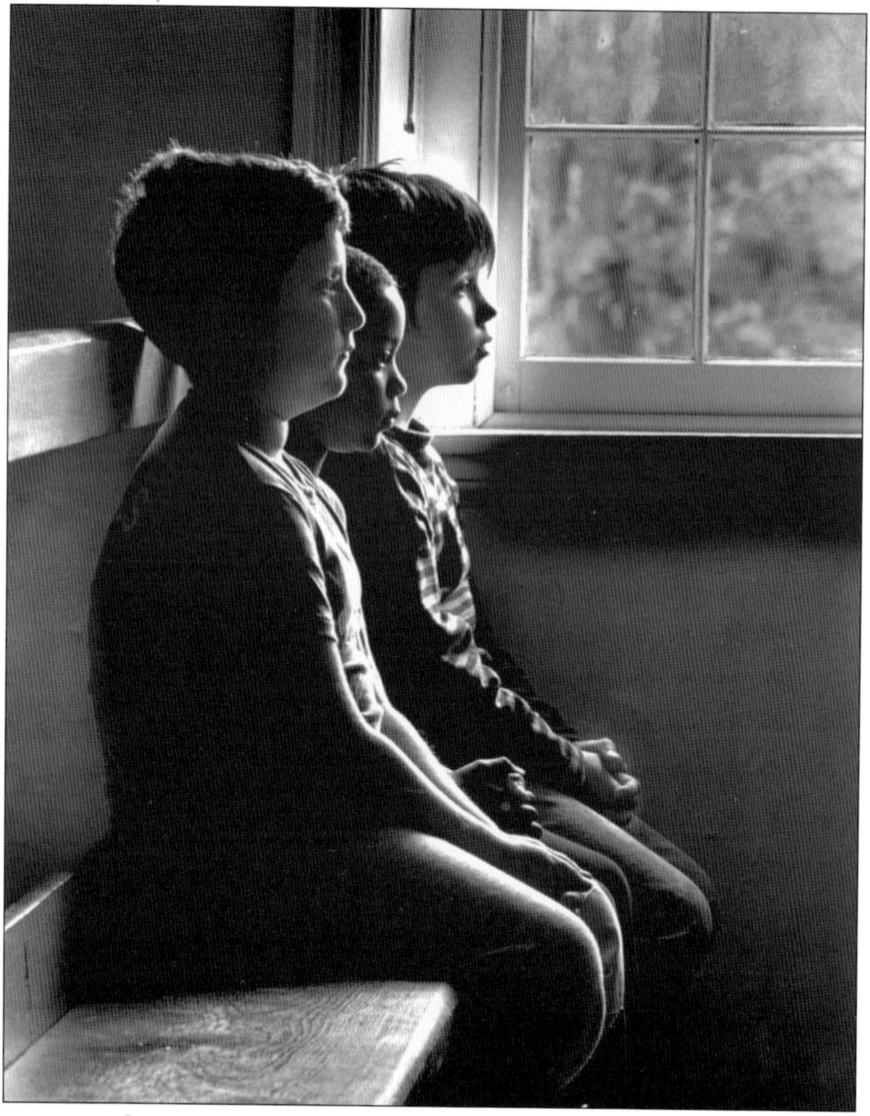

CONVICTION AND COMPASSION. Friends schools spend time preparing students for meeting for worship. Older students in each division often help run orientation programs for new students. Throughout the year, Friends schools also apply the central concepts of meeting for worship to other educational contexts, such as worship sharing (worshipping in small groups, generally following a theme or query), all-school meetings for worship, meetings in response to a tragedy or a troubling event, and meetings for leaving (celebratory meetings, usually nearing graduation, that are attended by parents and family). The meeting is a powerful pedagogical tool. The practice helps students to become spiritually centered by sensitizing individuals to the needs and experiences of others. Meeting affords school communities with regular times to reflect in silence and periodically listen to how people of all ages deal with issues of fairness, justice, and compassion. Meeting works on many levels at once by affirming the goodness of each person, the potential of the group, and the shared and limitless currency of compassion. Pictured above, lower school children are taking part in meeting for worship, around 1980. (Courtesy of Abington Friends School.)

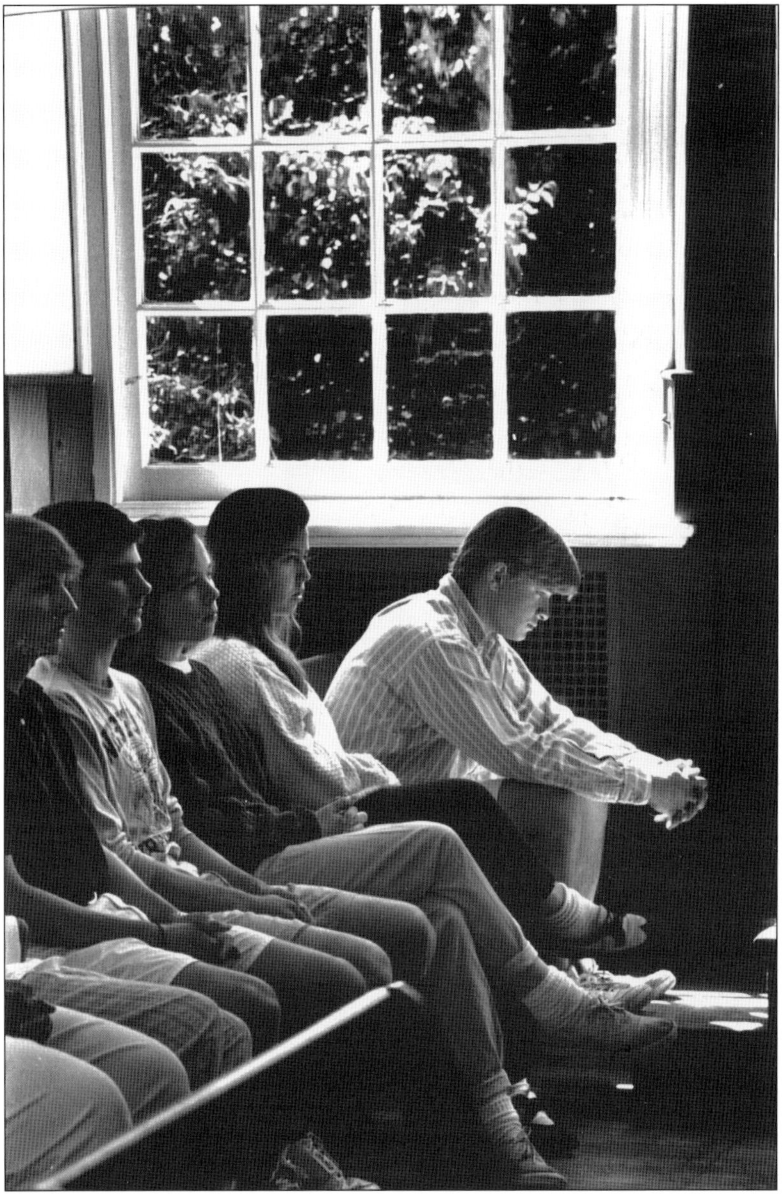

**The Individual and the Community.** Studies show that students learn best in an environment where expectations are high and where spiritual and moral growth is emphasized within a caring community. Friends schools encourage students to look within themselves for better answers, for what is good, and for what is true; often these answers emerge out of the silence. Friends schools also reinforce the notion that a greater sense of purpose is best realized within the context of collective goals. Friends, as seekers, believe that there are many valid ways of understanding a concept, or of understanding or thinking about God. Quaker worship respects the wide range of religious backgrounds in the school community by affirming the dignity of all people and all faiths. Here Westtown students and faculty gather in the meetinghouse around 1990. Meeting helps students grow in their appreciation of silence, aids them in their journeys of self-discovery, and includes them in the powerful experience of shared truths. (Courtesy of Westtown School.)

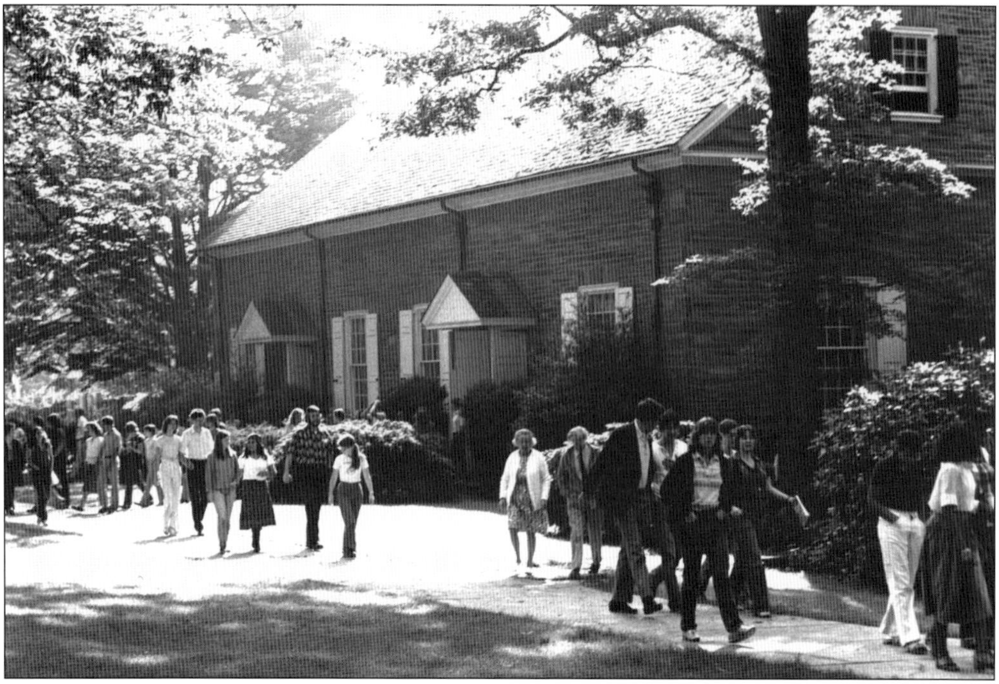

**Leaving the Meeting Room.** The core values of Quakerism are practiced in various ways by Friends schools, and their defining center is meeting for worship. At their best, Friends schools take the lessons learned and modeled in meeting and apply them wherever and whenever students and faculty congregate. Here Westtown School students and faculty exit the meeting room and return to class in the 1970s. (Courtesy of Westtown School.)

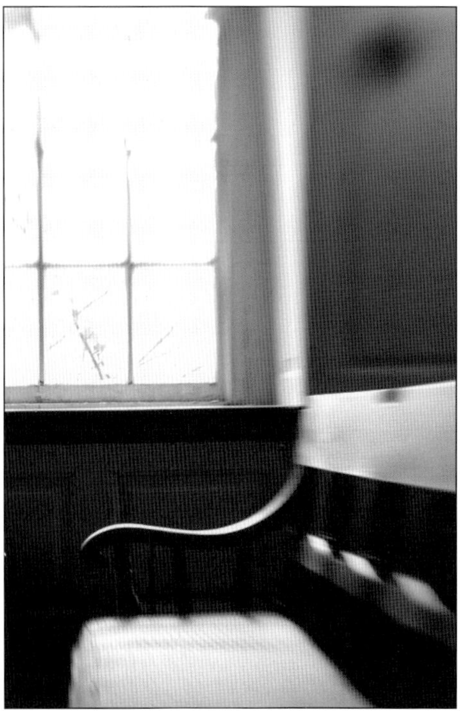

**Bench in Sunlight.** Outside the meeting room at the William Penn Charter School, where this photograph was taken, are these words of guidance from the Friends General Conference: "We are met in a great task when we meet in worship, no less than to realize the divine presence and to create an atmosphere in which that presence and power can touch us to fuller life. . . . It is something holy and wonderful we are trying to build up together." (Courtesy of the William Penn Charter School.)

# *Three*

# Inquiry and Innovation

*Quaker virtues—equality, community, simplicity, and peace—describe an environment, not a person. Education at Friends schools encourages a process of eternal searching.*

—Kim Hays, Quaker educator

Inquiry and innovation are obviously not unique to Friends schools, but the Quaker learning environment and theological foundation that drive the wheels of inquiry and innovation are. Friends schools believe in the power of communal discovery and shared search for knowledge, valuing the challenge of competing ideas. These beliefs are really values at work. Open-ended questions are powerful tools that stretch children's curiosity, reasoning ability, creativity, and independence. Inquiry learning, or query-based learning, allows each person in the classroom to benefit from multiple perspectives, building knowledge in a collaborative exploration. Friends schools invite students and faculty members into inquiry learning in corporate worship and in the classroom in a unique expression of continuing revelation within diverse communities. Paul Lacey describes the learning environment this way:

> It is a commitment to making connections, making contacts, encouraging risk, and experimentation, becoming inter-related, intimately "involved" together as companions in learning, reducing the prompts in the name of greater independence and autonomy for students, integrating thought with action and ethical convictions with ethical behavior.

Seeking truth is not only a shared endeavor at Friends schools, it is a sacred enterprise of continuing revelation. The images on the following pages demonstrate the Quaker values and practices that inspire communities of inquiry and innovation.

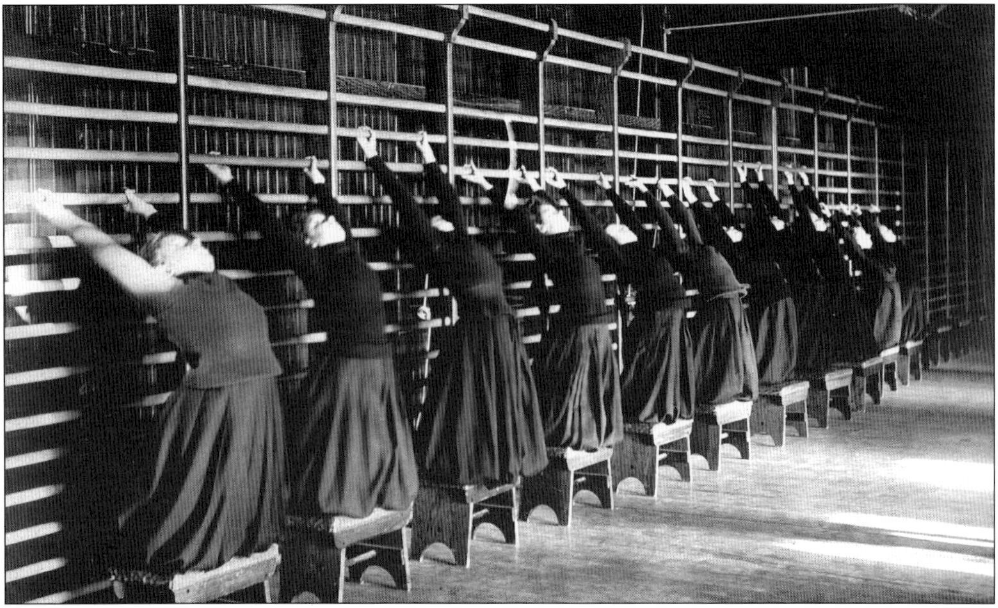

**SPAN BENDING IN GYM CLASS.** Friends schools have always sought to "stretch" their understanding to fit the changing needs of their students and the world, and sometimes these explorations produced unusual results. In this photograph, girls at Westtown School during the 1901–1902 school year practice stretching, or "span bending," along ribbed stalls. A fully equipped gymnasium was built at Westtown in 1899 as part of the school's expansion of "physical culture," as it was known then. (Courtesy of Westtown School.)

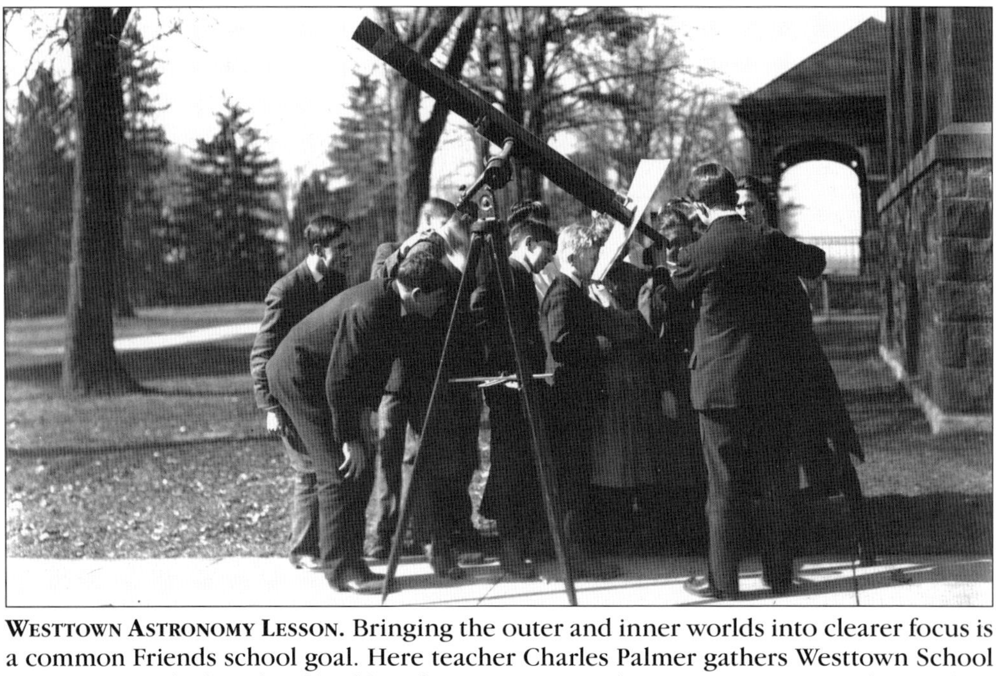

**WESTTOWN ASTRONOMY LESSON.** Bringing the outer and inner worlds into clearer focus is a common Friends school goal. Here teacher Charles Palmer gathers Westtown School students outside the school building for an astronomy lesson in 1908. An understanding of the natural world through the study of science has been an important part of the curriculum since the school's opening in 1799. (Courtesy of Westtown School.)

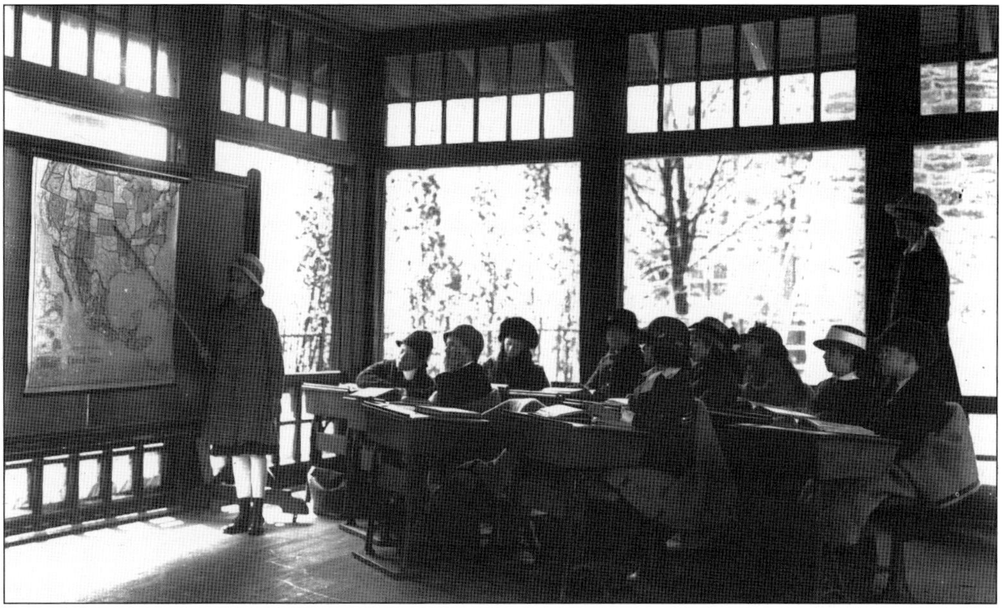

**Greene Street Friends School, *c.* 1915.** As part of a progressive educational concept promoting the salutary effect of fresh air, all classes spent a part of each day in one of the two open-air classrooms. According to Bruce Jones, "The School purchased sitting-out bags for use when the weather was chilly. The child climbed completely in, the bag was closed up to the neck with snaps down the front—and there they were, looking like a colony of over-grown caterpillars!" (Courtesy of Greene Street Friends School.)

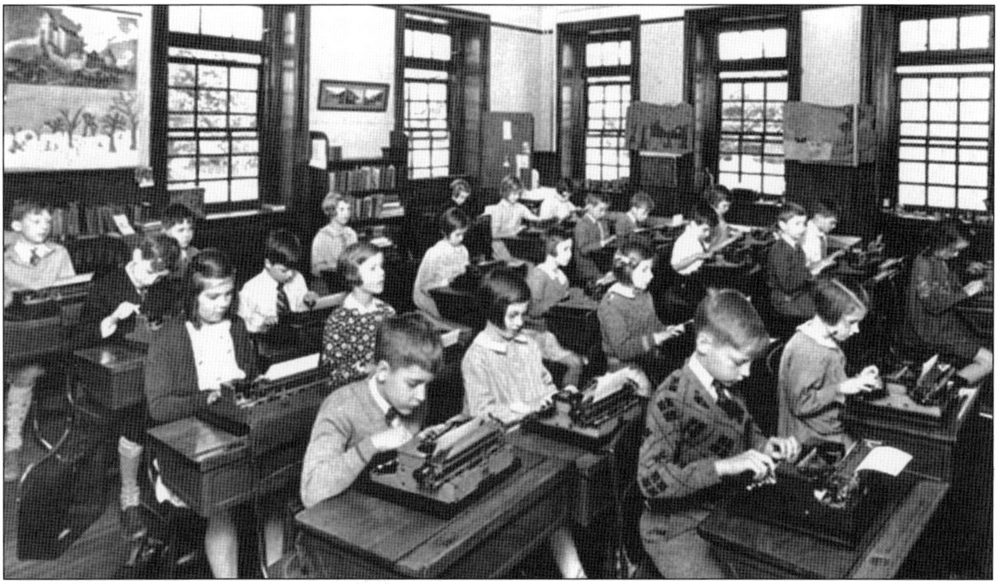

**Typewriters across the Curriculum.** Students at Germantown Friends School in May 1930 participate in the "typewriter experiment," which was used across disciplines. A *New York Times* article during the period states, "The typewriter places before the child neat, clean-cut letters which always look the same, and in a short time he comes to despise sprawling, irregular writing and seek to improve his work with the pen as well as with the machine." (Courtesy of Germantown Friends School.)

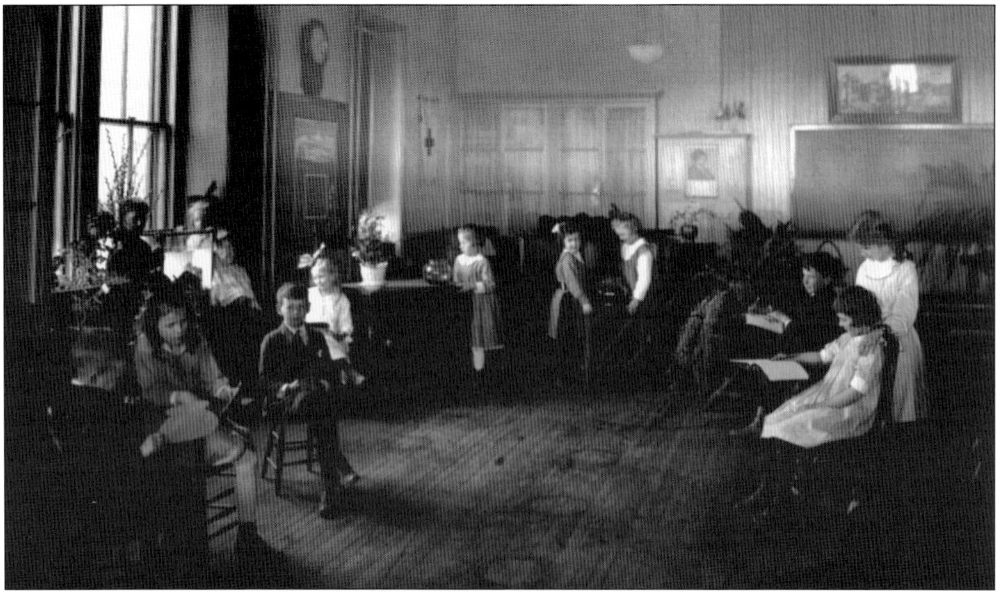

**EARLY DIFFERENTIATED INSTRUCTION.** This 1918 photograph of Abington Friends School illustrates a classroom environment using differentiated instruction, a concept from the progressive educational movement that is still valued today. At the time, Abington Friends School was a small coed school, competing against the increase in public schools in the area. By 1931, the school had become an all-girls college preparatory school and was to remain as such until the mid-1970s. (Courtesy of Abington Friends School.)

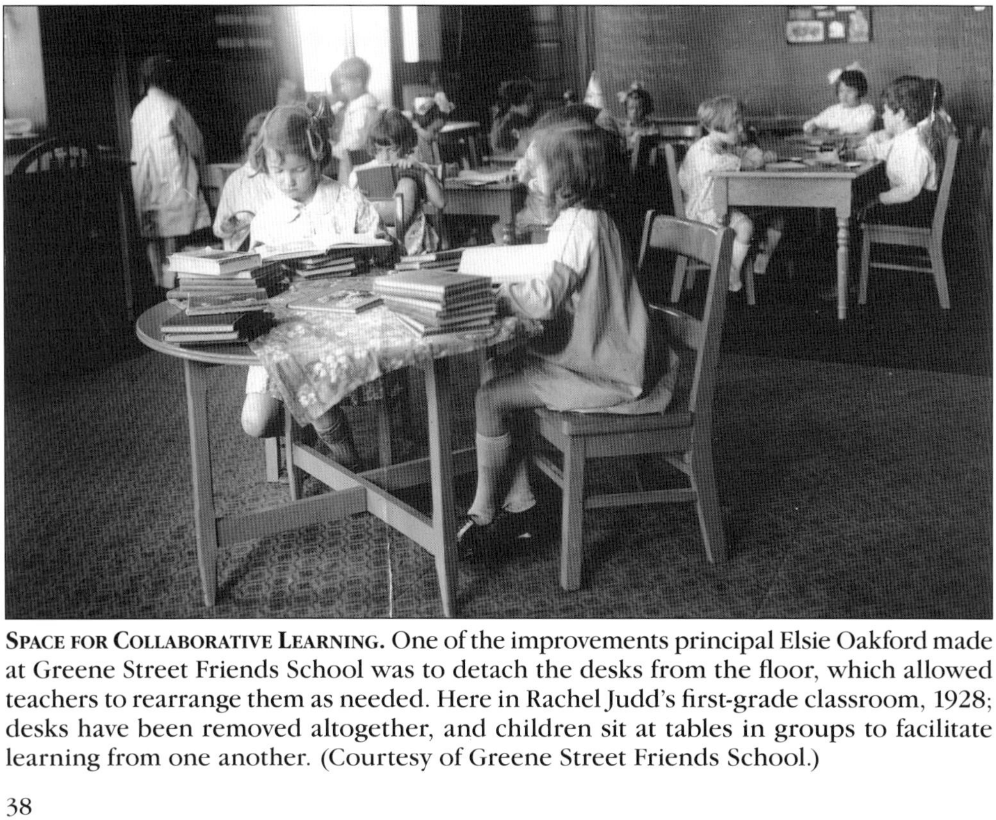

**SPACE FOR COLLABORATIVE LEARNING.** One of the improvements principal Elsie Oakford made at Greene Street Friends School was to detach the desks from the floor, which allowed teachers to rearrange them as needed. Here in Rachel Judd's first-grade classroom, 1928; desks have been removed altogether, and children sit at tables in groups to facilitate learning from one another. (Courtesy of Greene Street Friends School.)

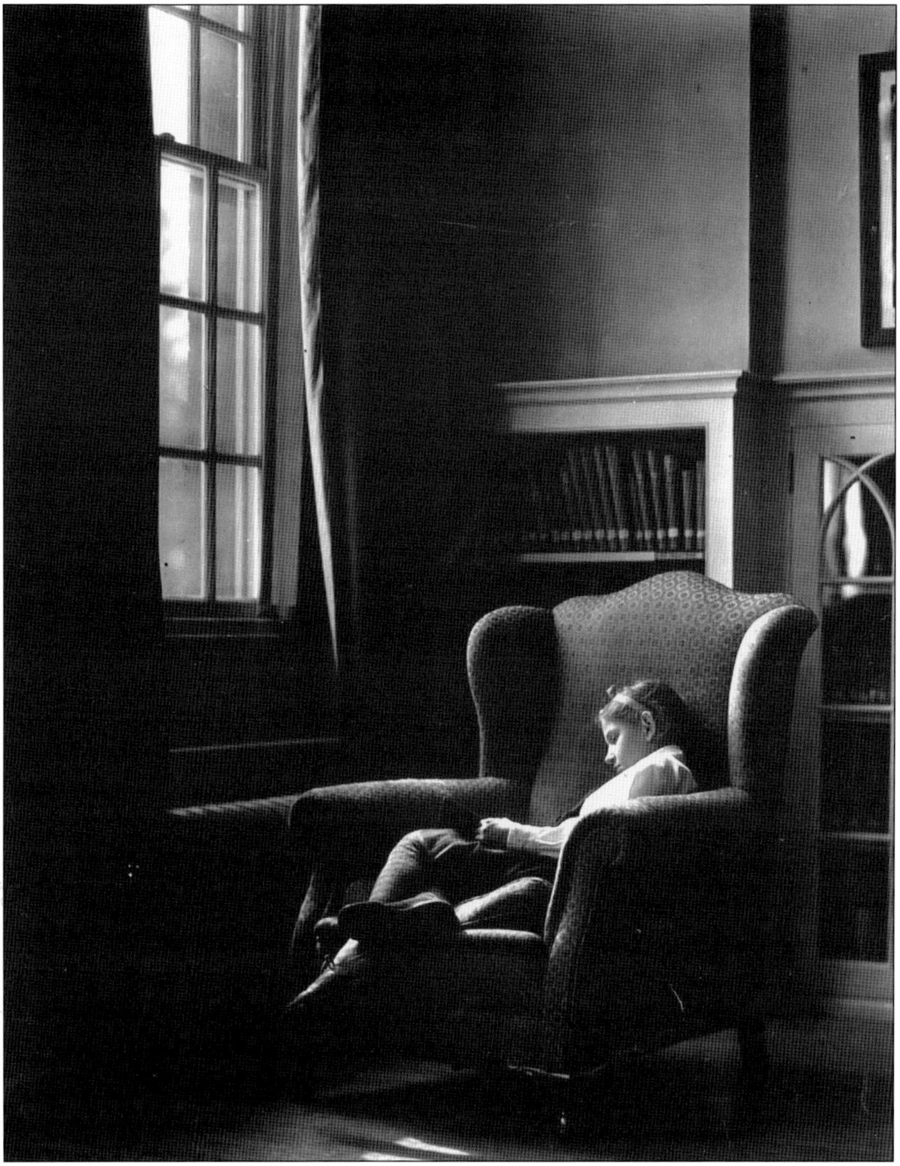

**Simplicity and Tranquility.** Quaker pedagogy places a high value on simplicity and tranquility. "The multiplication of time-saving gadgets seems, paradoxically, to increase the general busyness and complexity of life," wrote Howard Brinton in 1965. "The baton of some invisible conductor seems to be gradually increasing the tempo of life. The solution, as the sages and seers of all the great religions have pointed out, is not to increase our attainments but to decrease our desires; in other words, to follow the path of simplicity." Paul Lacey, in 1998, added, "When an object or a practice reduces the clutter and unnecessary business in our lives, at no unreasonable added cost, so we have more time and energy for what we think is worth doing, when our lives are so filled by satisfying work and recreation that fads, styles, and trivial amusements have no attractions, when we can enjoy living with less so that others can have enough, we are living simply." In this photograph, a young Westtown School student enjoys a quiet moment with a book in the school library in 1930. (Courtesy of Westtown School.)

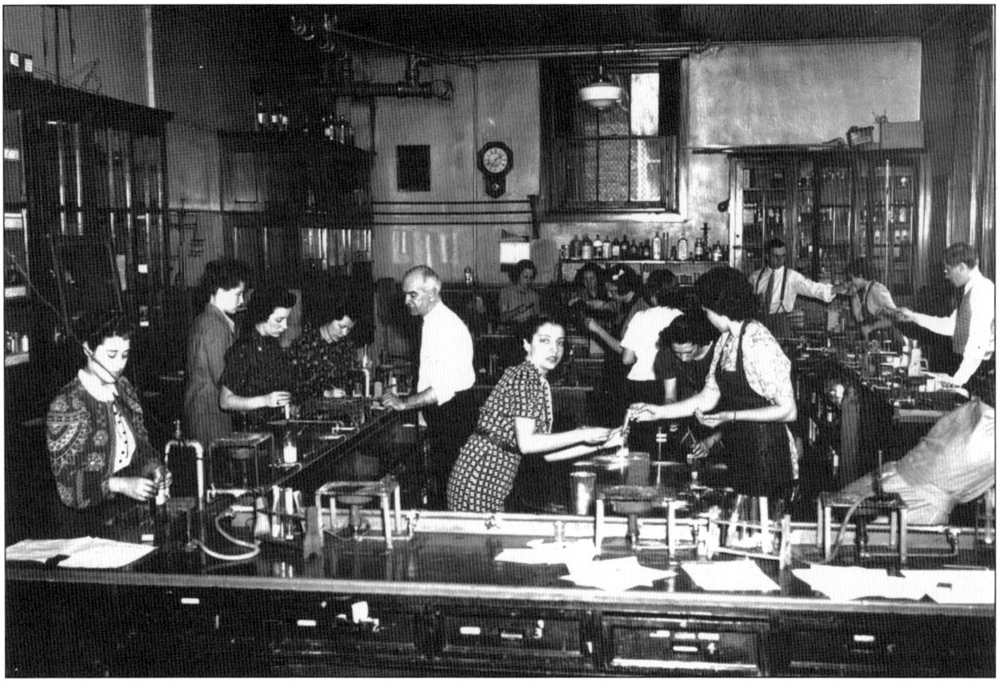

**Equality.** Master Lewis Cruikshank conducts a chemistry laboratory at Friends Select School. Male teachers were referred to as masters, and female teachers were known as teachers, until the late 1970s. Now students refer to all teachers as teacher, followed by the person's first name, demonstrating respect for their position. The testimony of equality informs the common practice at many Friends schools of all members of the school community addressing each other by first name. (Courtesy of Friends Select School.)

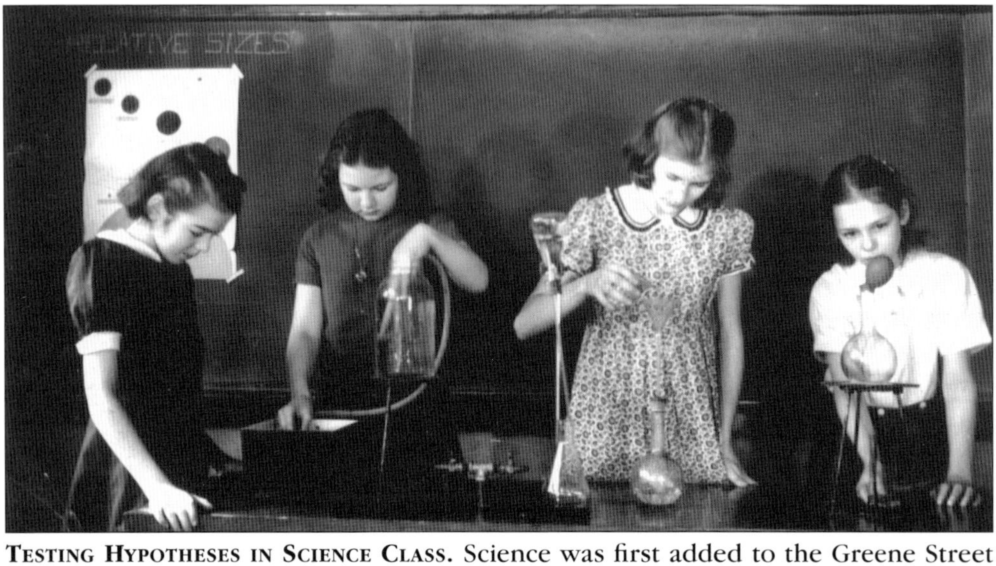

**Testing Hypotheses in Science Class.** Science was first added to the Greene Street Friends School curriculum in 1936. Learning from inquiry shifts the educational emphasis from the product, or "right answer," to the process, developing critical thinking skills and broadening students' engagement with the content. (Courtesy of Greene Street Friends School.)

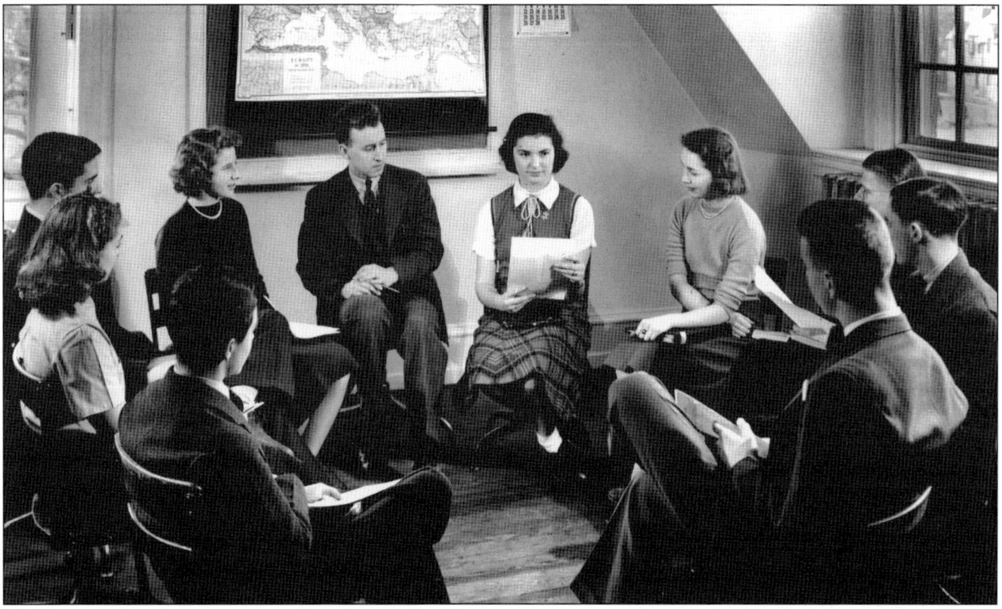

**Circles are the Norm.** In this 1939 Friends' Central School English class, teacher Robert J. Cadigan, under the map, leads a discussion in a circle—during a period of time when most classes in other schools were taught in rows of chairs, often bolted to the floor. (Courtesy of Friends' Central School.)

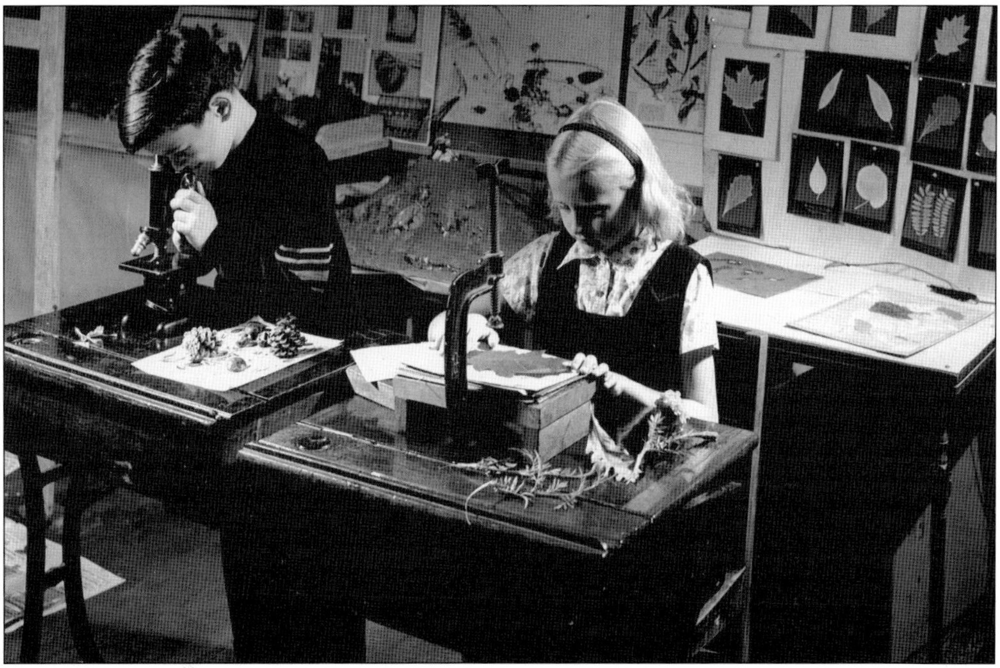

**Shared Discovery.** Friends' Central School students in this 1940s science class pore over leaves, ferns, and acorns. A central tenet of the Religious Society of Friends is the notion that truth is continually revealed and that every person has a shared part in discovering it. The implications of unfolding truth lead to learning that is open to the engagement of the spirit and the mind. (Courtesy of Friends' Central School.)

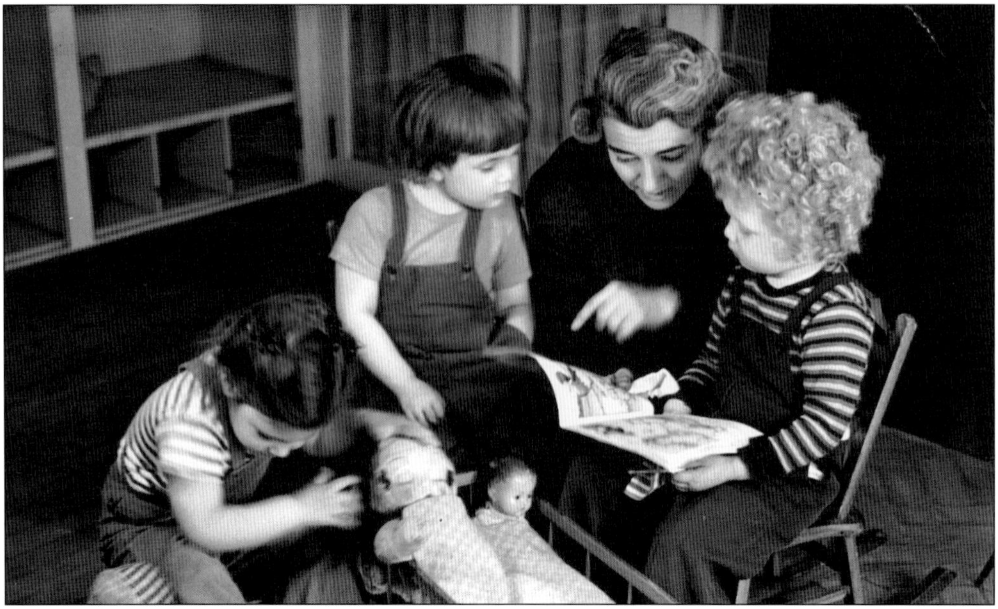

**An Early Prekindergarten Class.** In 1939–1940, Pearl Kerr started Greene Street Friends School's first prekindergarten class for four-year-olds in the meetinghouse, one of the first such programs in Philadelphia. "She directed her students' energies in the right channels," writes Bruce Jones, "and by the end of a year with her, young children had learned to play, sing, work and rest happily with their peers." (Courtesy of Greene Street Friends School.)

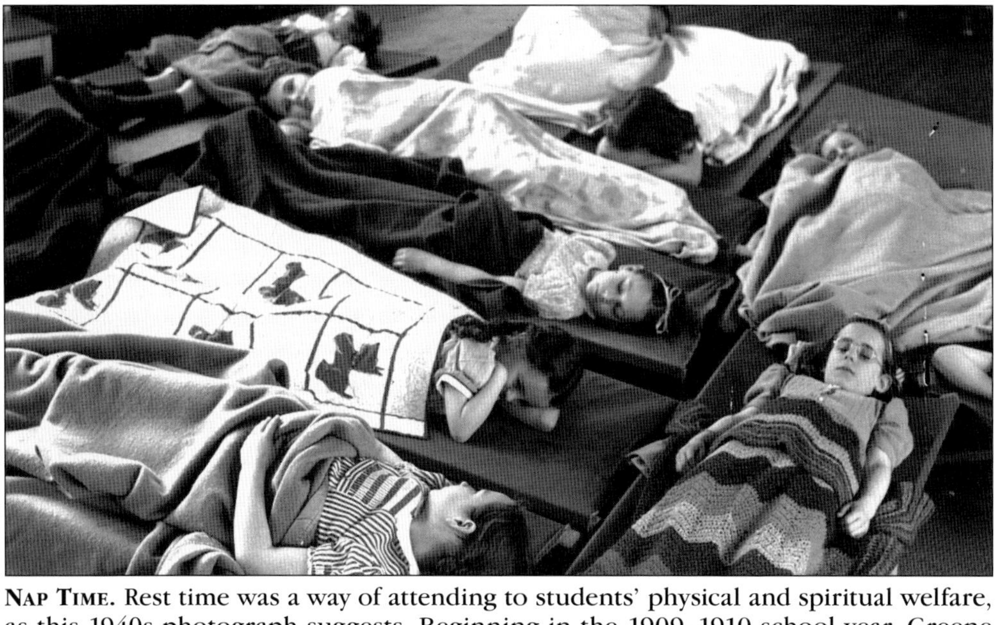

**Nap Time.** Rest time was a way of attending to students' physical and spiritual welfare, as this 1940s photograph suggests. Beginning in the 1909–1910 school year, Greene Street engaged a physician to provide yearly physical exams. Friends schools believe in supporting a child's physical, moral, and social development. Developing "a sense of the value of health" and "a sense of social responsibility" were program highlights in the 1936–1937 admission brochure. (Courtesy of Greene Street Friends School.)

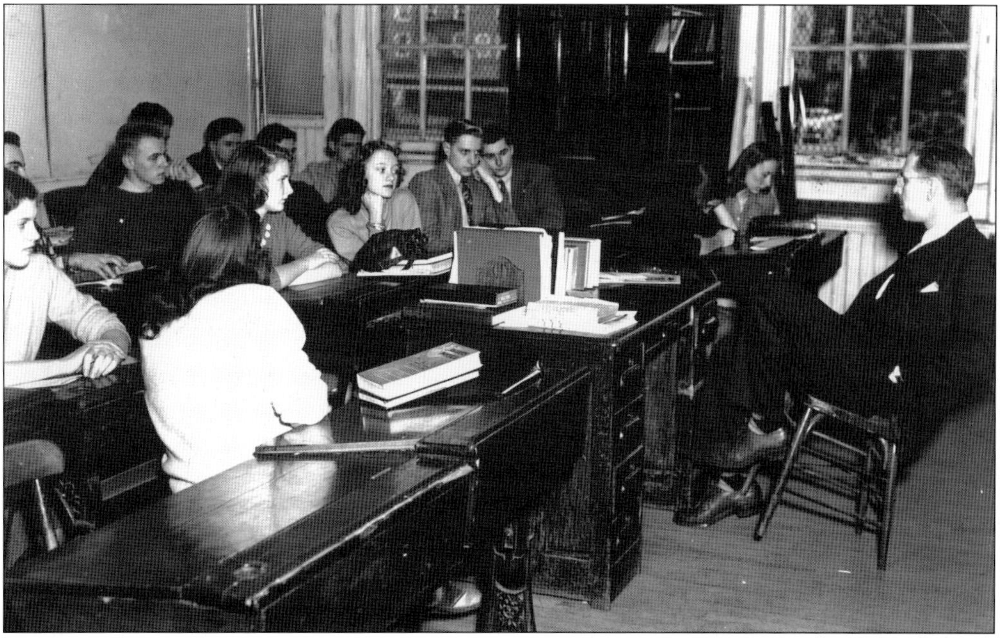

**A Vigorous Pursuit of Knowledge.** A hallmark of Quaker education is an open exchange of ideas, where every person's voice is honored. In this 1940s photograph, Friends Select School headmaster Harris Haviland leads a discussion in English class. (Courtesy of Friends Select School.)

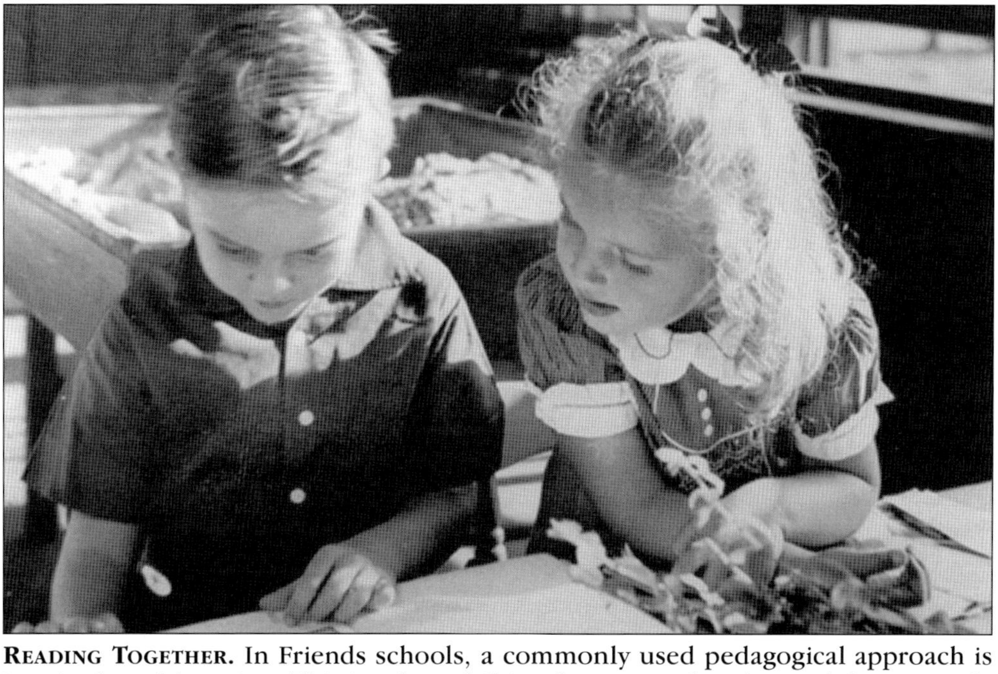

**Reading Together.** In Friends schools, a commonly used pedagogical approach is inquiry-based learning. This involves shifting from a teacher-directed, lecture-style approach to a child-centered, inquiry-based approach. In this 1950s photograph, two Germantown Friends School kindergarten students share a book. (Courtesy of Germantown Friends School.)

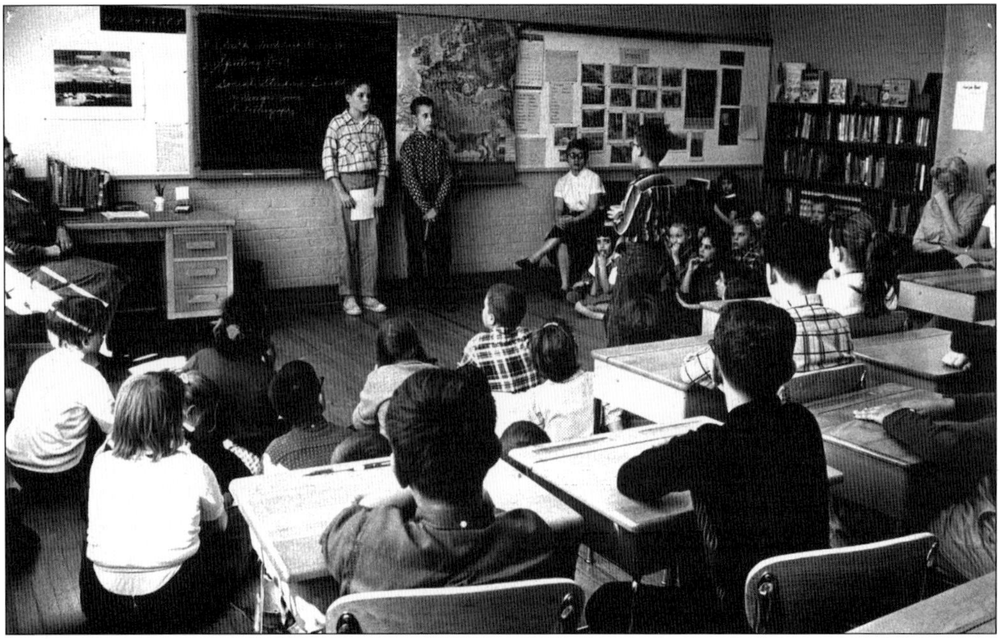

**Developing Student Leadership.** During the 1950s, under the direction of principal Reba Lammey, Frankford Friends School Student Council meetings were held for students in third through sixth grades. Reba Lammey said it was "really the governing body of the school." It established "rules for the playground and lunchroom," and the council operated on an "odd mixture of Roberts' Rules of Order and Quaker practice." (Courtesy of Frankford Friends School.)

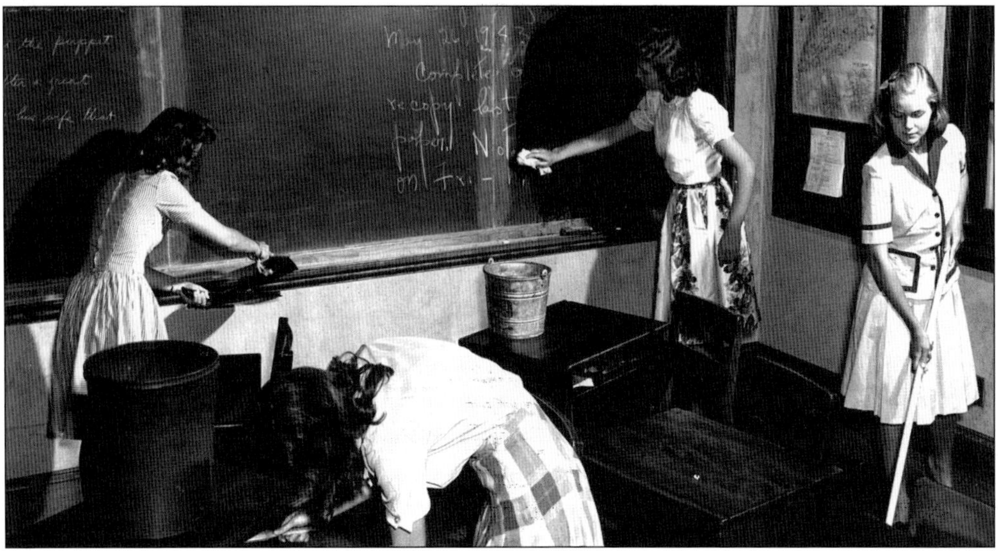

**Value of Hard Work.** In this 1950 photograph, girls at George School are performing their cooperative work assignment for the semester. Jobs ranged from cleaning a classroom, to working in the horse barn, to filing reports in the dean's office, to shelving books in the library. Every student also performed shifts in the kitchen and dining room. Still a part of George School life today, co-op work is a Quaker way of teaching students to value honest labor. (Courtesy of George School.)

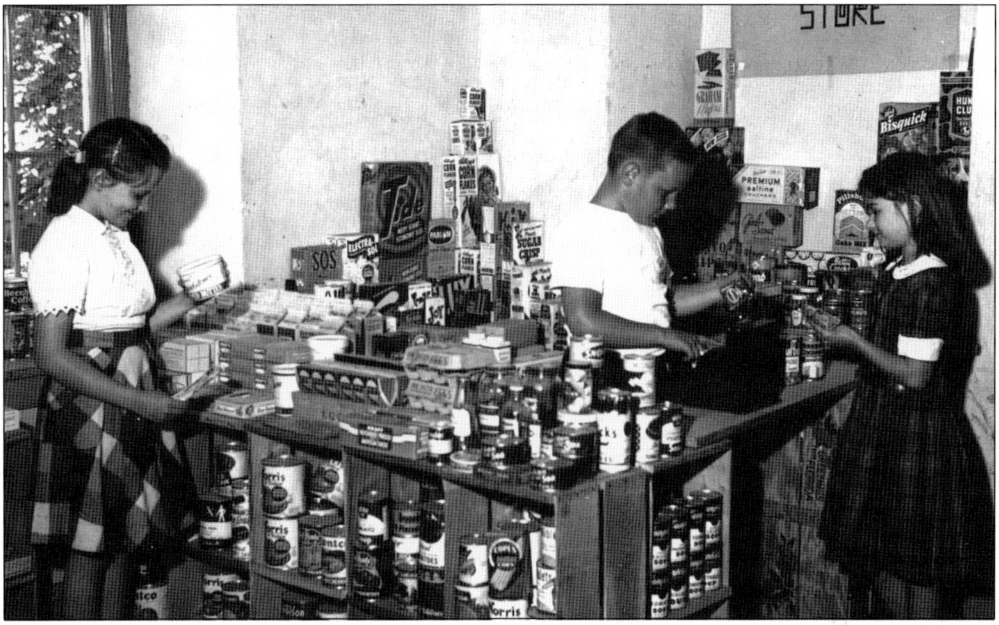


**TANGIBLE MATH.** The Friendly Store at Plymouth Meeting Friends School, pictured here in 1956, illustrates a hands-on, experiential approach that allows children to interact with and learn math concepts in tangible ways. (Courtesy of Plymouth Meeting Friends School.)

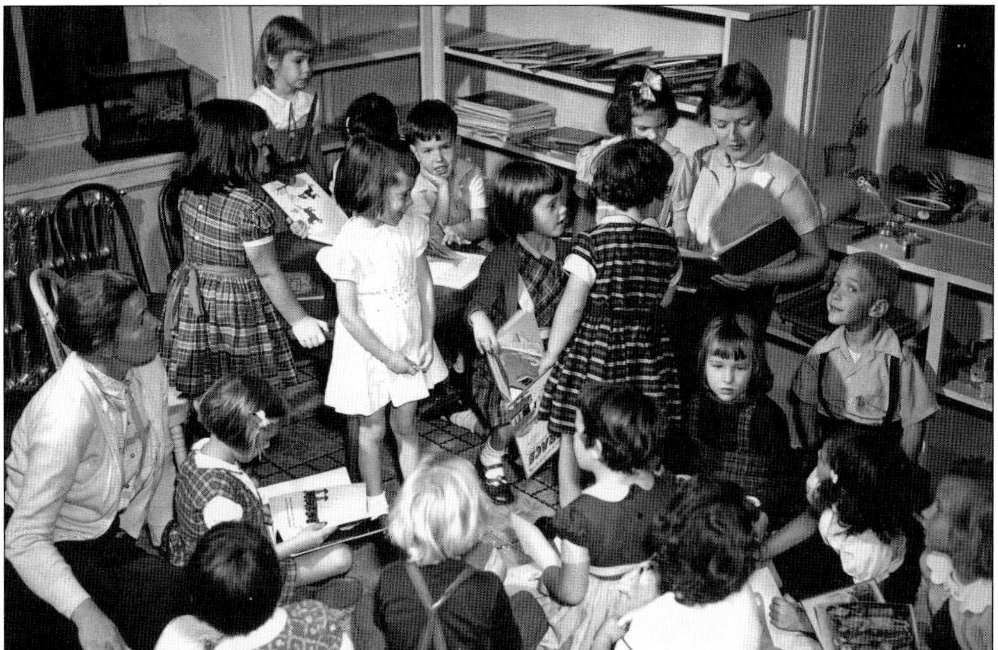

**EAGER YOUNG READERS.** As a way to develop critical thinking skills, Friends schools engage students with reflective and elaborative questions, or queries. The inquiry process engages students in observation, reflection, and then often a co-construction of ideas. This 1950s kindergarten class at Abington Friends School is an early example of inquiry-based instruction. (Courtesy of Abington Friends School.)

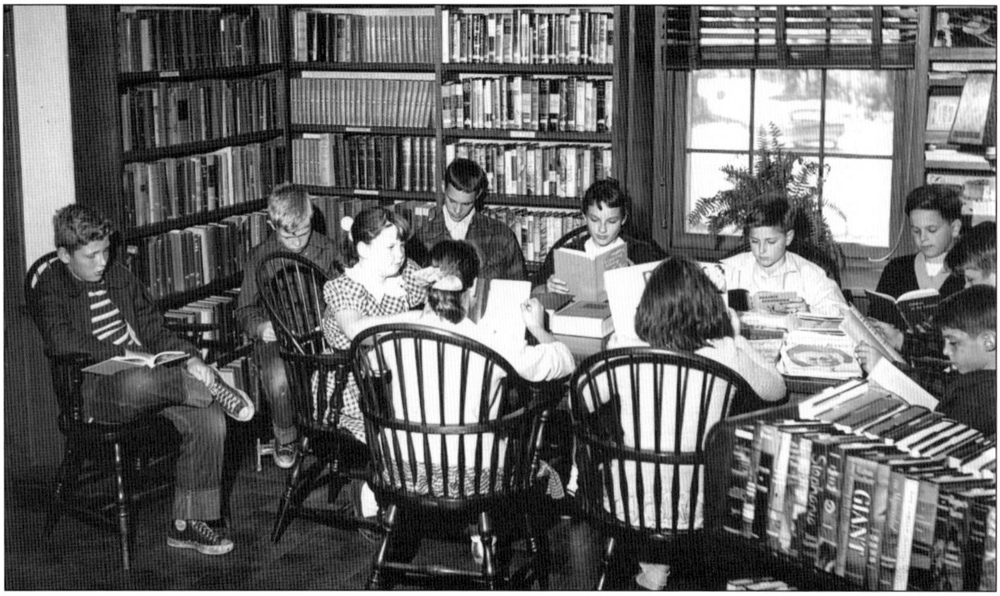

**Respectful Relationships.** A culture of respect permeates Friends schools. A 1998 study by the Friends Council on Education found that bullying, put-downs, and hurtful words are carefully dealt with, not with automatic consequences but with reaching out to those who are involved. All people and all groups are worthy of respect. These students in the William Jeanes Memorial Library at Plymouth Meeting Friends School enjoy a respectful moment in the library, around 1956. (Courtesy of Plymouth Meeting Friends School.)

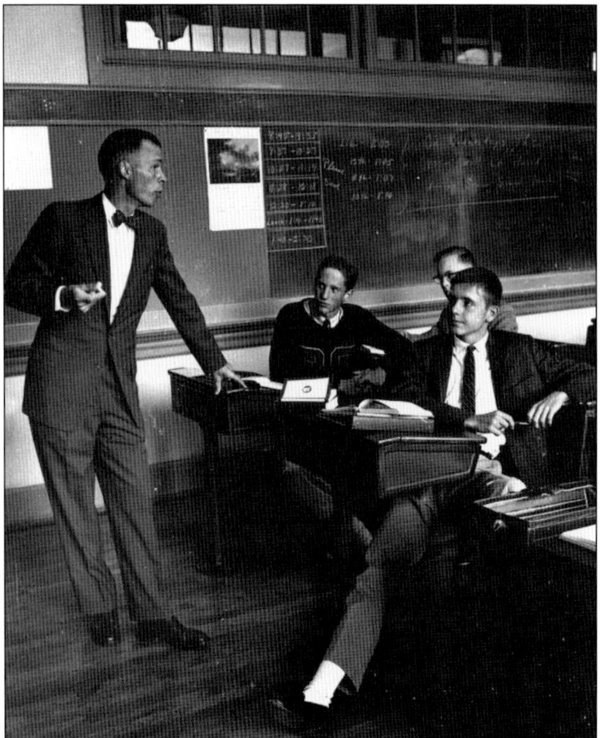

**Teaching to the Whole of Life.** Teacher-coaches have the strength and the skill to inspire young people year after year. Here M. Albert (Bert) Linton Jr. conducts a mathematics class in 1960. Like most faculty at Friends schools, Linton had additional responsibilities outside of the classroom, which included coaching soccer and golf. In this way, faculty and students got to know one another outside purely academic settings. (Courtesy of the William Penn Charter School.)

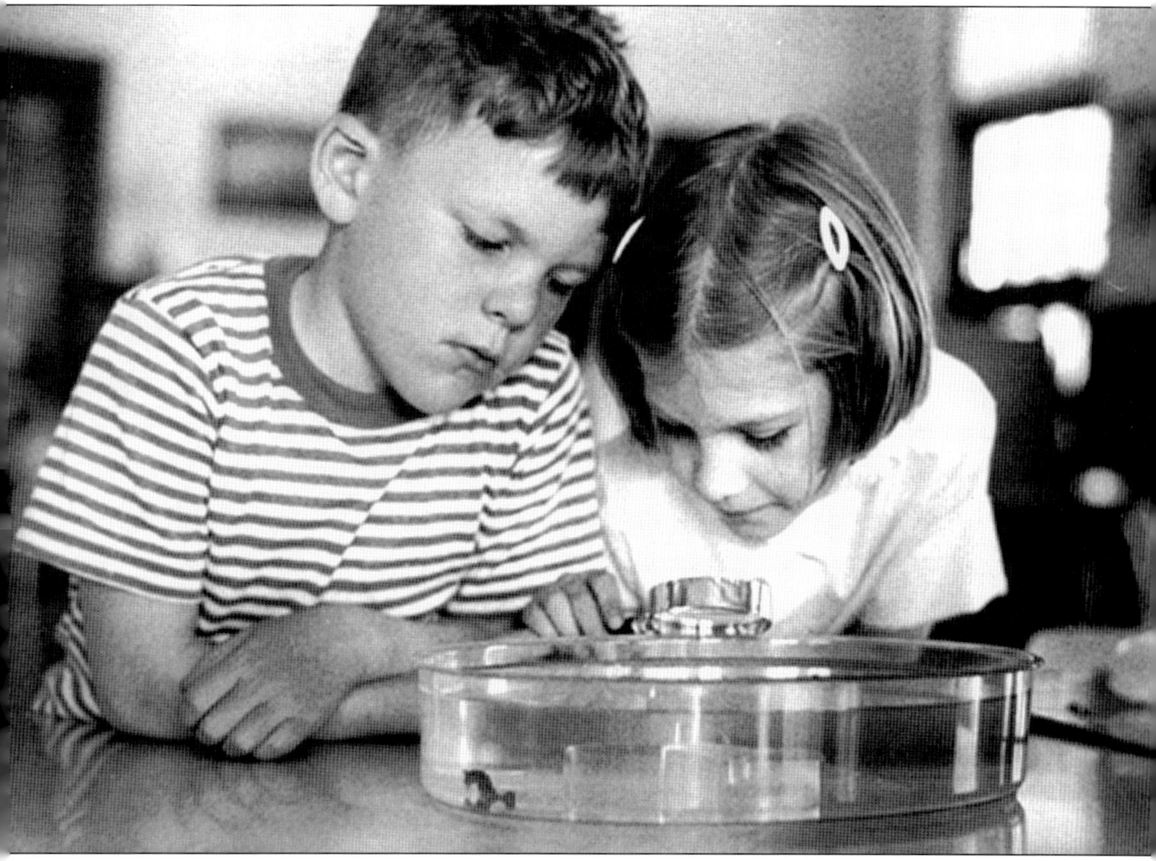

**The Power of Discovery.** In this 1962 photograph, a girl and a boy at the Germantown Friends School peer through a magnifying glass and into the contents of a petri dish. Vital to Friends school pedagogy is an inquiry process that leads to genuine insights and new ways of looking at the world. Rather than teaching the answers, the teacher's responsibility is to raise inspiring questions and create a space for learning that engages students in their own process of inquiry and discovery. Quakers trust that the sacred can be revealed through the physical world. Students develop the capacity for silent attention and observation during science experiences. Paul Lacey writes, "The child who learns how to sit still while waiting for a bird to land or a deer to emerge from the thicket is laying the foundation for greeting the sacred, for centering outside the self, for knowing herself as part of a world of beauty and order, as well as for learning how to collect data." (Courtesy of Germantown Friends School.)

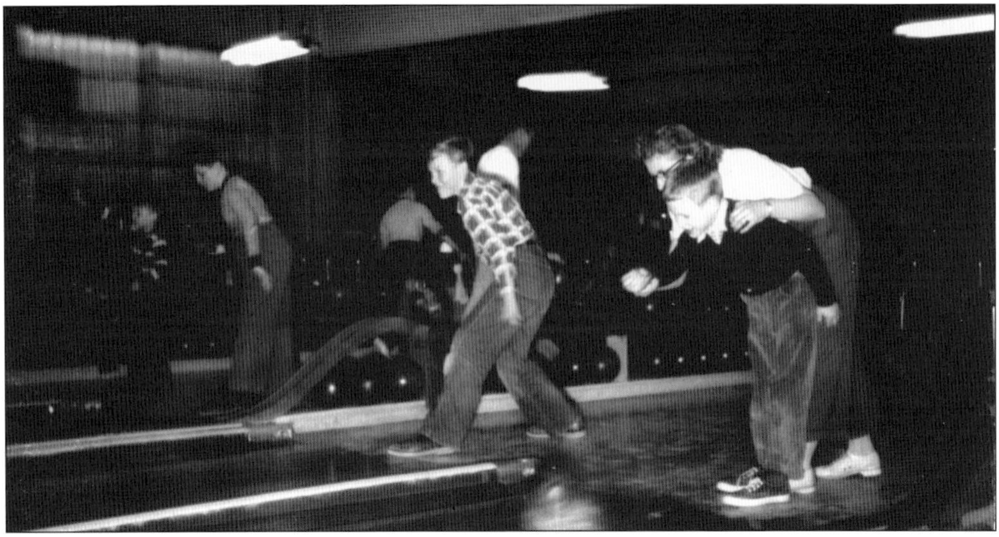

**Bowling for Community.** For many years at Plymouth Meeting Friends School, bowling was a regular and popular activity. These students, pictured at the local bowling alley in 1956, illustrate the school's aim of developing the individual child physically, as well as socially, academically, emotionally, and spiritually. (Courtesy of Plymouth Meeting Friends School.)

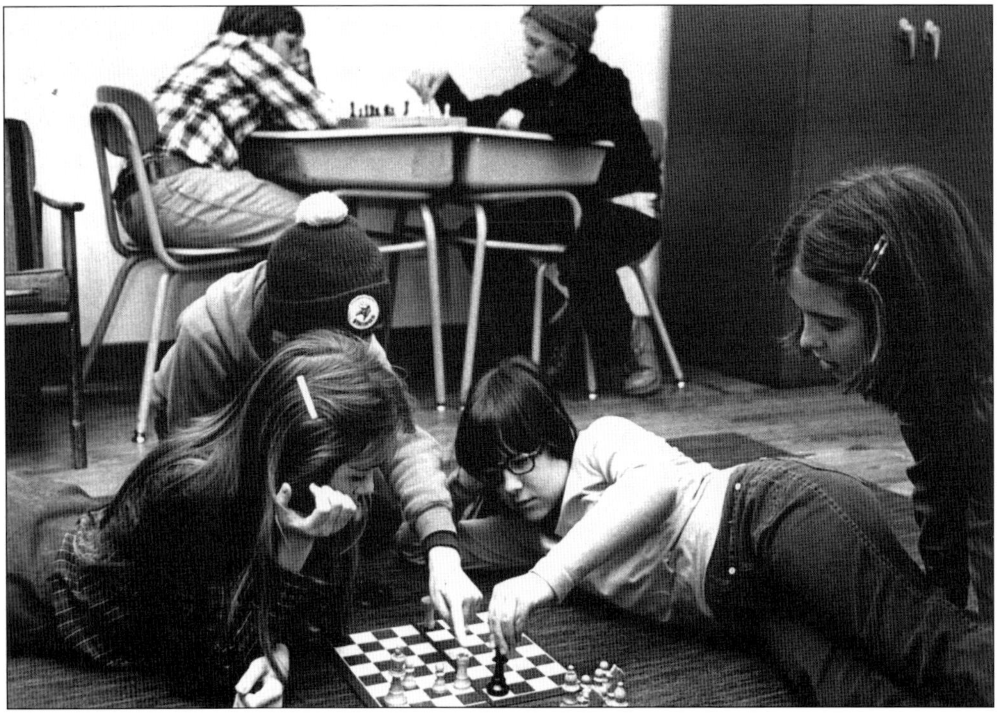

**Clubs for All.** Special interests, such as this chess club at the Frankford Friends School, were promoted to foster intellectual curiosity and growth. Students from fourth through sixth grades participated, allowing cross-grade friendships to flourish. It is common at many Friends schools for every person on campus to know one another by first name. (Courtesy of Frankford Friends School.)

**INSPIRING WONDER.** A Friends school alumnus, remembering his science teacher, wrote, "He could explain scientific data with magnificent clarity; but it wasn't filling our heads with facts that he had in mind. We remember a strange silence that he liked to keep, as if the important facts of Nature lay beyond the reach of names and explanations. His Silence was a way of inspiring wonder within us." In this photograph, Brian MacInnes, a 1970 William Penn Charter School graduate, conducts a chemistry experiment. (Courtesy of the William Penn Charter School.)

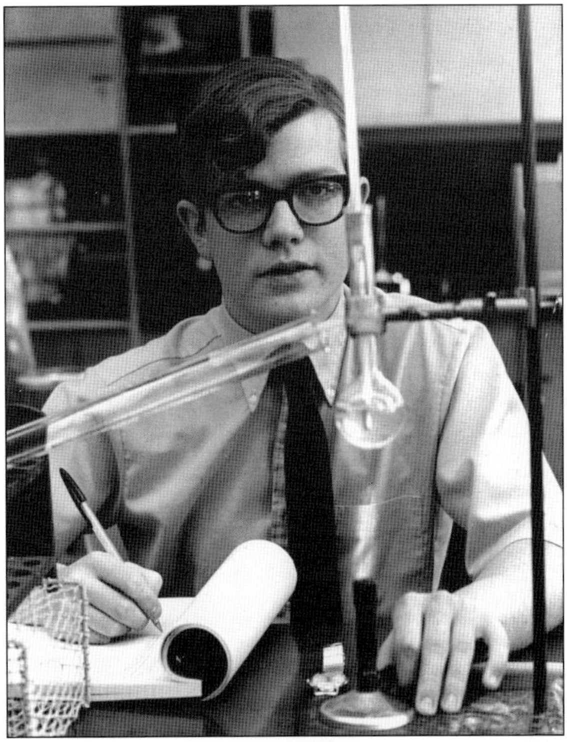

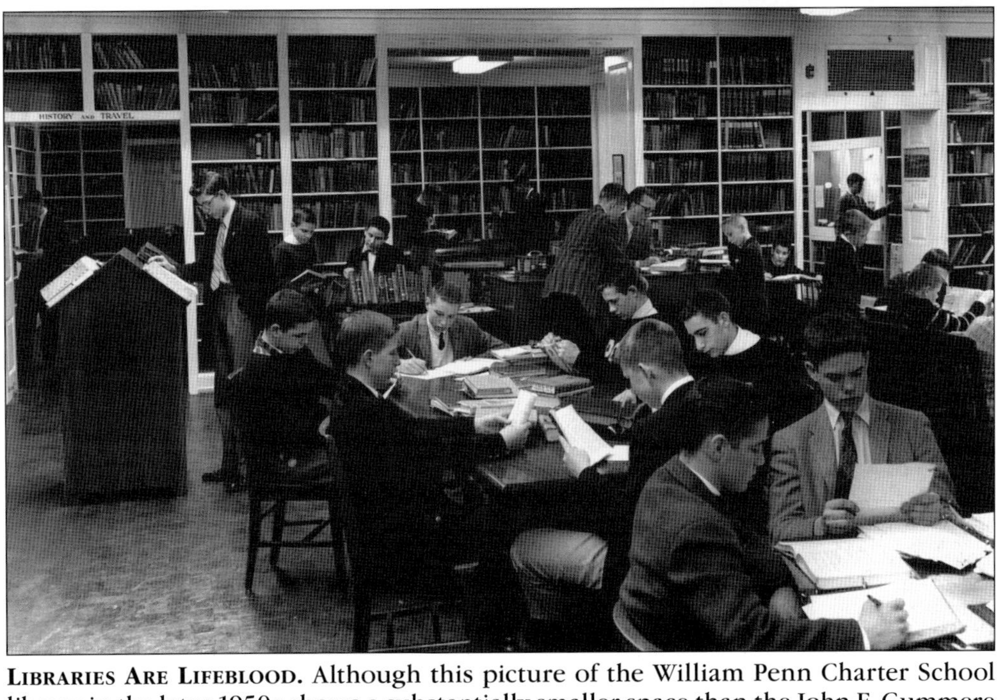

**LIBRARIES ARE LIFEBLOOD.** Although this picture of the William Penn Charter School library in the later 1950s shows a substantially smaller space than the John F. Gummere Library that replaced it in 1967, it does not change the fact that the library was and still is a central place in the educational development of students. (Courtesy of the William Penn Charter School.)

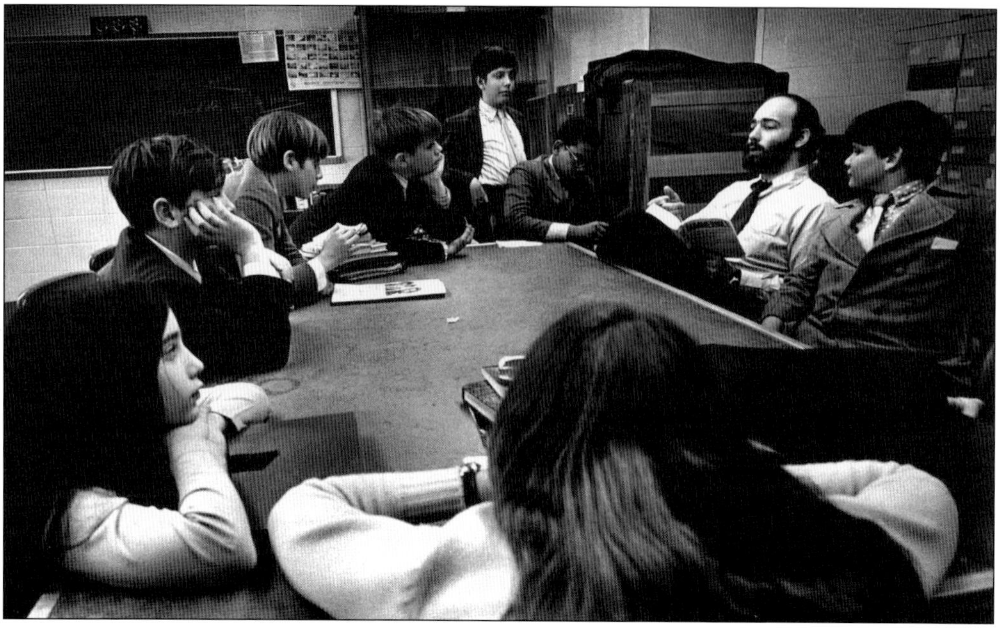

**Meeting for Learning.** Parker Palmer describes Quaker pedagogy as a "meeting for learning," in which "the individual is always in relationship, and knowledge emerges in dialogue." In this 1969 photograph, master Eric Berg teaches fourth graders, shortly after Friends Select School moved into its new building at Seventeenth Street and Benjamin Franklin Parkway. (Courtesy of Friends Select School.)

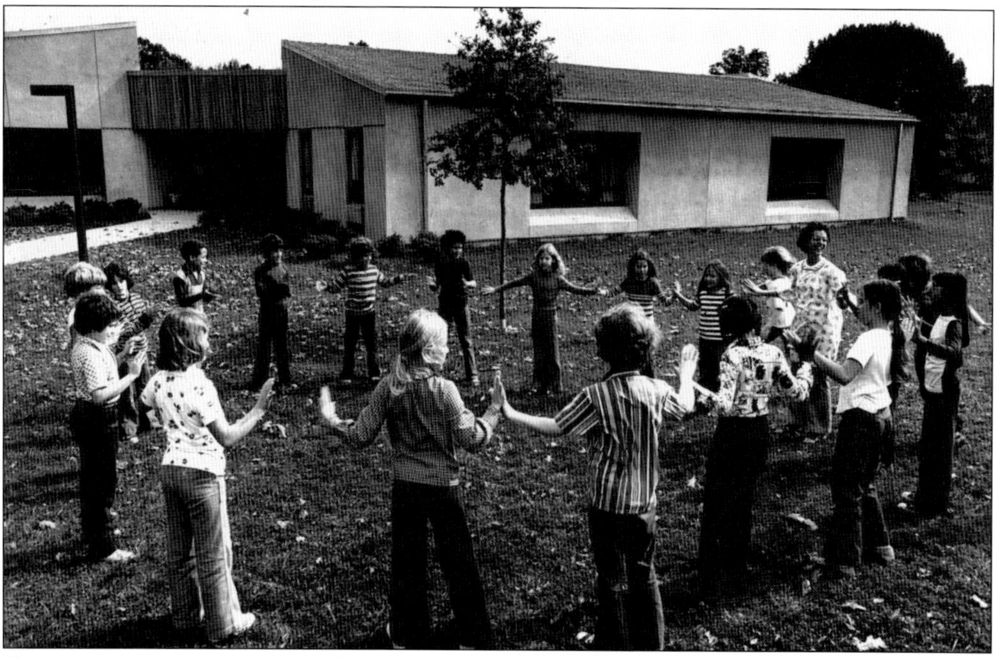

**Outdoor Music Class.** Whether it is to pursue an experiential-learning endeavor or merely to enjoy the natural beauty of the environment, teachers at Friends schools often take their students outdoors, as in this mid-1970s photograph of Abington Friends School students. (Courtesy of Abington Friends School.)

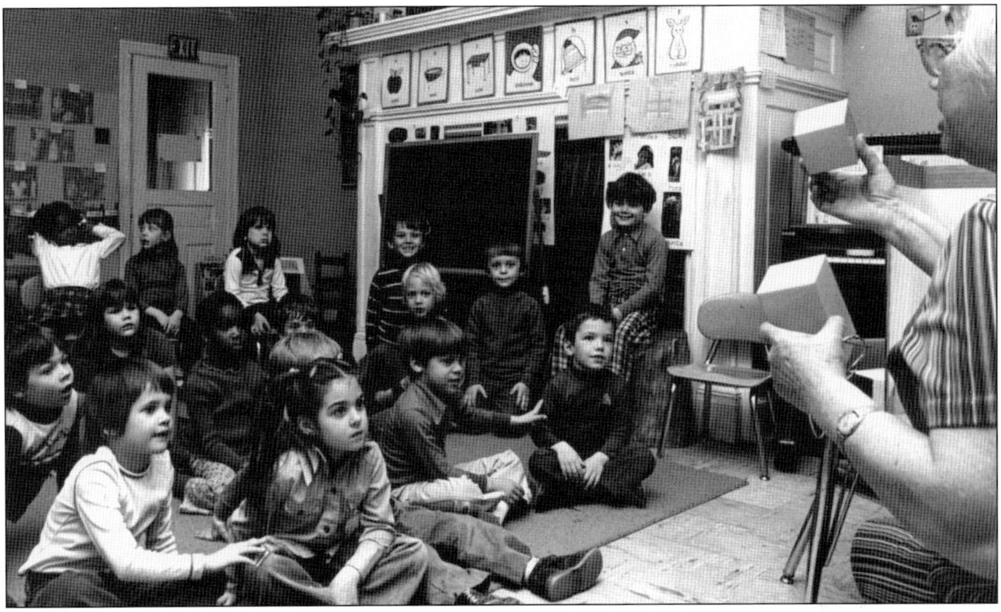

**TEACHING WITH PASSION.** Teachers in Friends schools are encouraged to bring their life experiences and passions into their work. In this 1970s photograph, Frankford Friends School teacher Helen Satterthwaite gives a science lesson for the kindergarten class. Satterthwaite was known to draw upon her experiences and artifacts from her world travels with every class, explaining how different cultures were influenced by climate and geography. (Courtesy of Frankford Friends School.)

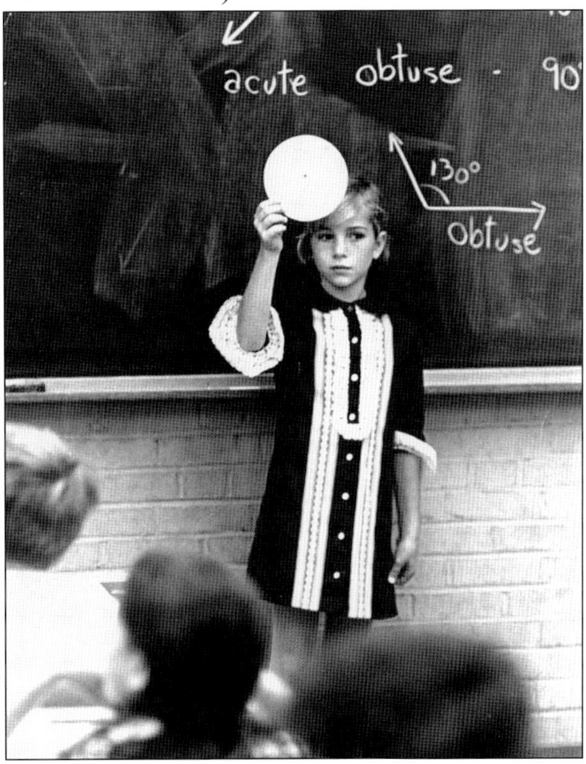


**INTRODUCTORY GEOMETRY LESSON.** An acute observer will recognize that learning is never obtuse when it is child-centered and set within a learning environment that involves collective truth seeking. In this 1970s photograph, a Frankford Friends School student presents a geometry lesson at the board. Eric Johnson writes, "In a Friends school, as in Meeting for Worship, wisdom can come from any corner in the room." (Courtesy of Frankford Friends School.)

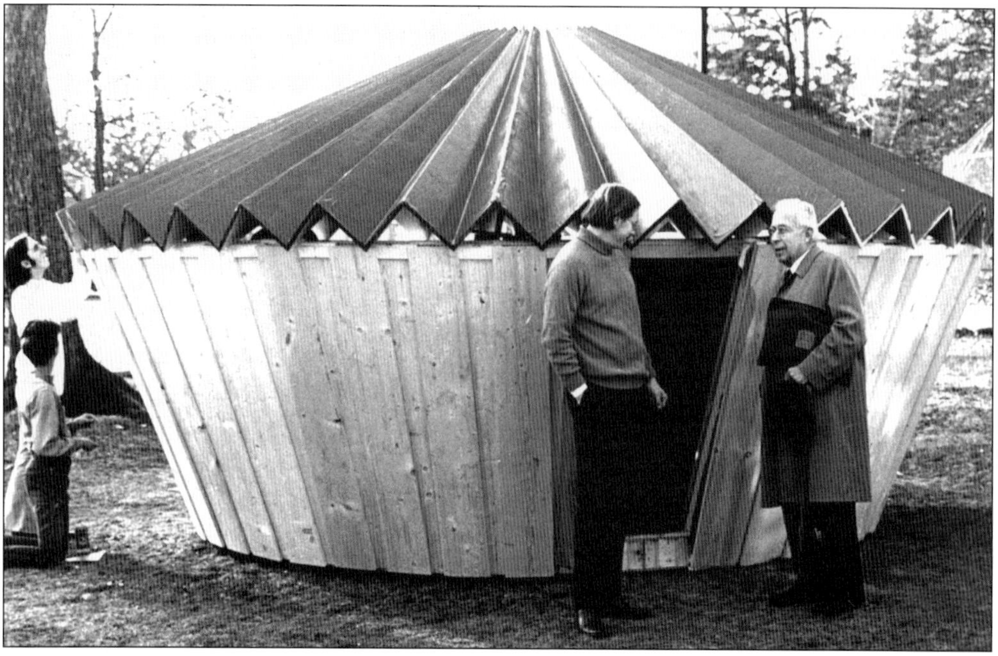

**The Yurt, an Experiment.** "The true method of knowledge," writes the English poet William Blake, "is experimentation"—an idea that resonates well with Quaker pedagogy. In contrast to the usual classroom and rows of desks, the yurt in this 1979 photograph provided a round classroom, encouraging an entirely different set of relationships than the traditional format. Here English teacher Myron Arms (left) explains the concept to board member Richard R. Wood. (Courtesy of the William Penn Charter School.)

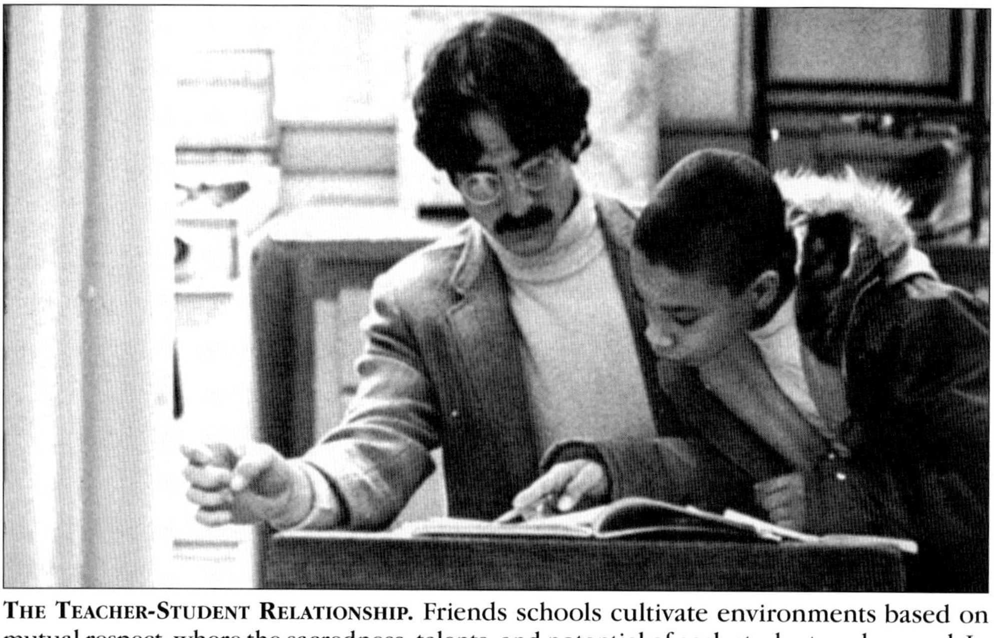

**The Teacher-Student Relationship.** Friends schools cultivate environments based on mutual respect, where the sacredness, talents, and potential of each student are honored. In this 1977 photograph, a Germantown Friends School student works with Tom Scattergood, teacher of history and English. (Courtesy of Germantown Friends School.)

**The Joy of Learning.** This photograph of James Lemonick, a 1976 William Penn Charter School graduate, was taken in the early 1970s in a middle school social studies class. Small class sizes make possible participation by all students in daily class discussions in all disciplines. (Courtesy of the William Penn Charter School.)

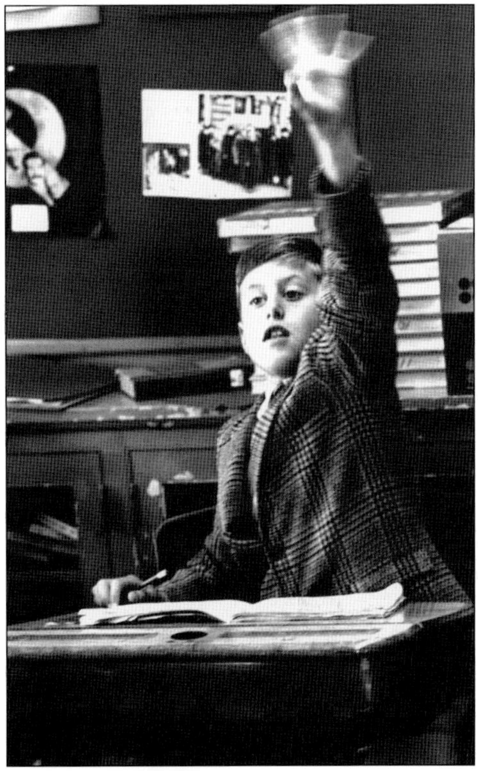

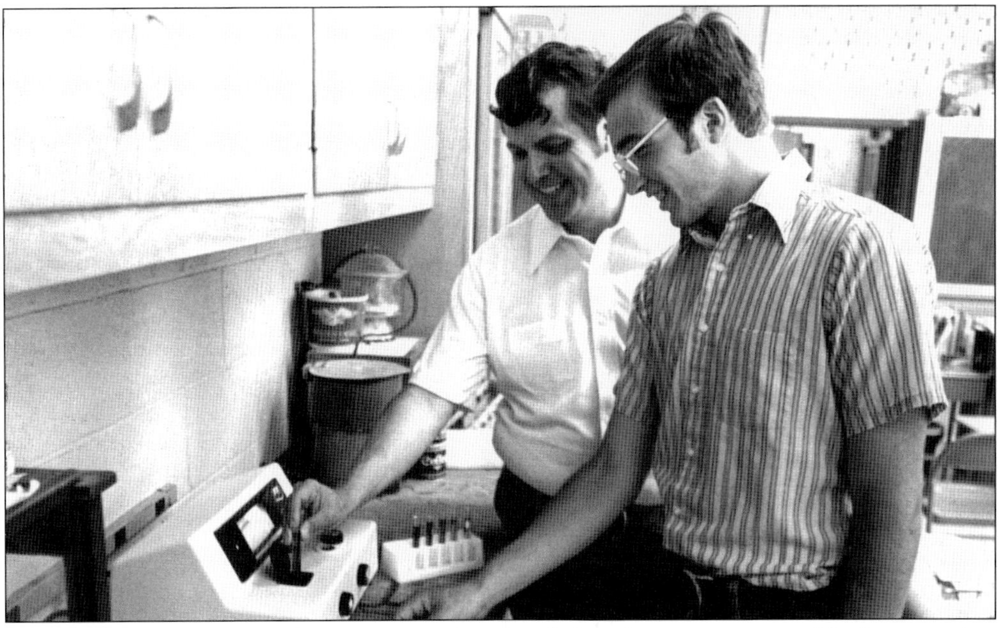

**Your Life's Work.** Here Abington Friends School chemistry teacher Carl Brehmer assists upper school student Nelson File with an experiment. Abington Friends School graduate and now professional writer Bill Kashatus said Carl Brehmer taught him that "a love for and a genuine commitment to your life's work is more important than society's standards of prestige or affluence." (Courtesy of Abington Friends School.)

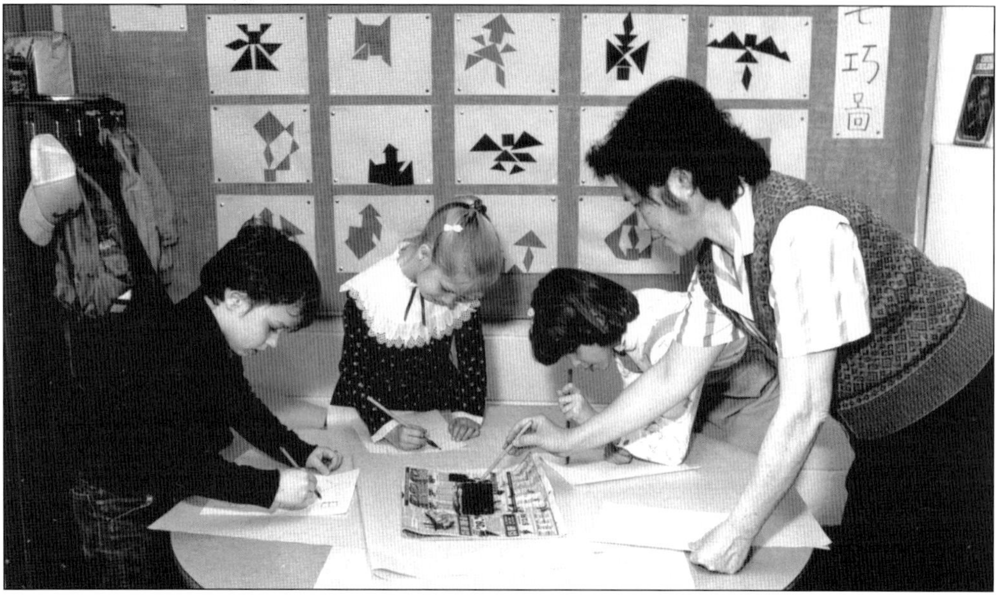

**Beauty and Discipline.** Tsu-Shan Chung, born and raised in China, shows her first-grade class at Frankford Friends School the beauty of and the discipline needed for the art of calligraphy in the 1980s. Learning about and appreciating diverse cultures is an important part of Friends schools' curricula. (Courtesy of Frankford Friends School.)

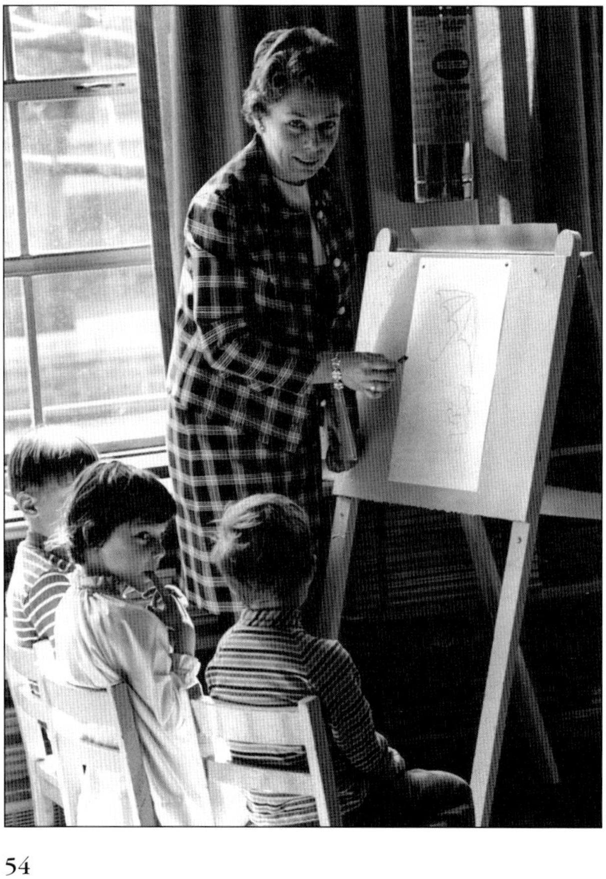

**A Call to Teach.** Paul Lacey writes, "In every generation there are people who are called to teach as ministry." Joan Costello, a devoted and spirited teacher, is pictured here with kindergarten students in 1960. (Courtesy of the William Penn Charter School.)

# *Four*

# Community and Collaboration

*The important affinities between Quakerism and various philosophies of education [is that they] all spring from an idealism about human possibilities and a conviction that individuals grow into their best selves when supported and sustained by a healthy community.*

—Paul Lacey, Quaker educator

Quakers believe that the insight of the individual is tempered by the collective understanding and wisdom of the group. Alone individuals can lose sight of deeper spiritual truths; similarly, as a collective, individual contributions help to raise new insights when a community is stagnant or afraid of risks. In Friends schools, as in Friends meetings, the community is supported by the twin pillars of meeting for worship and meeting for business. These long-standing Quaker practices do more than support the classroom; they provide a pedagogical model for the role of students and teachers and the collaborative nature of the entire learning environment. Teachers and learners at Friends schools often engage together in researching and co-constructing meaning in the various curricular areas. The text or task at hand is an opportunity for the class to seek a deeper understanding through the sharing of ideas and a winnowing to the surface of the answer, or other possible answers—or even better questions. Friends schools teach students that knowledge is not fixed. Knowledge, like wisdom, is always expanding and being altered by new and changing facts and perspectives. The best way to pursue knowledge is in a community that recognizes the power of collaboration and appreciates the process of continuing revelation. The model, indeed the constitutive metaphor for the learning environment, is meeting for worship. Ideally the community is fully realized in classrooms, playing fields, theater stages—indeed, wherever students assemble. Quaker educator Thomas Farquhar calls it "worship across the curriculum"; Parker Palmer calls it "meeting for learning"; and Jane Fremon describes it as "the transcendent Spirit lies not within any one of us, but among us, transforming us daily as we live together in this meeting for learning that is our school." The images on the following pages demonstrate vibrant Friends school learning communities at work, at play, and at rest.

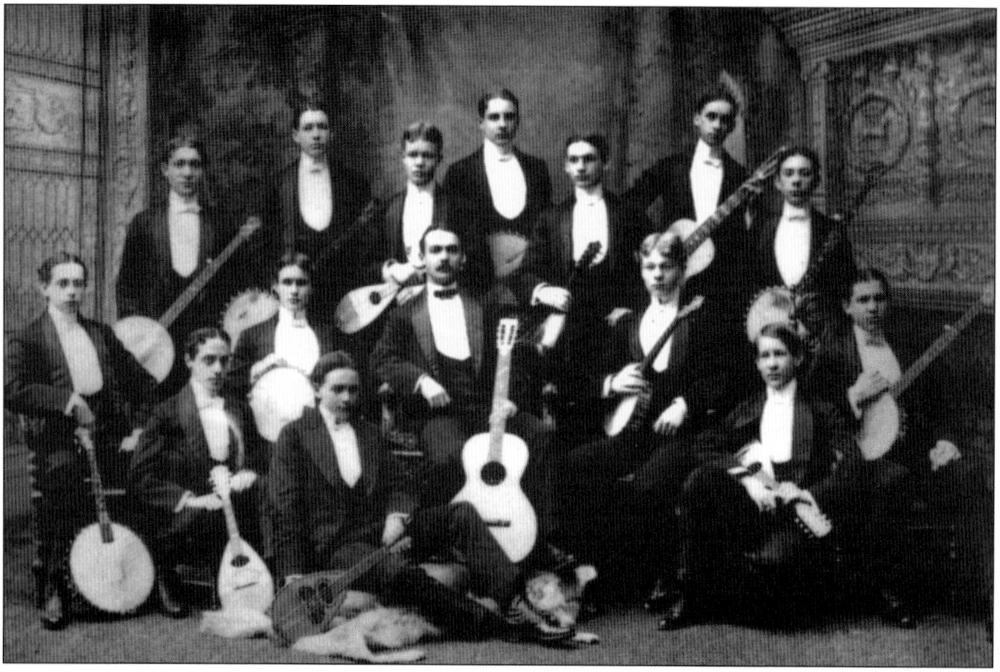

**Mandolin Music.** The Mandolin Club was one of several musical clubs that existed at the William Penn Charter School around 1900. Instruments included the violin, banjo, guitar, piano, and drums as well as various mandolins. Every March students performed in an event called the Annual Entertainment, which featured music, gymnastics, and a declamation contest. (Courtesy of the William Penn Charter School.)

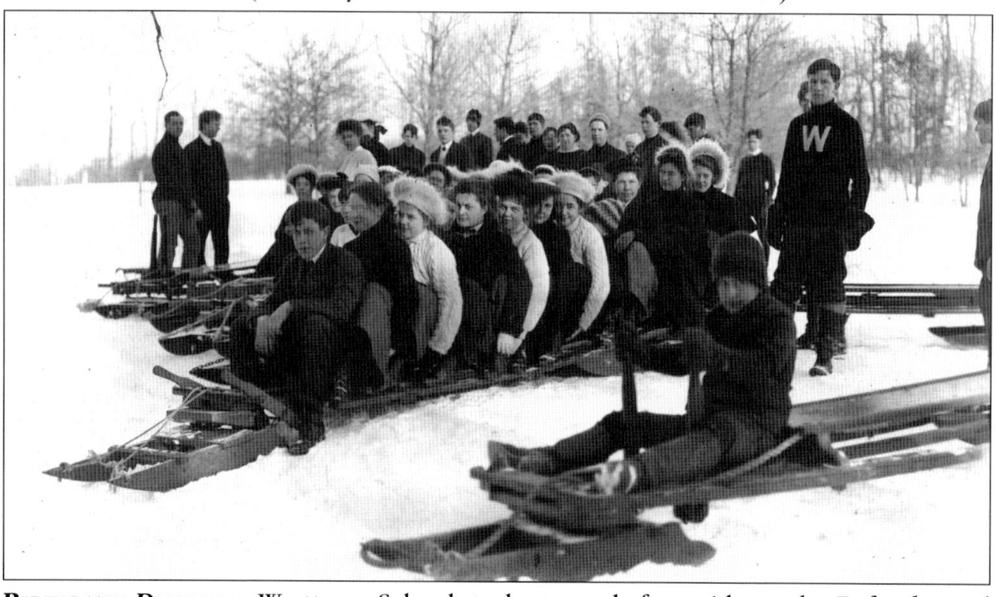

**Riding the *Defender*.** Westtown School students ready for a ride on the *Defender* and other bobsleds, winter 1903–1904. Sledding was a popular winter pastime on the rolling hills of Westtown's campus. Large wooden bobsleds carried students down the snowy track for many years until the smaller, steerable Flexible Flyer sled became popular. (Courtesy of Westtown School.)

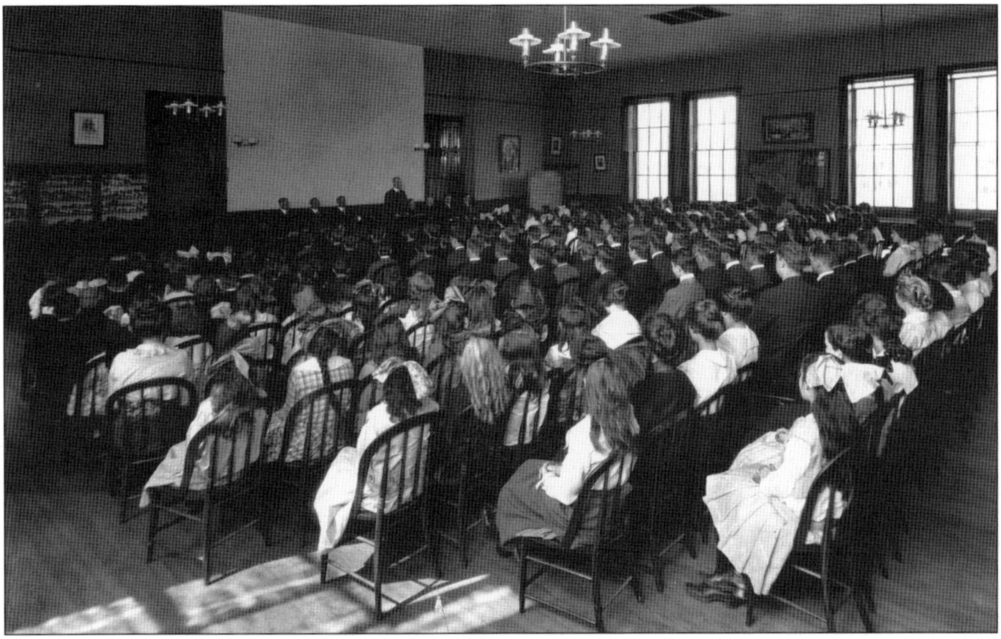

**MORNING COLLECTION.** Students gather in community to share a moment of silence, then hear announcements and prepare for the upcoming week, around 1915. Now known as devotions, these meetings continue today in all three divisions at Friends Select School. Meetings, like the one pictured here, are the building blocks of all Friends schools; they foster healthy communities. (Courtesy of Friends Select School.)

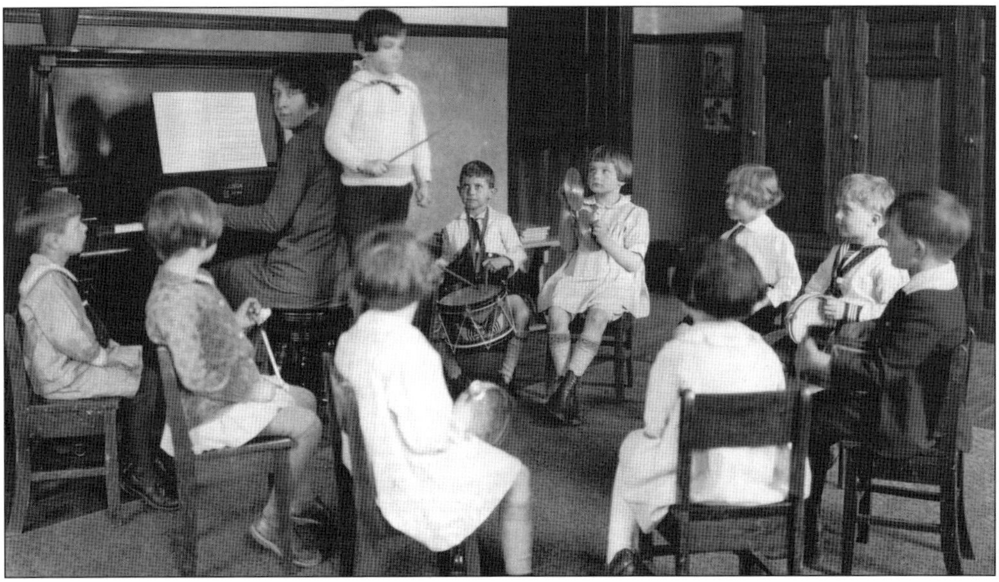

**A STUDENT CONDUCTOR.** Friends pedagogy decentralizes the role of the teacher and inspires children to seek the "teacher within." Theodora Melcher, pictured here with students at Greene Street Friends School, around 1920, was one of the best-loved teachers in the school. She inspired students by telling stories and playing music by great artists and orchestras; often she encouraged the children to act out the stories as they listened. (Courtesy of Greene Street Friends School.)

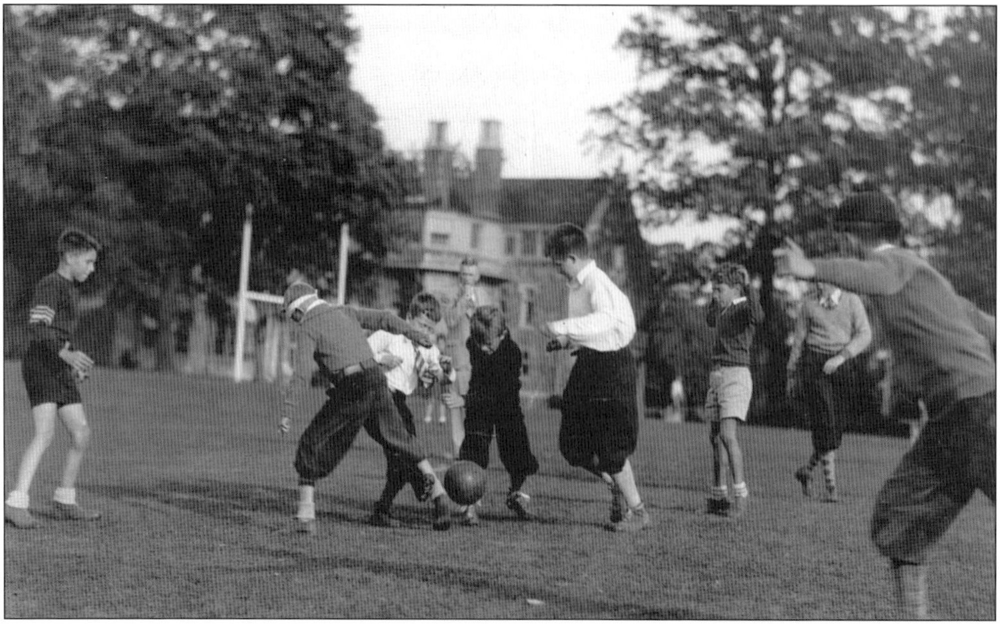

**Recreation and Play.** Collaboration rather than competition is the norm at Friends schools. Here Friends' Central Middle School students enjoy a game of soccer while a teacher looks on in the 1930s. Notice the range of apparel, from gym clothes to dangling ties. (Courtesy of Friends' Central School.)

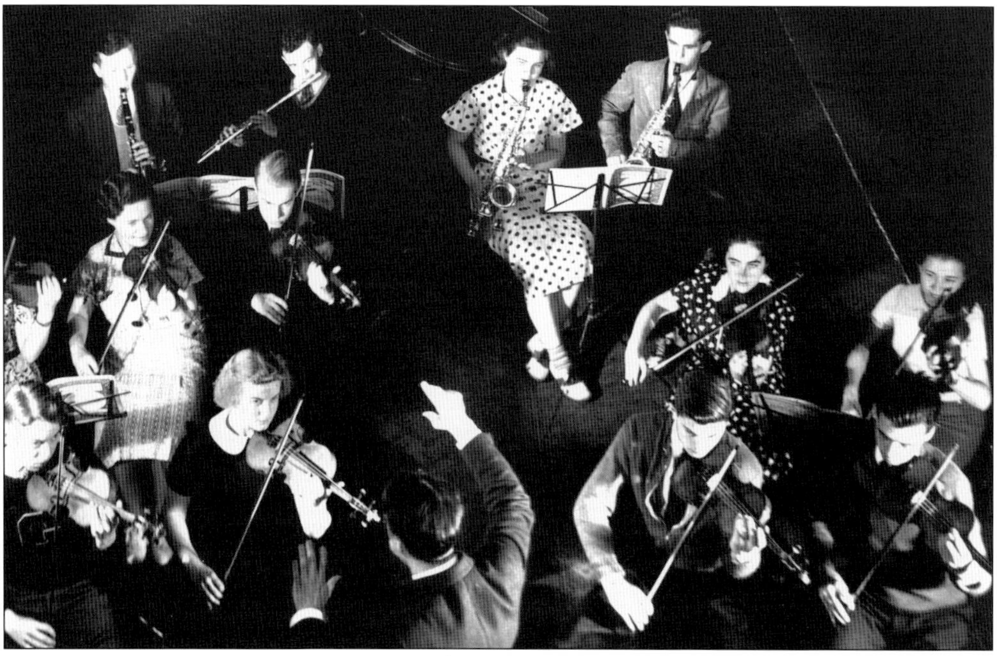

**The George School Orchestra.** Friends schools are proud of their commitment to the arts, realizing that a mix of curricular and cocurricular endeavors help shape students' attitudes and beliefs about themselves and their community. The George School orchestra, shown here in 1937, was a popular venue for students, spurring some to pursue and establish themselves in the professional ranks. (Courtesy of George School.)

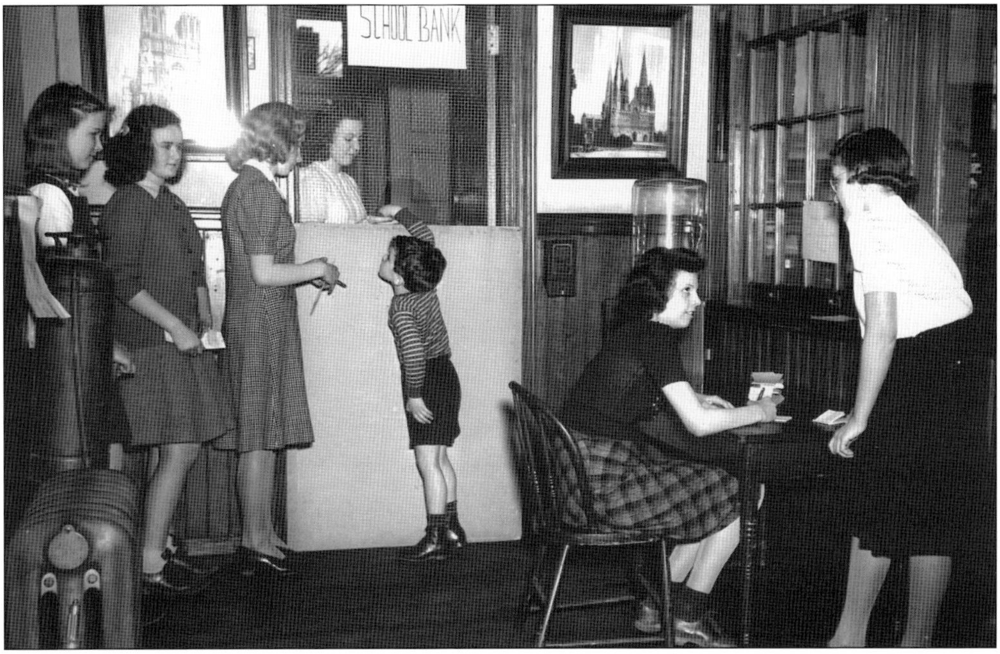

**THE SCHOOL BANK.** Friends schools seek ways of teaching personal responsibility through experiential learning across the grades. At Greene Street Friends School, the school admission brochure from 1936–1937 shows that the students learned banking skills through managing their own school supply accounts. The supply fee ($3) was deposited in the school bank; students then purchased supplies from the school store using checks from the school bank. (Courtesy of Greene Street Friends School.)

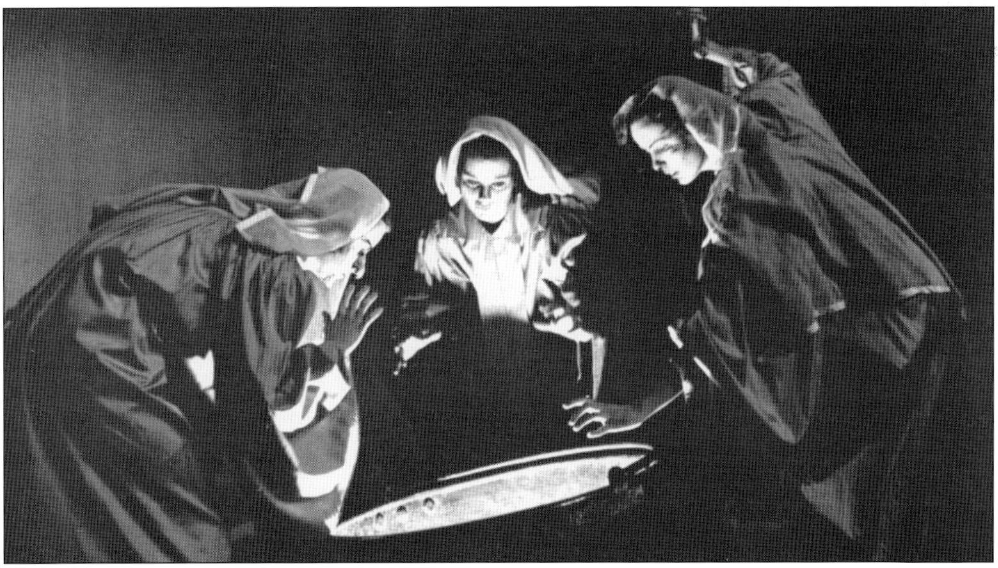

**THREE WITCHES AND A CAULDRON.** Germantown Friends School students perform the three witches scene from William Shakespeare's *Macbeth* in a 1931 school production. During the 20th century, Friends schools began integrating visual and performing arts into the life of school communities. Friends schools' curricula blend the best of traditional with the best of emerging educational pedagogy. (Courtesy of Germantown Friends School.)

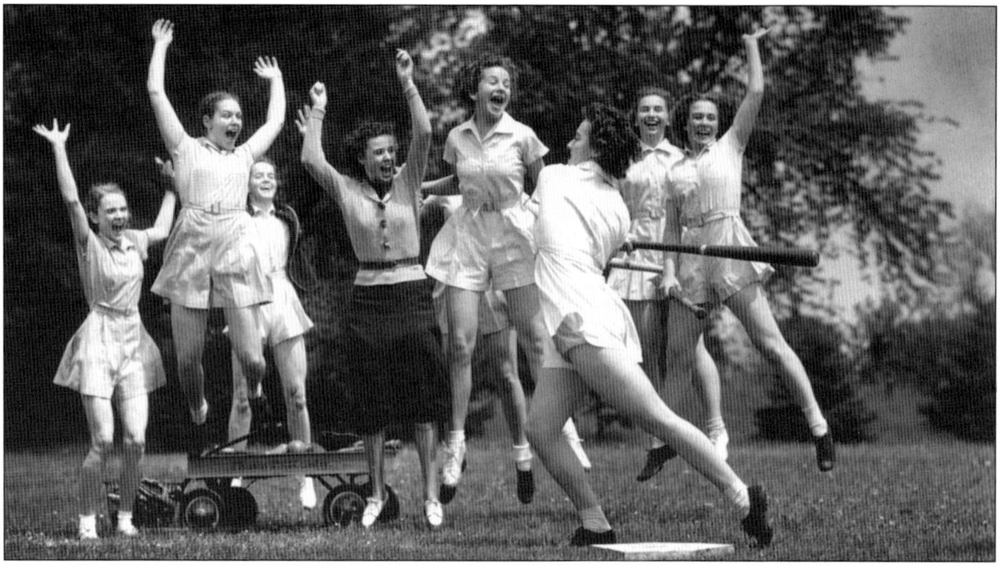

**Joy in Collaboration.** In this 1937 softball game, one of the George School girls has just made a hit and everyone pictured is excited. Friends schools value the joy that can be found in group effort and teamwork while emphasizing a philosophy of participation rather than competition. (Courtesy of George School.)

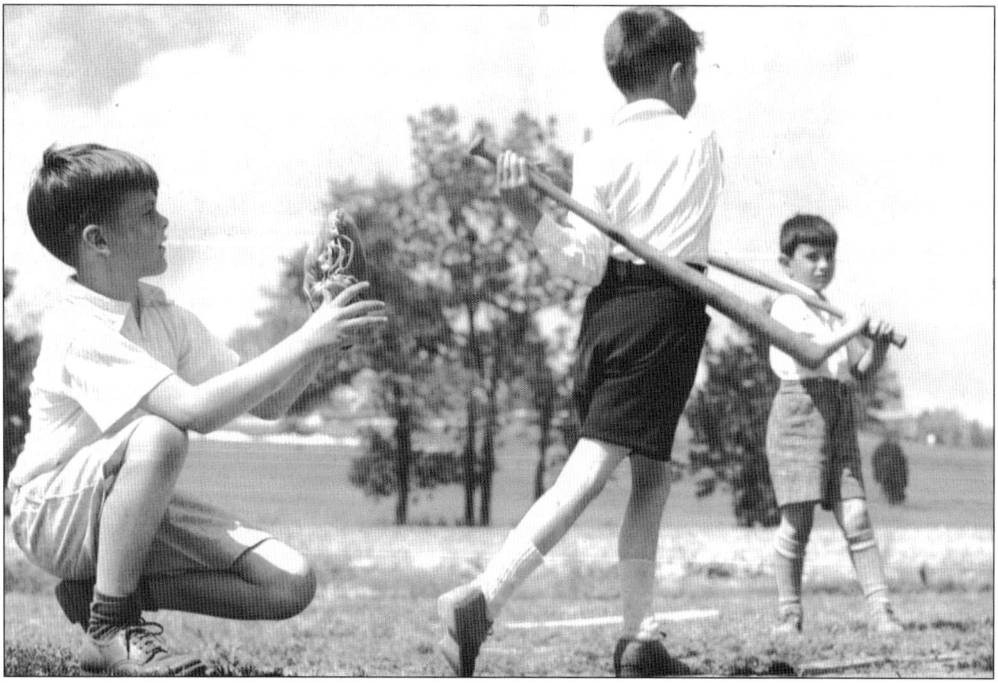

**Playing Ball, c. 1930.** The location of Friends' Central School at Fifteenth and Race Streets meant that students often traveled in order to play sports. In 1925, the school moved to City Avenue in Overbrook. The editor of the school publication *Blue and Gray* wrote, "It will be infinitely better for all of us. Acres of [grass] all around us, ready just outside the windows and the doors. Good for our eyes, good for our feet, good for our minds and our souls." (Courtesy of Friends' Central School.)

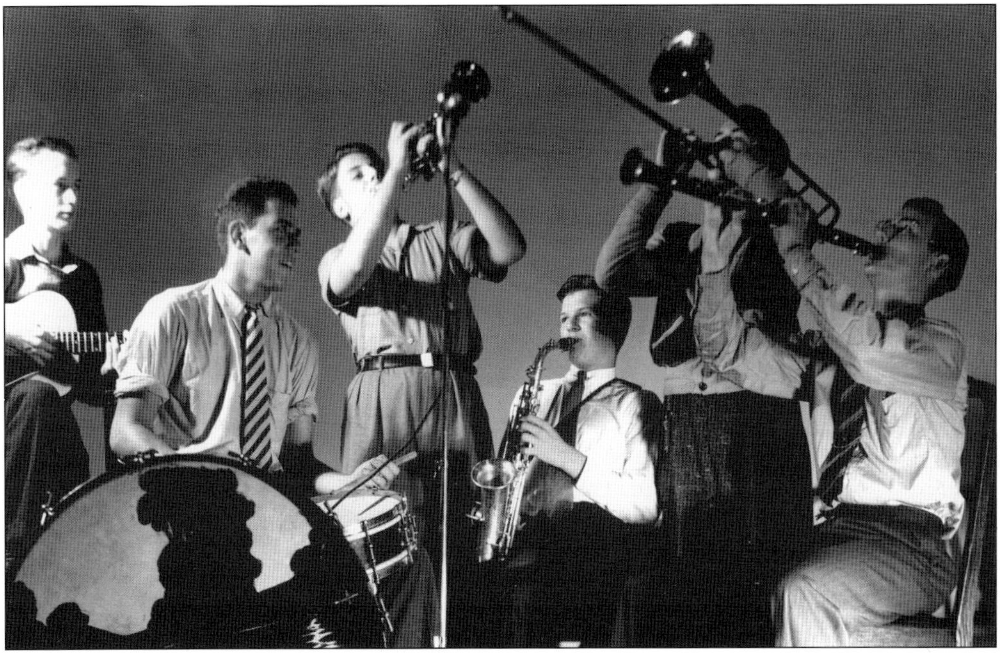

**Jazz—Lively in Spirit.** Jazz—lively in spirit, improvisatory, and marked by melodic freedom—has sometimes been used to describe the collaborative spirit at work in the teaching and learning process at Friends schools. Pictured is the George School jazz band around 1940. (Courtesy of George School.)

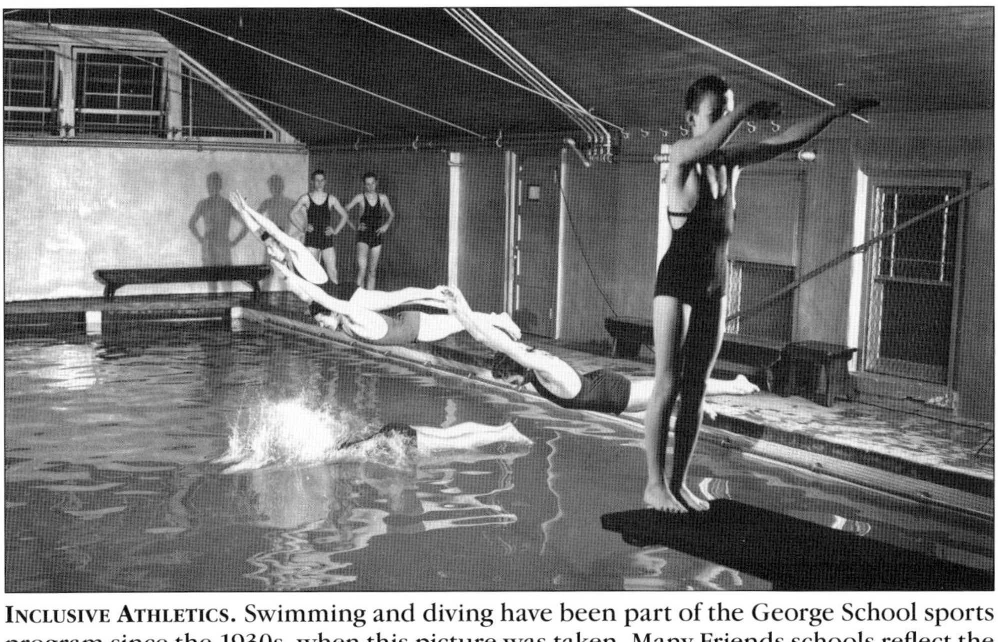

**Inclusive Athletics.** Swimming and diving have been part of the George School sports program since the 1930s, when this picture was taken. Many Friends schools reflect the Quaker testimony of equality through their inclusive athletic policies, such as no-cut, no experience necessary, and scheduling of appropriate competitions for all levels of expertise. (Courtesy of George School.)

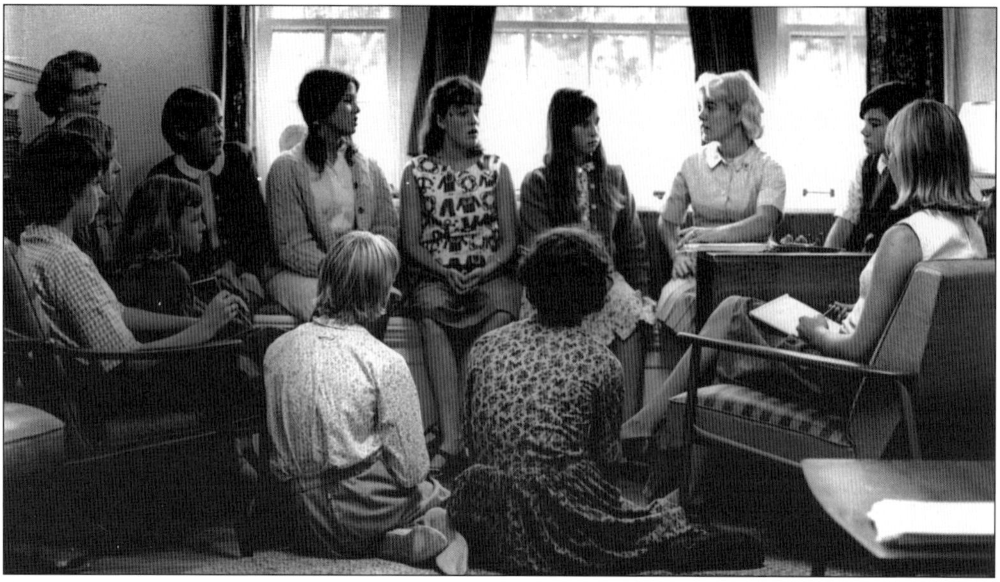

**Student Leadership.** The teacher is present, at far left, but this meeting of the Abington Friends School Student Council in the 1950s is being run by the students. Student leadership is encouraged at all grade levels in Friends schools. Students learn how to participate in and lead the Quaker process for consensus decision making, "coming to unity," an important component of Friends education. (Courtesy of Abington Friends School.)

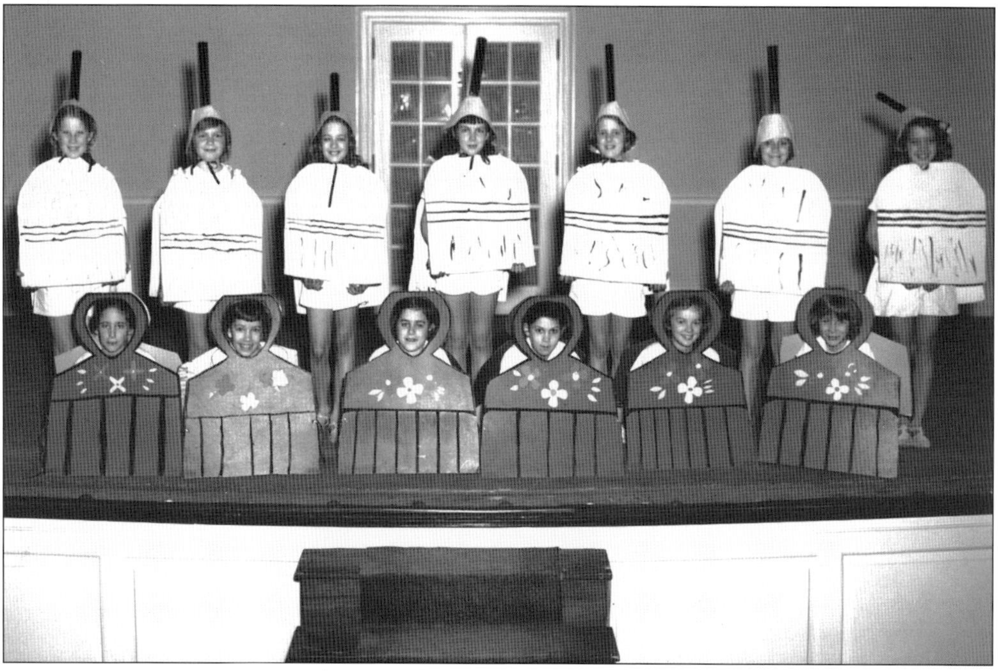

**Found Objects into Art.** This production of *The Kitchen Clock* at the Greene Street Friends School in March 1952 featured student-written segments based on items found around the house, such as the "brooms" and "dust pans" pictured here. Friends schools encourage student-centered projects and student-led productions. (Courtesy of Greene Street Friends School.)

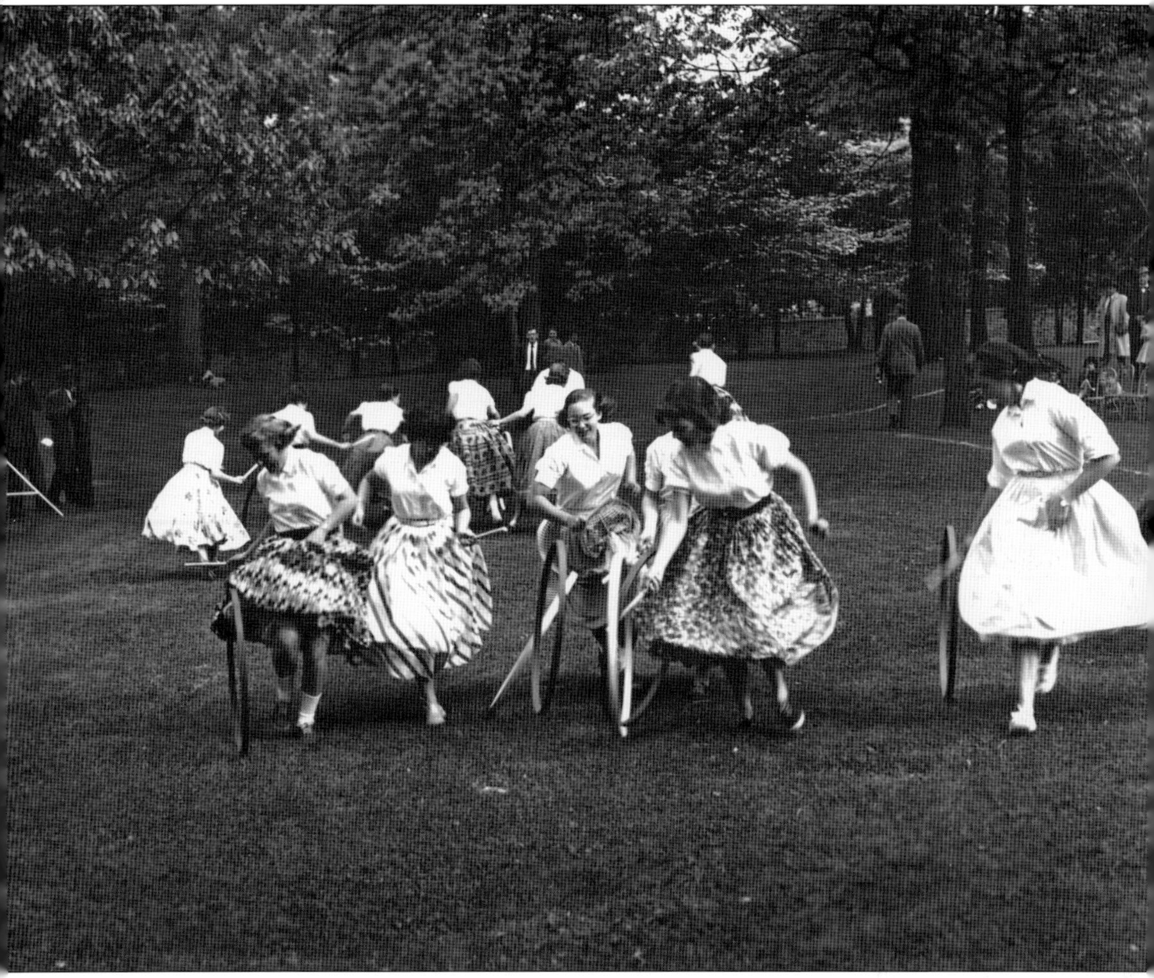

**Joie de Vivre.** Hoop racing in the grove behind the meetinghouse was a May Day tradition, later woven into Abington Friends School's current Arbor Day celebration. Affirming, protecting, and celebrating the natural world are important Friends school goals that flow directly from the Quaker testimony on stewardship of the earth. At the time of this 1950s picture, Abington Friends was an all-girls school. Celebrations of the earth's changing seasons have inspired events at Friends schools for generations. (Courtesy of Abington Friends School.)

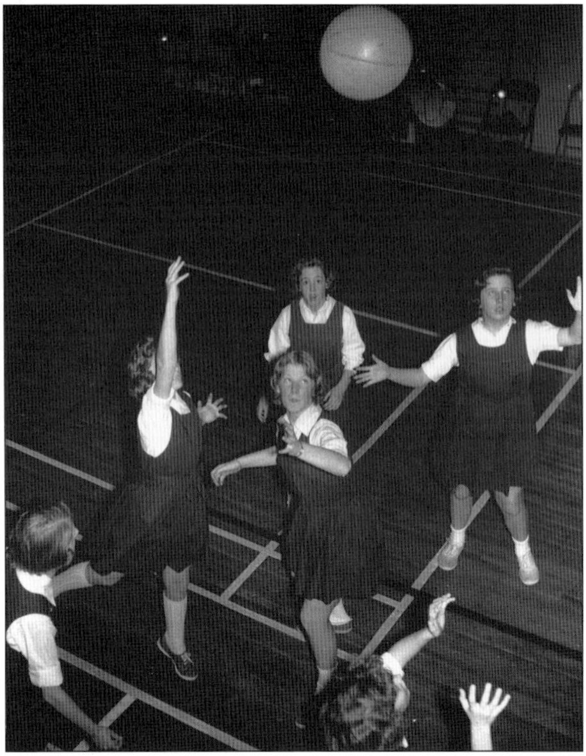

**Good Sportswomanship.** Basketball was introduced at Greene Street Friends School in 1902 for boys and girls to foster the love of healthy exercise. By the 1920s, it was part of a robust intramural sports program. The girls in this photograph are playing in the gymnasium in the basement of the lower school in the 1950s. (Courtesy of Greene Street Friends School.)

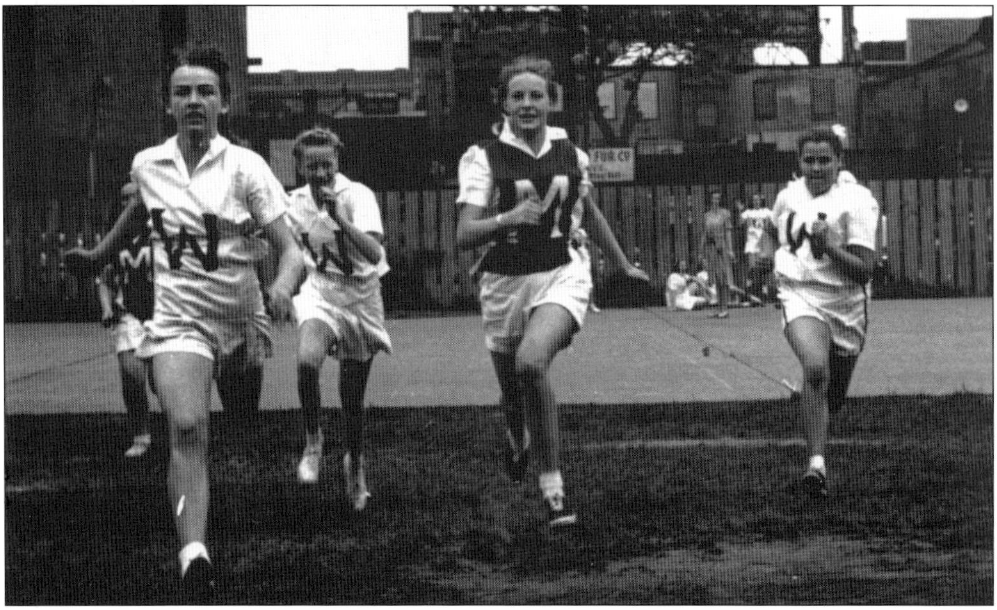

**Field Day Celebration.** Greene Street Friends School's first field day, now called Color Day, was held in the spring of 1909. The upper grades played before an audience of appreciative parents and friends in various and exciting relay races and broad-jump challenges. In this 1950s photograph, girls divided into their school colors—team maroon, *M*, and team white, *W*—to compete in a spirited race. (Courtesy of Greene Street Friends School.)

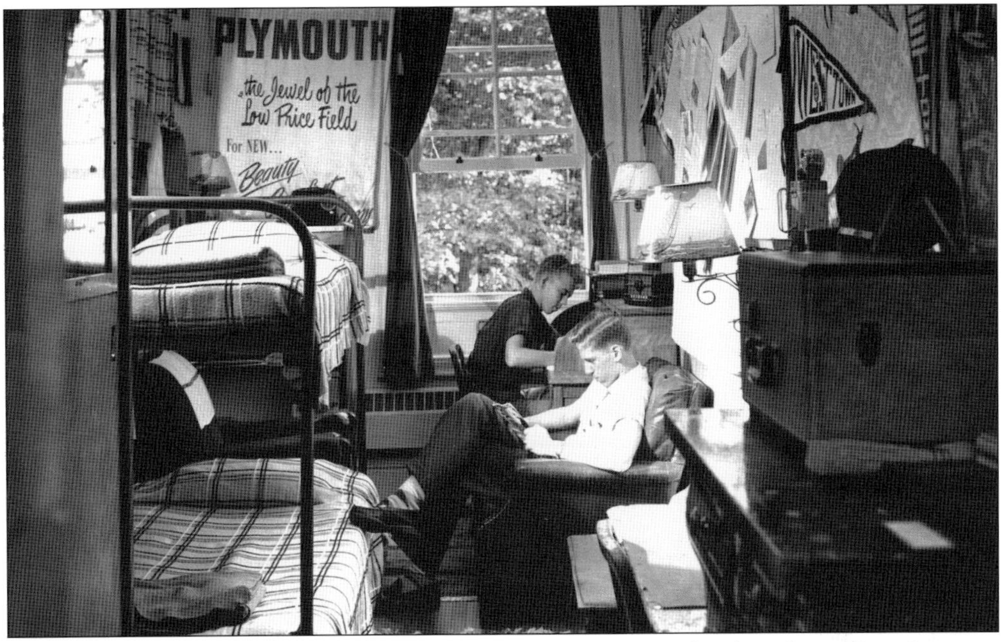


**Westtown's Formative Experience.** Pictured are Westtown School students Hans Lawaetz and Don Perera in their boys' dormitory room around 1955. Westtown School's boarding program, in place for the entire 200 years of the school's operation, reinforces the school's commitment to a living community grounded in wholesome and simple values, such as honesty, openness, and respect. The boarding setting makes possible the formative experience of living in a diverse community. (Courtesy of Westtown School.)

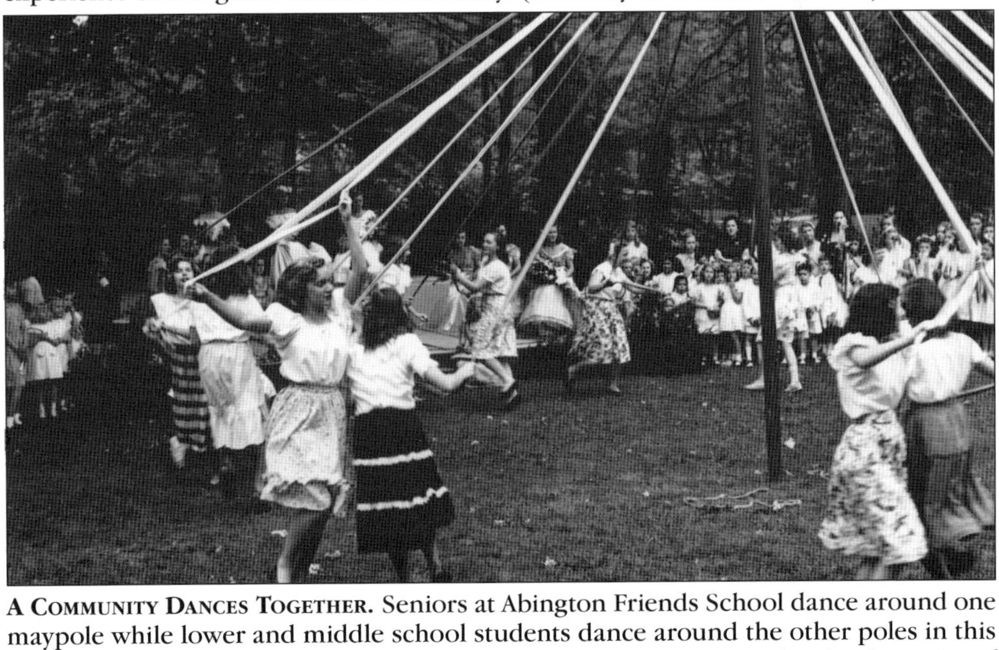

**A Community Dances Together.** Seniors at Abington Friends School dance around one maypole while lower and middle school students dance around the other poles in this May Day celebration in 1961. This event illustrates the common Friends school practice of bringing students together across grades and divisions to create a community of learners that engages together in work and play. (Courtesy of Abington Friends School.)

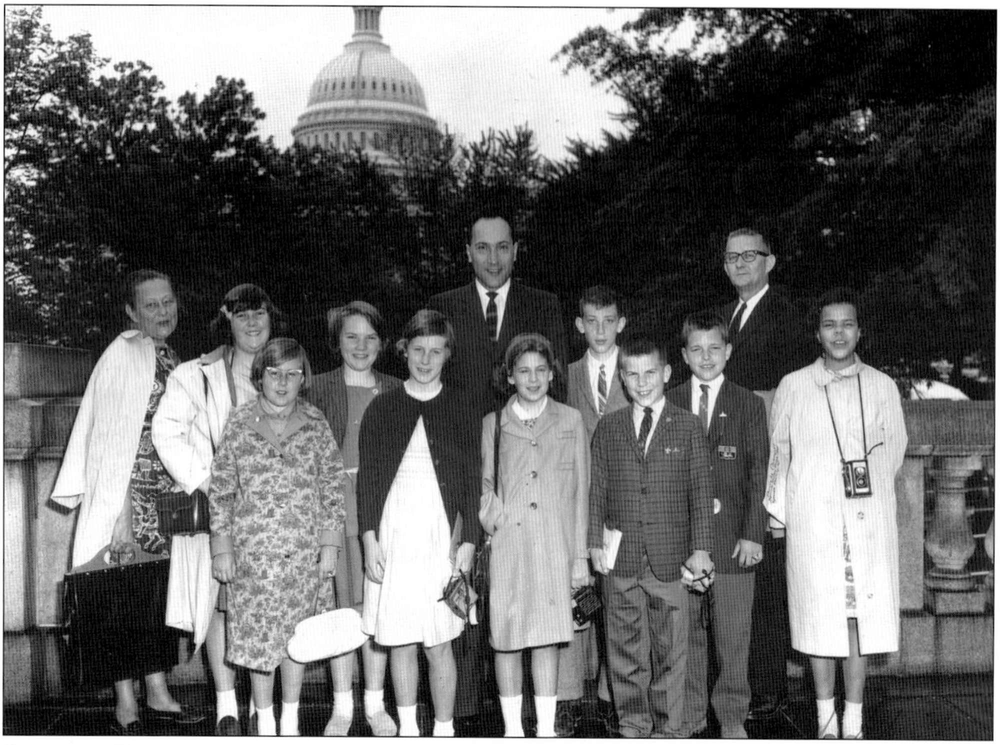

**Students Engaged in Democracy.** Travel that enables children to engage with the world is an important part of Friends education. Plymouth Meeting Friends School students travel to Washington, D.C., every year. In this 1960 photograph, the class is accompanied by head of school LaRue Taliaferro as they meet with Pennsylvania congressman Richard Schweiker (center). (Courtesy of Plymouth Meeting Friends School.)

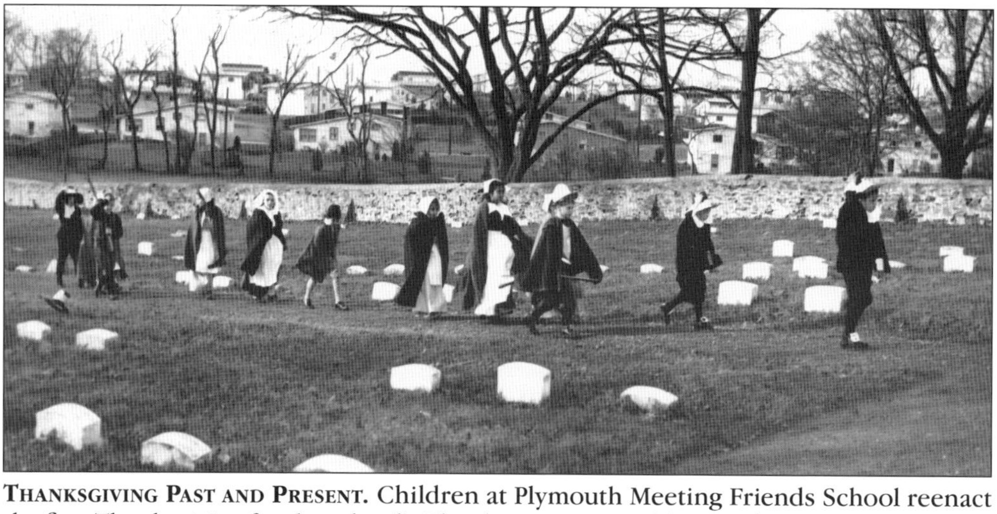

**Thanksgiving Past and Present.** Children at Plymouth Meeting Friends School reenact the first Thanksgiving for the school's Thanksgiving assembly in 1963. Verbal expression, including dramatic arts, has long been a part of the Plymouth language arts program. In costume, the children journey through the meeting graveyard, reflecting on the historic influences that led to the first Thanksgiving with gratitude for the fullness of their present lives. (Courtesy of Plymouth Meeting Friends School.)

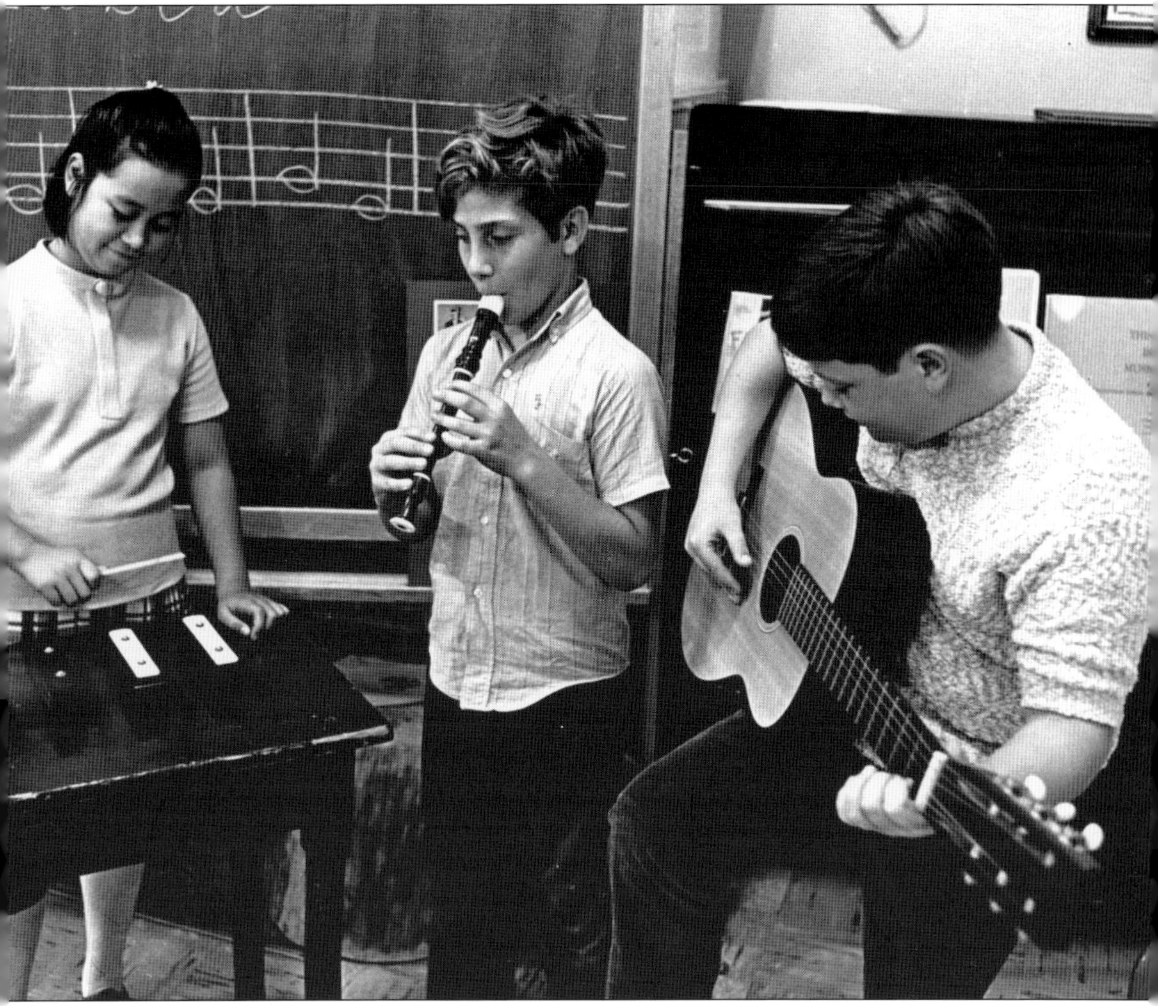

**MUSIC APPRECIATION.** At Frankford Friends School, a wide variety of creative expressions and aesthetic appreciation was fostered under the care of principal and music teacher J. Terrence Farley (1967–2005) and continues today. In this 1969 photograph, students learn together to play the xylophone, recorder, and guitar. (Courtesy of Frankford Friends School.)

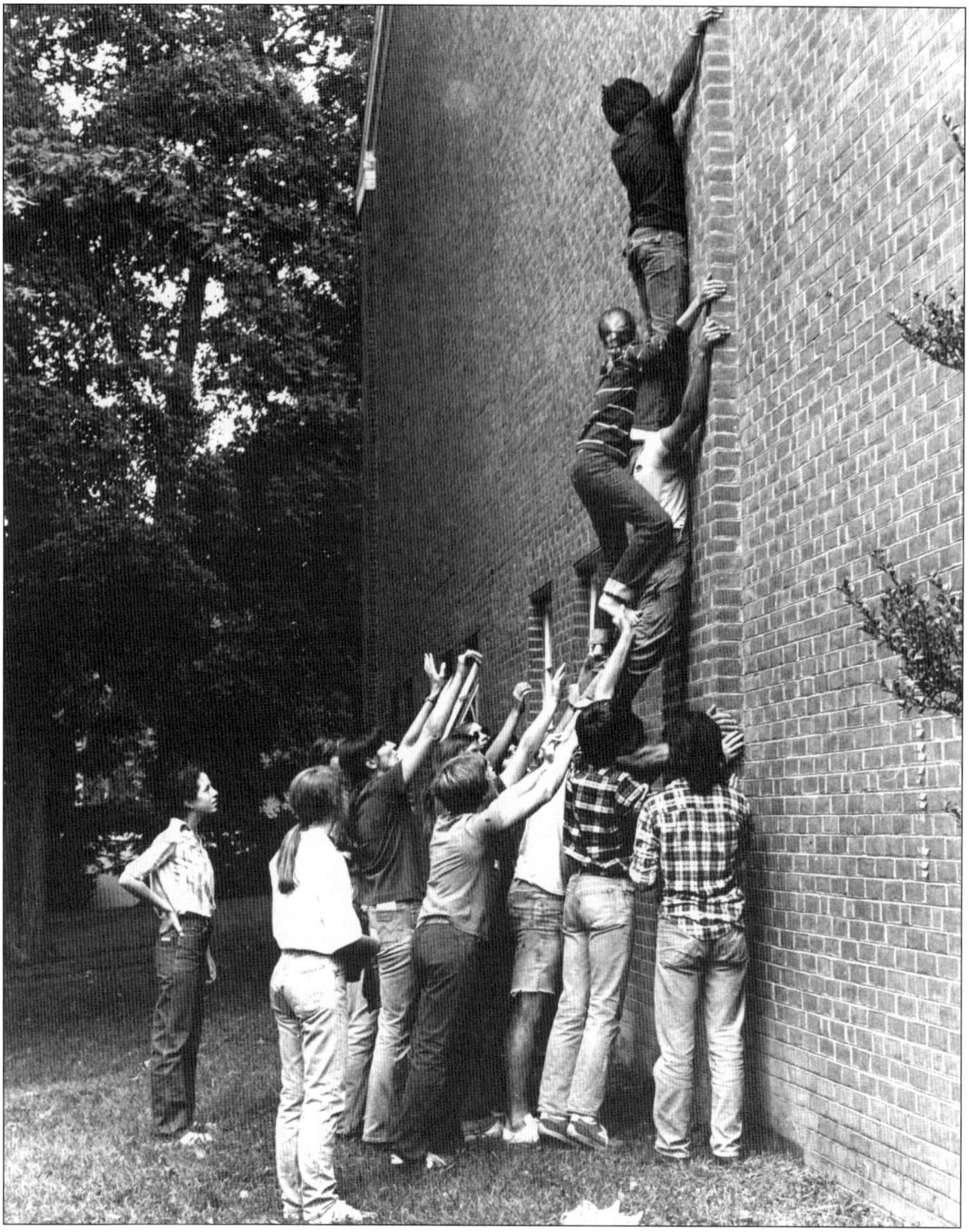

**TRUST AND COLLABORATION.** Friends schools have unique orientation programs for students and faculty that focus on community building, as healthy community relationships are at the core of Quaker pedagogy. This photograph shows group games at Westtown School's student orientation in the 1970s. Many Friends schools begin each school year by building strong community relationships through bringing students and faculty together for cooperative work and play. (Courtesy of Westtown Friends School, photograph by Donald H. Byerly.)

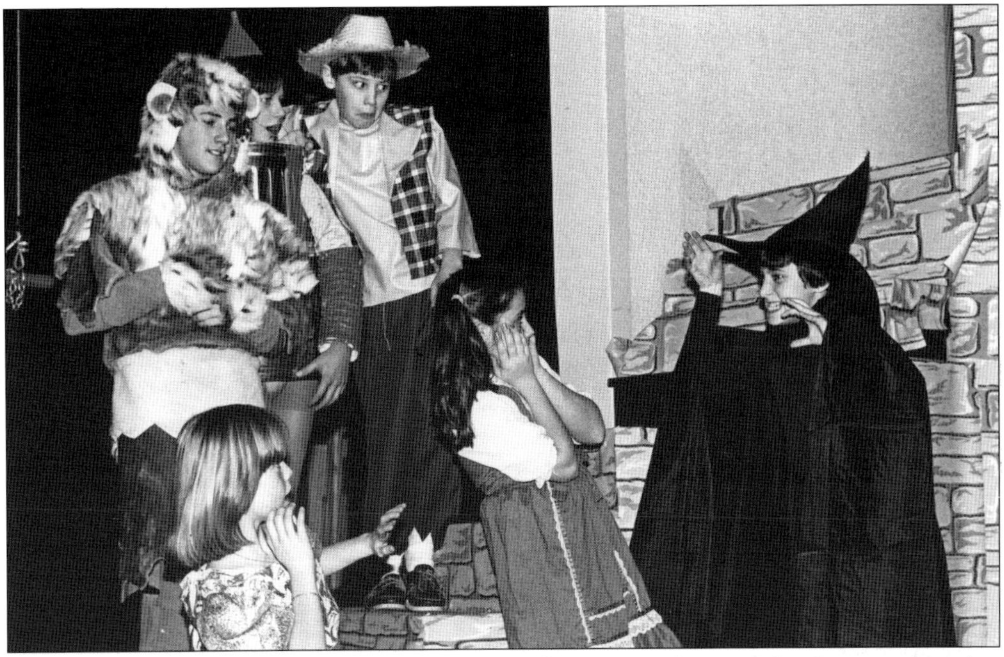

**The Wizard Goes Coed.** In the mid-1980s, the William Penn Charter School was undergoing a conversion from an all-boys school to a coeducational institution. In this middle school production of *The Wizard of Oz*, a fifth-grade student, Susan Bunch, was recruited to play Dorothy. (Courtesy of the William Penn Charter School.)

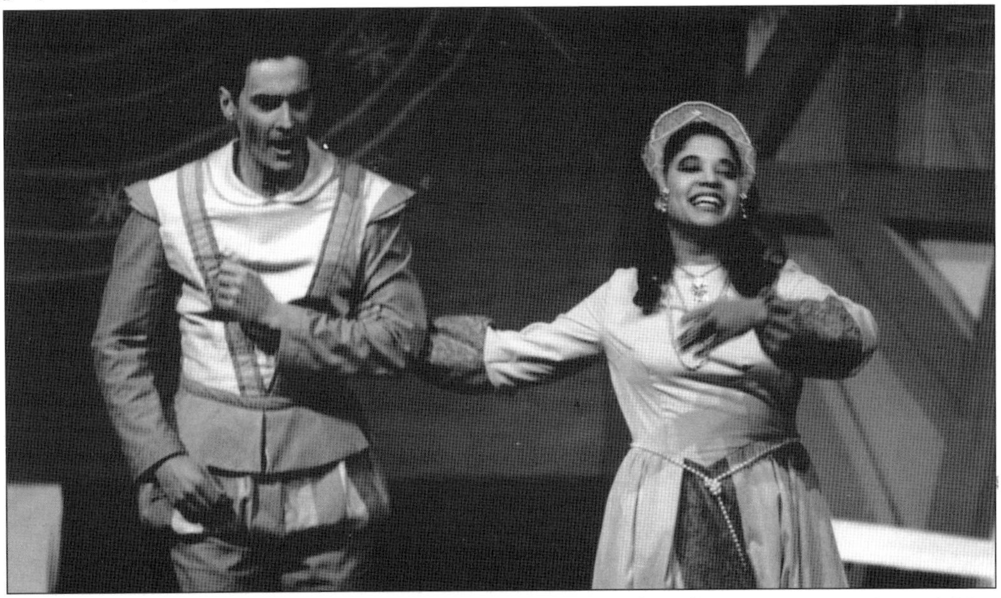

**Faculty on Stage.** Integrating teachers, administrators, and students in community activities has long been a Friends school hallmark. In this 1972 Westtown School performance of *Ralph Roister Doister*, head of school Earl Harrison and teacher Terrell Nash enjoy their teamwork for theatrical brilliance. Faculty plays performed for students and their families are just one way in which adults are engaged in the school community outside of the classroom. (Courtesy of Westtown School, photograph by Theodore Hetzel.)

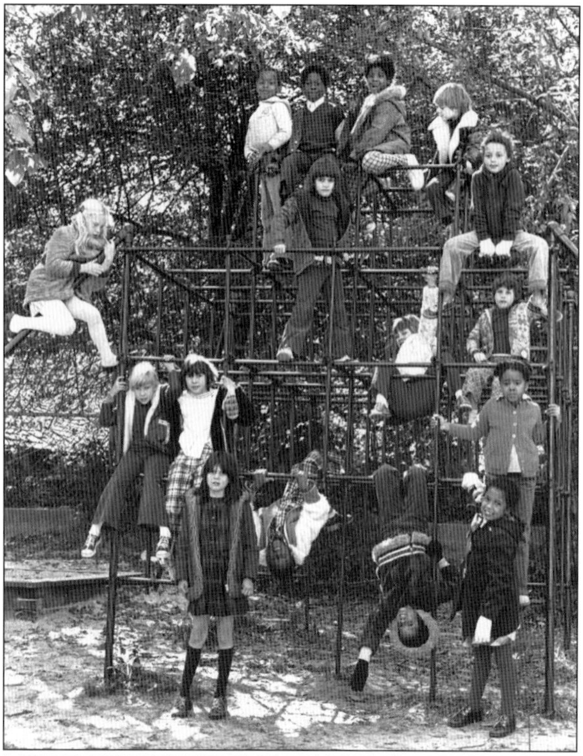

**Playing on Jungle Gym.** The structure in this photograph was a gift of Thomas H. Shoemaker to Greene Street Friends School. He bought the jungle gym around 1914 at the request of principal Elsie Oakford. The racial balance of the second-grade class, pictured here in 1975, reflects the diversity that continues to flourish today in this urban school. (Courtesy of Greene Street Friends School, photograph donated by Wanda Will.)

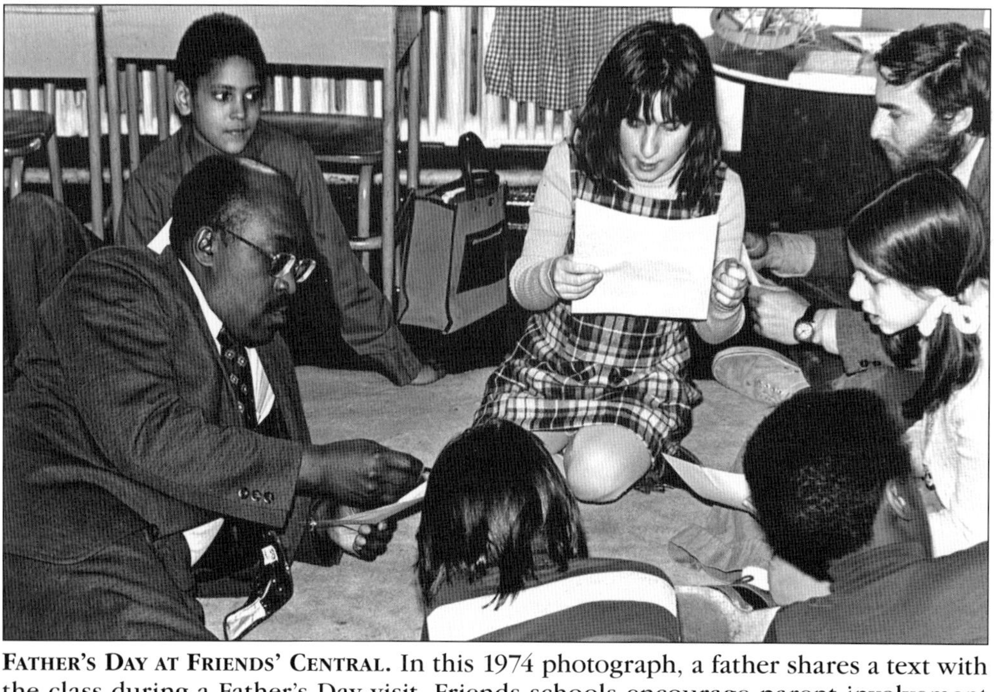

**Father's Day at Friends' Central.** In this 1974 photograph, a father shares a text with the class during a Father's Day visit. Friends schools encourage parent involvement through a variety of parent-child activities embedded in the curricula, as well as through special visiting days for parents, grandparents, and "grand friends." (Courtesy of Friends' Central School.)

**Smiles All Around.** Germantown Friends School students in this 1974 photograph attend the Fun Day school fair organized by the school's parents' association, which raised funds for the school. Involving families in school spirit through special parent-sponsored events contributes to community building and resource enrichment. (Courtesy of Germantown Friends School.)

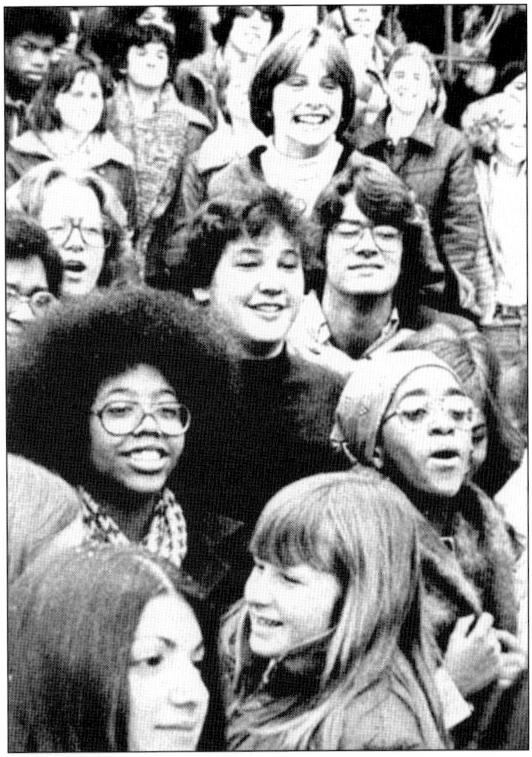

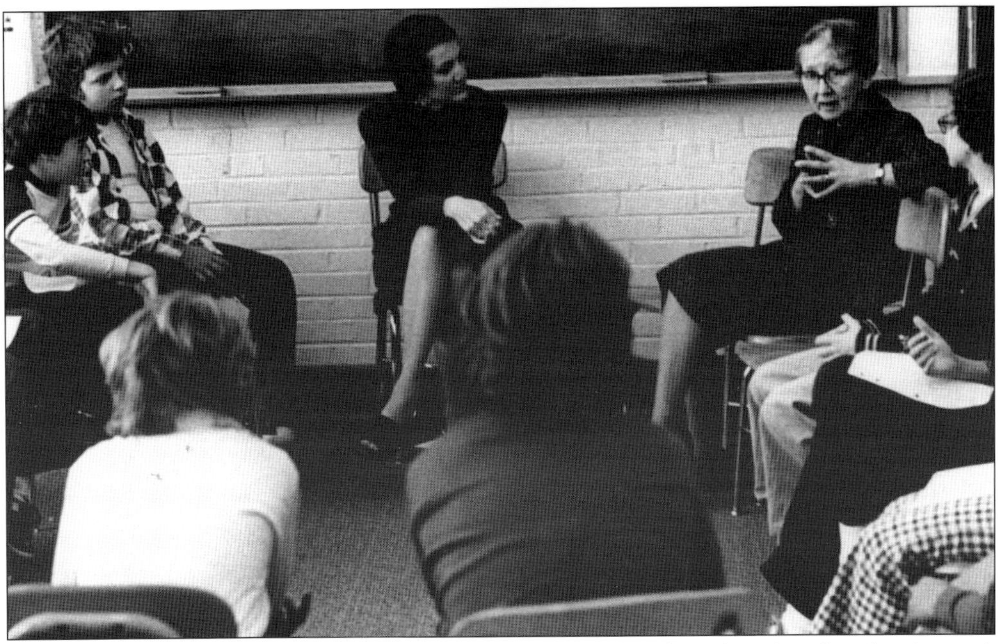

**Sharing Stories, Braided Lives.** Frankford Friends School teacher Carol Farley (center) and Elfrida Vipont (right), a famous British author and frequent visitor to Frankford Friends School, lead a sixth-grade class discussion in 1977. Author Vipont often shared spellbinding stories of the early Quakers, their hardships, imprisonments, and triumphs. (Courtesy of Frankford Friends School.)

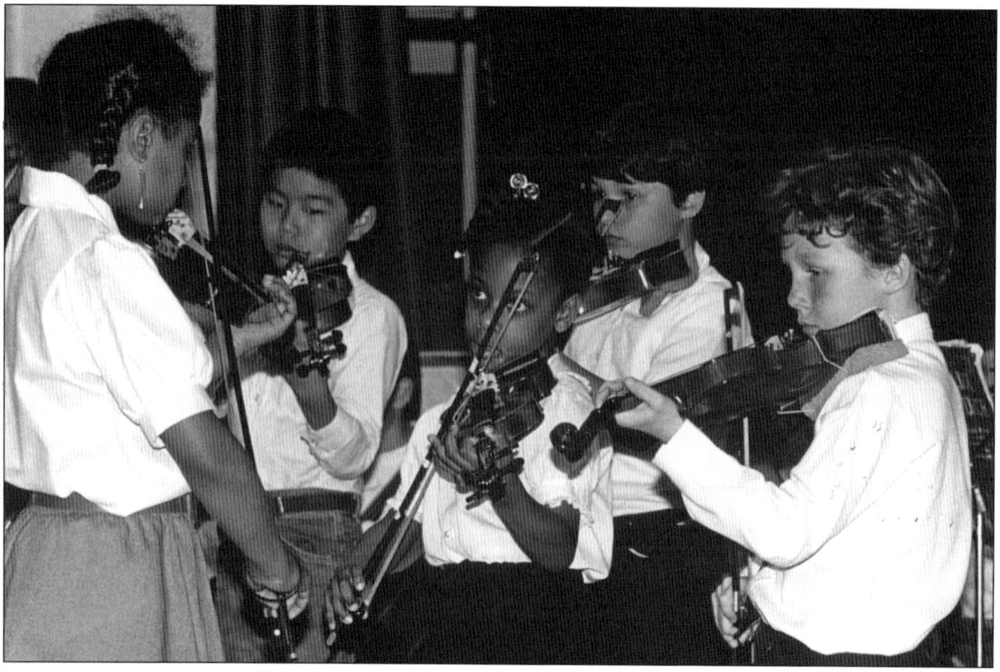

**Young Musicians.** In this *c.* 1980 photograph, musicians from Friends Select School's lower school student body perform together. Music became an official part of the Friends Select School curriculum about 1923 and thrives there today. (Courtesy of Friends Select School.)

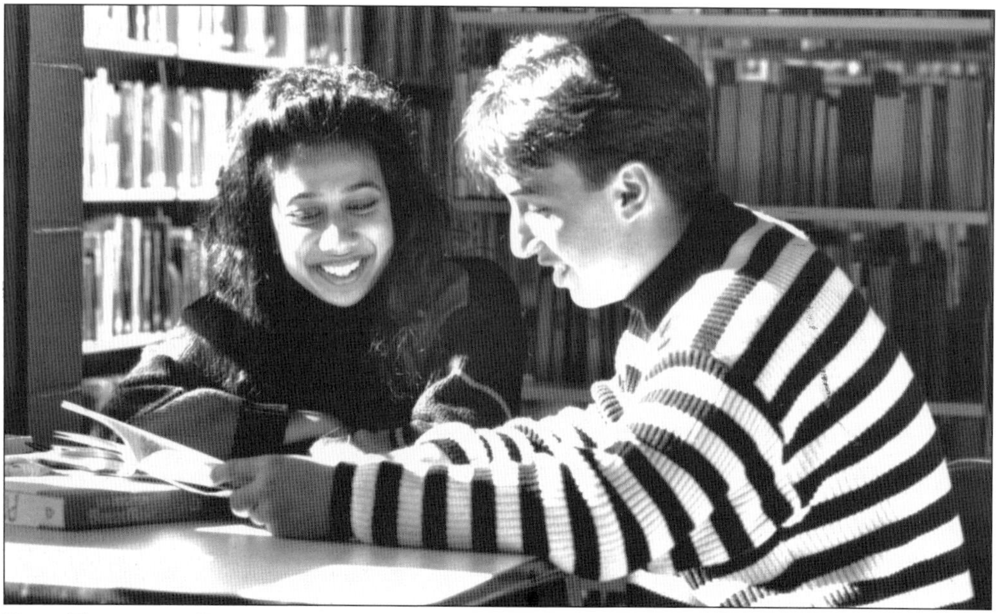

**Peer Tutoring, Enriching the Community.** Abington Friends School has long had a tradition of peer tutoring, like this session, around 1980, where students who are particularly strong in one area volunteer to help those who may be struggling. Peer-tutoring programs at Friends schools help students learn how powerful partnerships can be and how each person's gifts enrich the community. (Courtesy of Abington Friends School.)

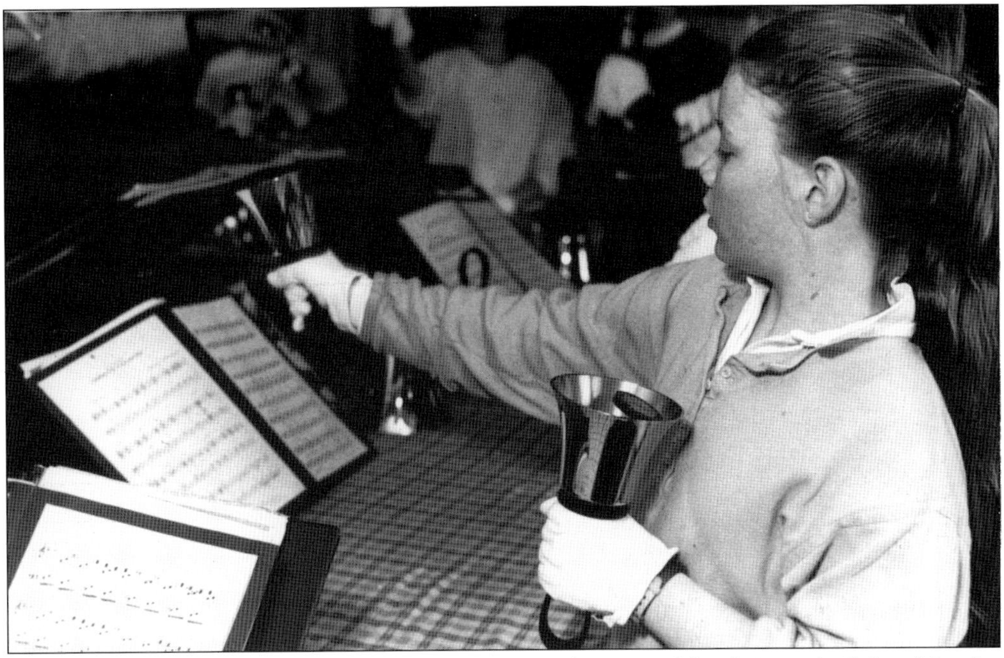

**In Concert.** English handbells were introduced to Frankford Friends School in the 1980s. Handbells teach children to read music and perform cooperatively. Erin Woods, a 1996 Frankford Friends School graduate, offers, "Playing handbells made me feel that we were in some way pulled together by a special bond." (Courtesy of Frankford Friends School.)

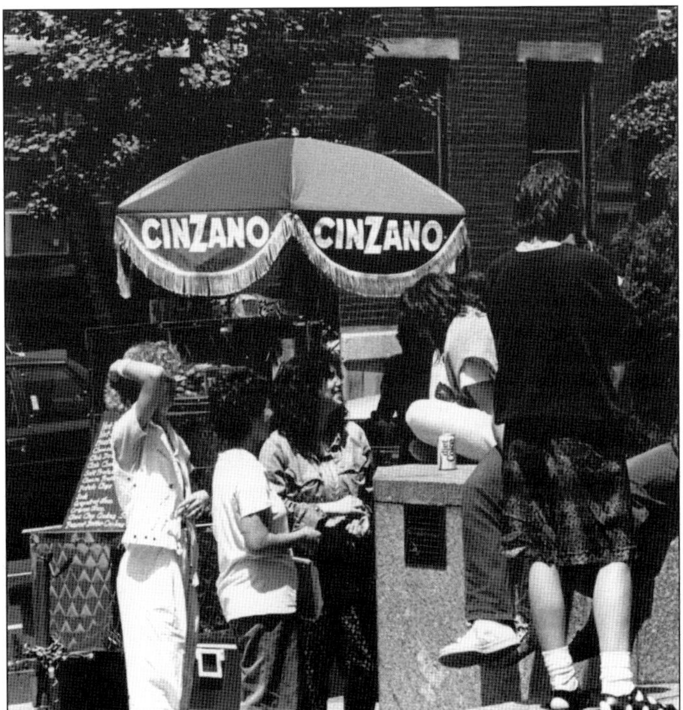


**Lunch in the City.** Upper school students at Friends Select School cherish the opportunity to leave the school campus during lunch or breaks, a privilege that is earned anew each year. Each grade organizes itself and petitions the school administration to be granted this privilege, which can be revoked at any time, if even one member of the class behaves in an irresponsible manner. (Courtesy of Friends Select School.)

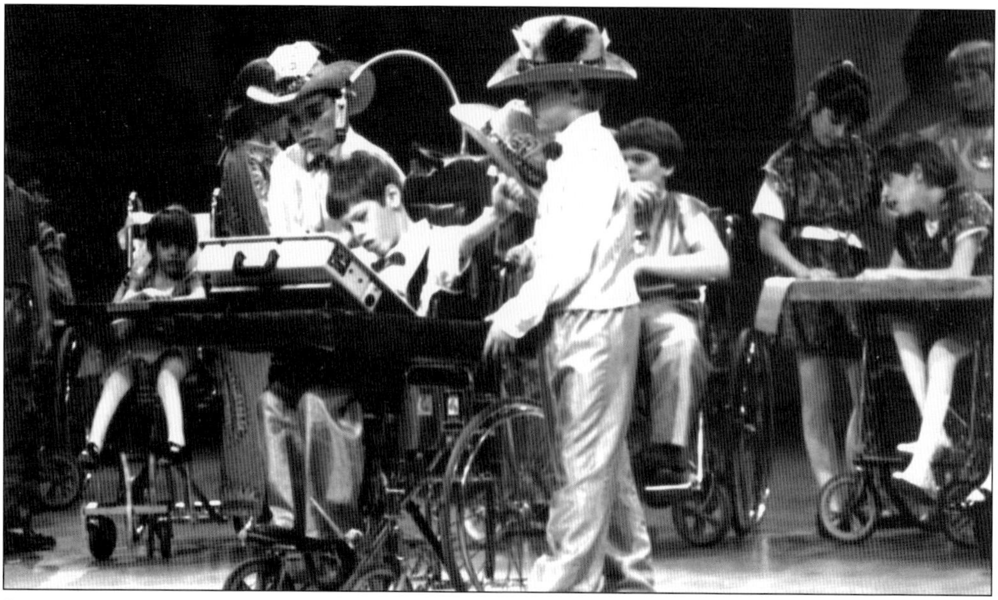

**Partnership.** Germantown Friends School students have partnered to develop musical performances with students from the HMS School for Children with Cerebral Palsy annually for the last 25 years. This 1998 production, *The Return of Halley's Comet*, shows, from left to right, Danny Magaziner, Germantown Friends School; Michael Randis, HMS; and Scott McWilliams, Germantown Friends School. They sing as Lumians and Earthlings emphasizing the need to learn and understand the differences among beings. (Courtesy of Germantown Friends School.)

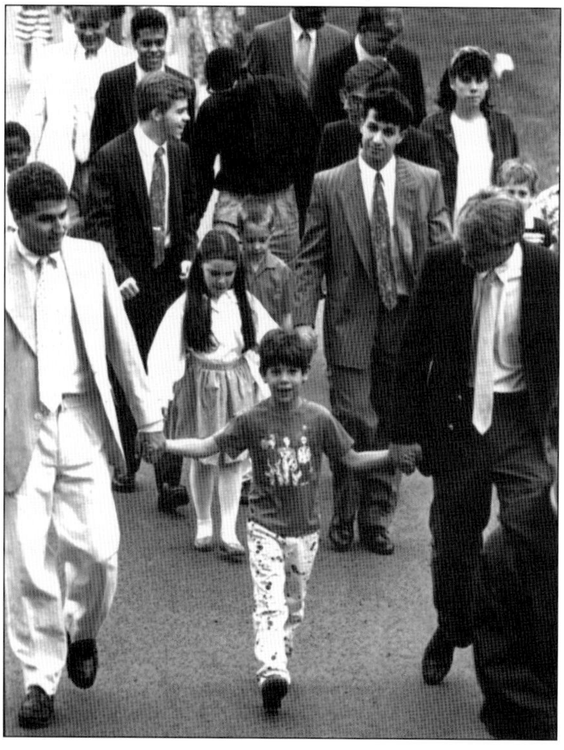

**Power in Community.** As part of a long tradition, seniors at Abington Friends School begin the year by pairing up with first-grade students. Throughout the year, they engage in activities together; then, at commencement, the first-grade pages play an active role in the graduation ceremonies, pictured here in the 1980s. This is one example of valuable intergenerational friendships that prosper within the supportive atmosphere of Friends schools. (Courtesy of Abington Friends School.)

# *Five*

# EXPERIENTIAL LEARNING

*I entered the classroom with the conviction that it was crucial for me and every other student to be an active participant, not a passive consumer . . . education as the practice of freedom . . . education that connects the will to know with the will to become. Learning is a place where paradise can be created.*

—bell hooks, progressive educator

Although the phrase *experiential learning* originates in the progressive movement, Friends schools embraced hands-on education long before the dawn of the 20th century. In the 17th century, George Fox, founder of Quakerism, called for Friends schools to provide training in all "things civil and useful in the creation," a view that resonated with American Quakers. William Penn, Quaker founder of Pennsylvania, highlighted learning a useful trade or skill as one of his three central educational principles. Consequently, most Philadelphia Friends schools provided direct, hands-on training in the practical arts, such as woodshop, gardening, and sewing, from their very founding. This concern for the practical was coupled with a deep appreciation for the natural world and a willingness to regard the outdoors as a worthy space for learning. In the 20th century, American schools witnessed the rise of many pedagogical movements, most notably John Dewey's progressivism. Educators from Friends schools both influenced and were influenced by this movement in an ongoing dialectical process. Several Philadelphia-area Friends schools were involved in research studies of progressive education. With this burgeoning of energy around hands-on approaches, experiential learning at Friends schools had a new renaissance, including field trips, archaeological digs, science experiments, foreign exchange programs, camping excursions, and even thematic approaches that integrated material rather than parceling it out. Experiential learning continues to emerge in myriad ways in today's Friends schools.

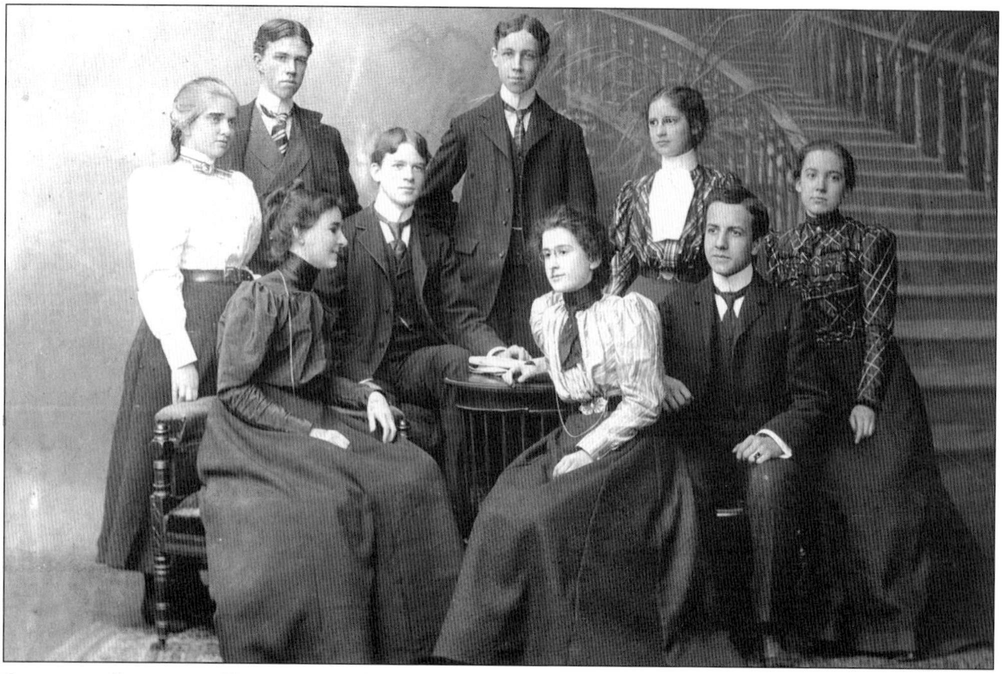

**Student-Centered Publishing.** Even prior to the start of the 20th century, students at Friends schools engaged directly in creating their own publications. Girls and boys at Friends' Central School published a periodical, the *Blue and Gray*, beginning in 1892; a yearly subscription cost 50¢ in advance. (Courtesy of Friends' Central School.)

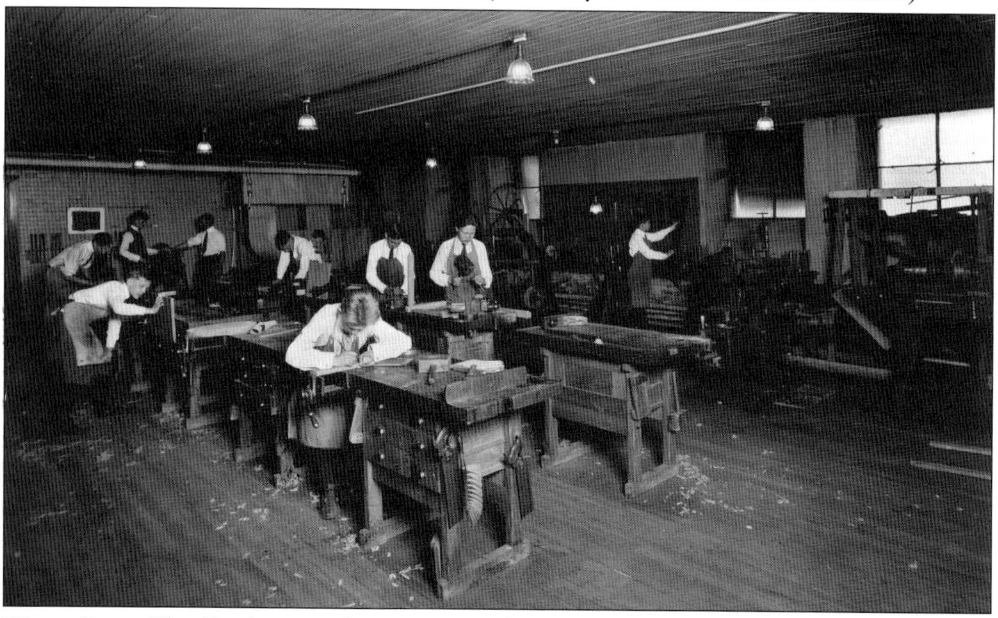

**Wood Shop.** The Quaker emphasis on "productive work with one's hands" sometimes emerged in ways that reflected societal norms in American culture. At Friends Select School, boys engaged in wood shop, while girls participated in domestic science; these sex-segregated classes continued through the 1960s. (Courtesy of Friends Select School.)

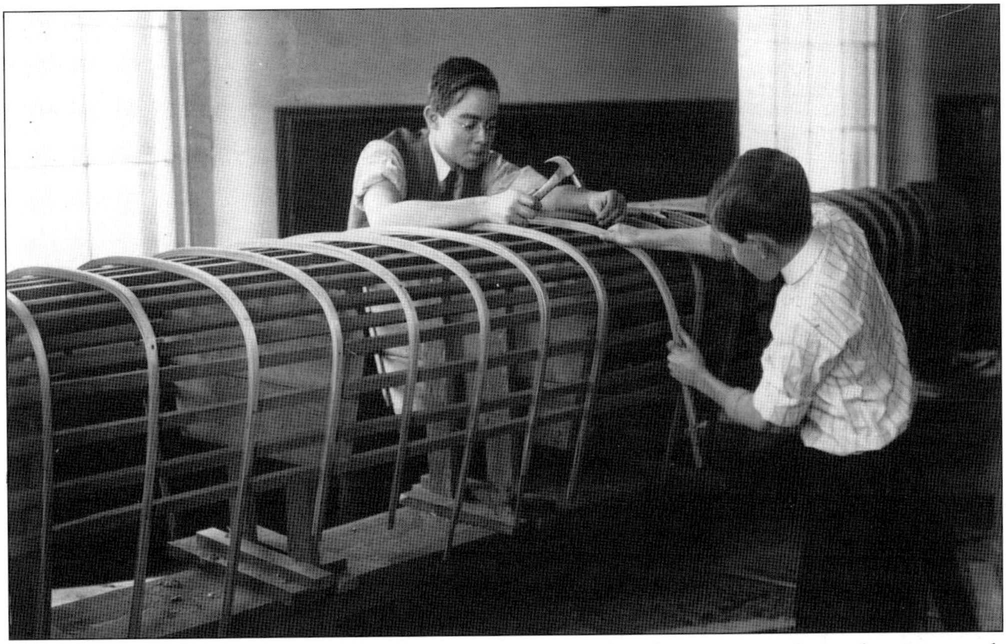

**Crafting.** Some pedagogical projects at Friends schools connected productive work with one's hands directly to exploration of the natural world. In the photograph above, young Westtown School students are bending and affixing the ribs in the early stages of constructing a canoe frame, as part of manual training class. Teacher Thomas K. Brown built the first canoe at Westtown in 1884; between 1900 and 1910, seven or eight canoes were constructed per year. While most canoe builders were boys, girls participated as well. In the photograph below, children from Greene Street Friends School hold a variety of birdhouses, which they made in school. Children at Friends schools learn to show respect for the natural world, correlating with the long-standing Quaker emphasis on stewardship of the earth. (Above, courtesy of Westtown School; below, courtesy of Greene Street Friends School.)

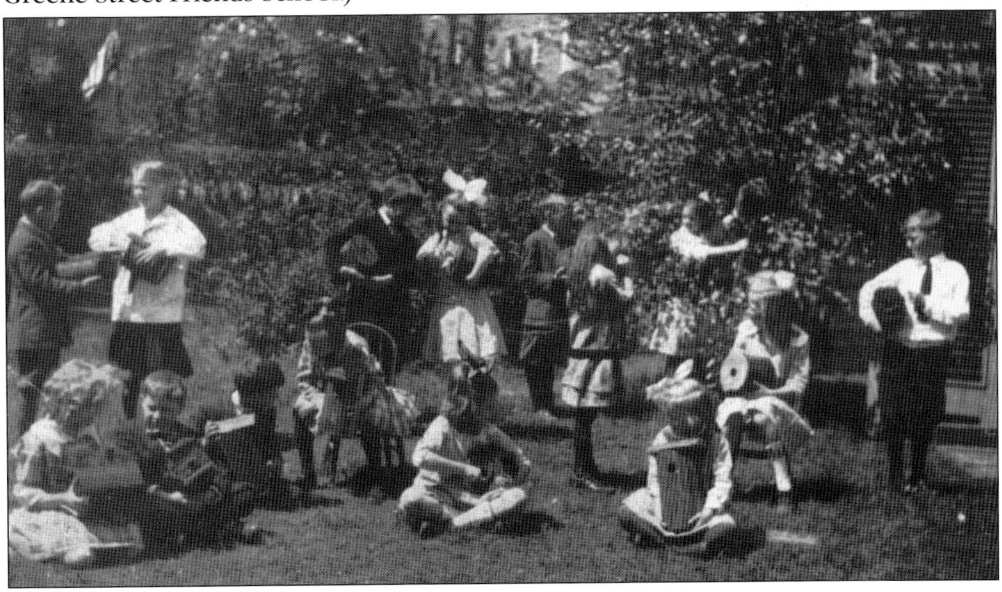

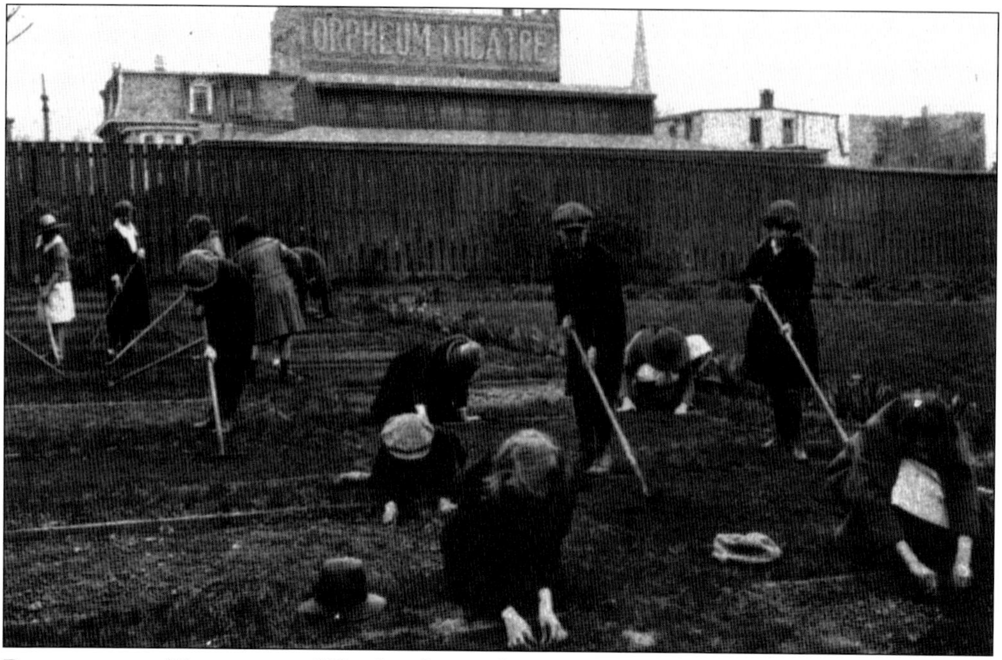


**Planting and Harvesting.** Whether located in a crowded urban area or on a campus with vast spaces of greenery, many Philadelphia-area Friends schools offered gardening programs in the 19th and 20th centuries. The importance of tilling the soil echoes Quakers' rural beginnings and their understanding that education should have practical value in the world. At Greene Street Friends School in the early 20th century, students planted and tended small garden plots behind the meetinghouse. Vesta Haines, together with an average of eight young gardeners, tended the plots through the summer. Crops included beans, lettuce, tomatoes, and carrots. The photograph below depicts the gardening program at Friends' Central School in the 1950s. (Above, courtesy of Greene Street Friends School; below, courtesy of Friends' Central School.)

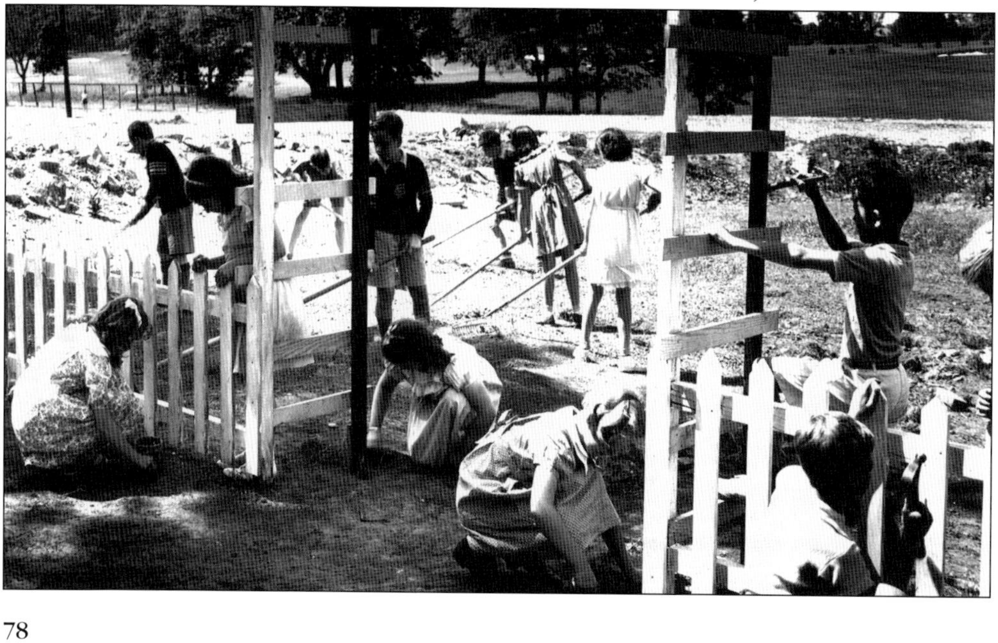

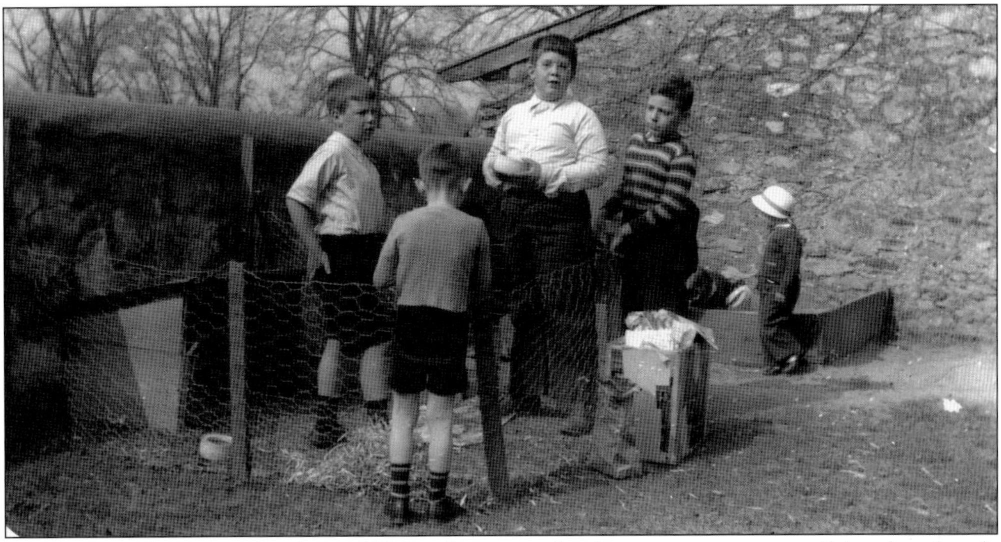

**CARING FOR ANIMALS.** As these 1930s photographs demonstrate, many Friends schools provide children with direct, hands-on experience caring for animals. In the photograph above, Plymouth Meeting Friends School students are tending rabbits on school grounds, next to a stable shed. In the image below, children from the City Line Campus at Friends' Central School are learning through observation and interaction. At the time, this aspect of education was known as animal husbandry. At many Friends schools, these direct experiences tending animals often occurred indoors, as well, with children learning to feed and care for classroom pets. In fact, this meaningful practice was emphasized by progressive educational philosophers such as Nel Noddings in the latter part of the 20th century. (Above, courtesy of Plymouth Meeting Friends School; below, courtesy of Friends' Central School.)

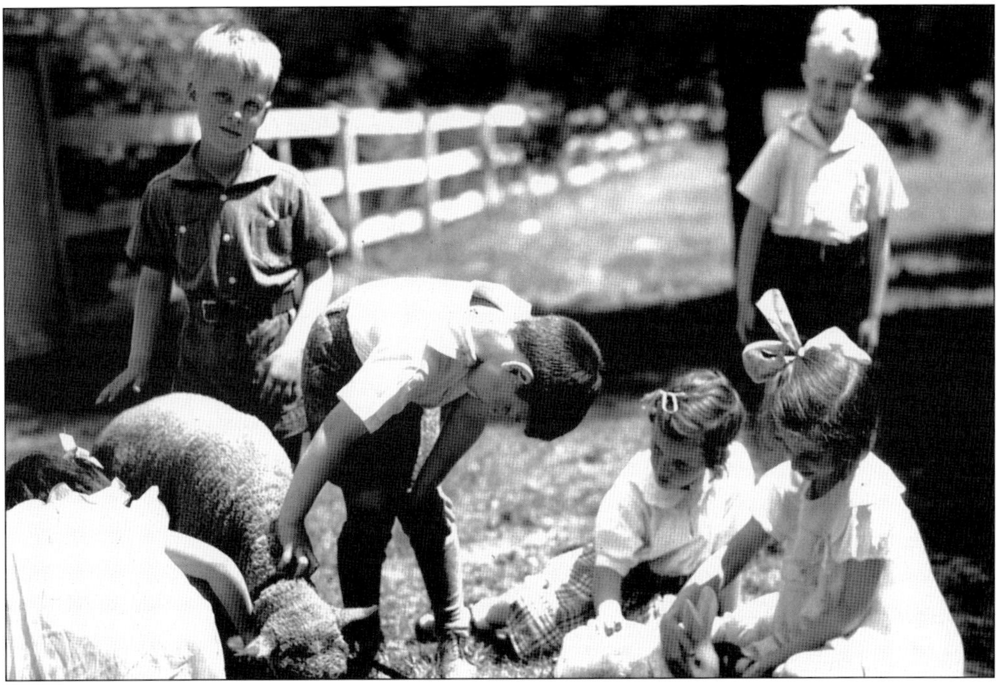

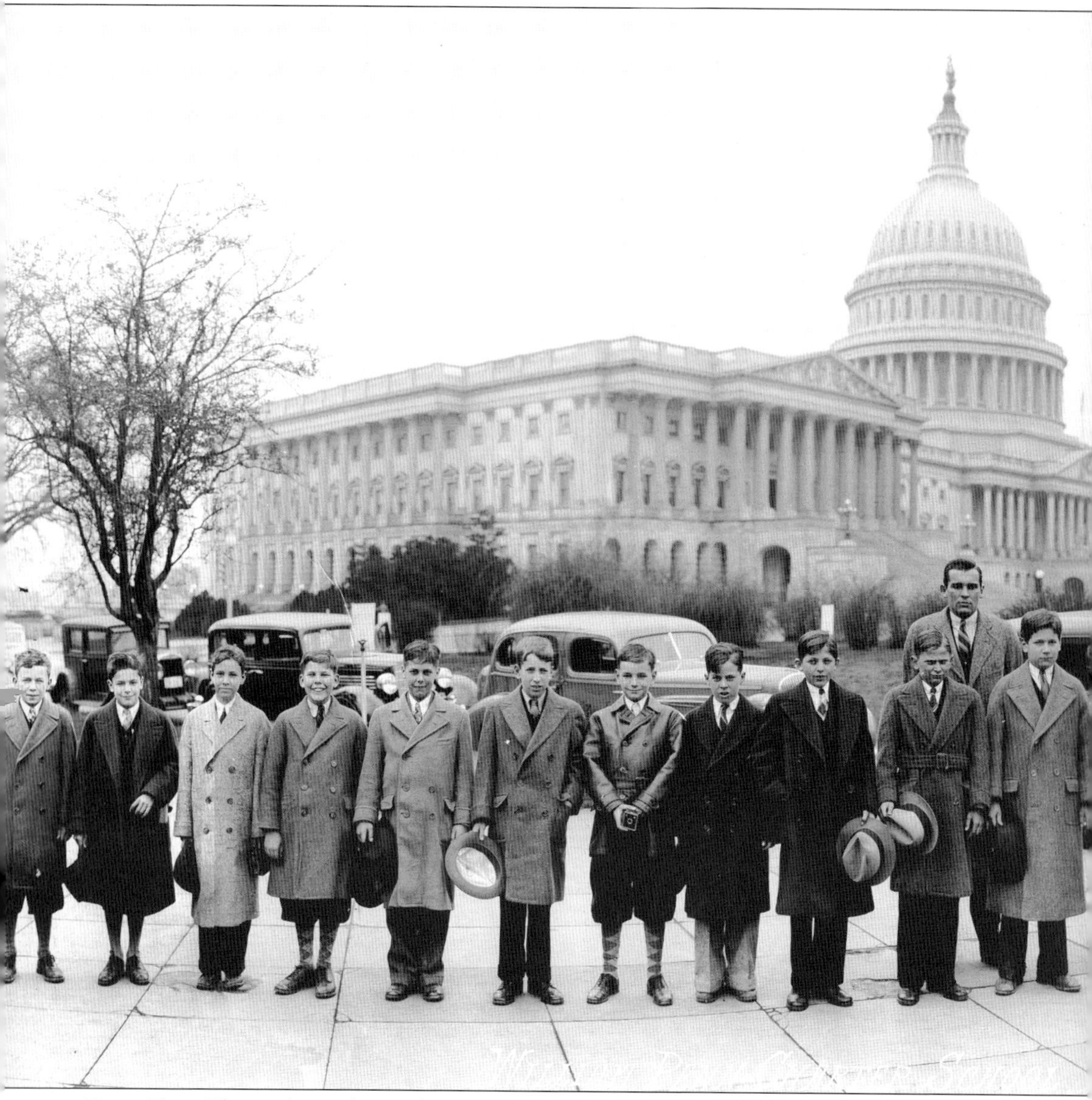

**Field Trip.** Throughout the 20th century, Friends schools enthusiastically planned field trips as a way to extend the curriculum beyond classroom walls and embrace experiential learning that deepened a student's understanding of the world. At the William Penn Charter School, students traveled to Washington, D.C., each year in conjunction with

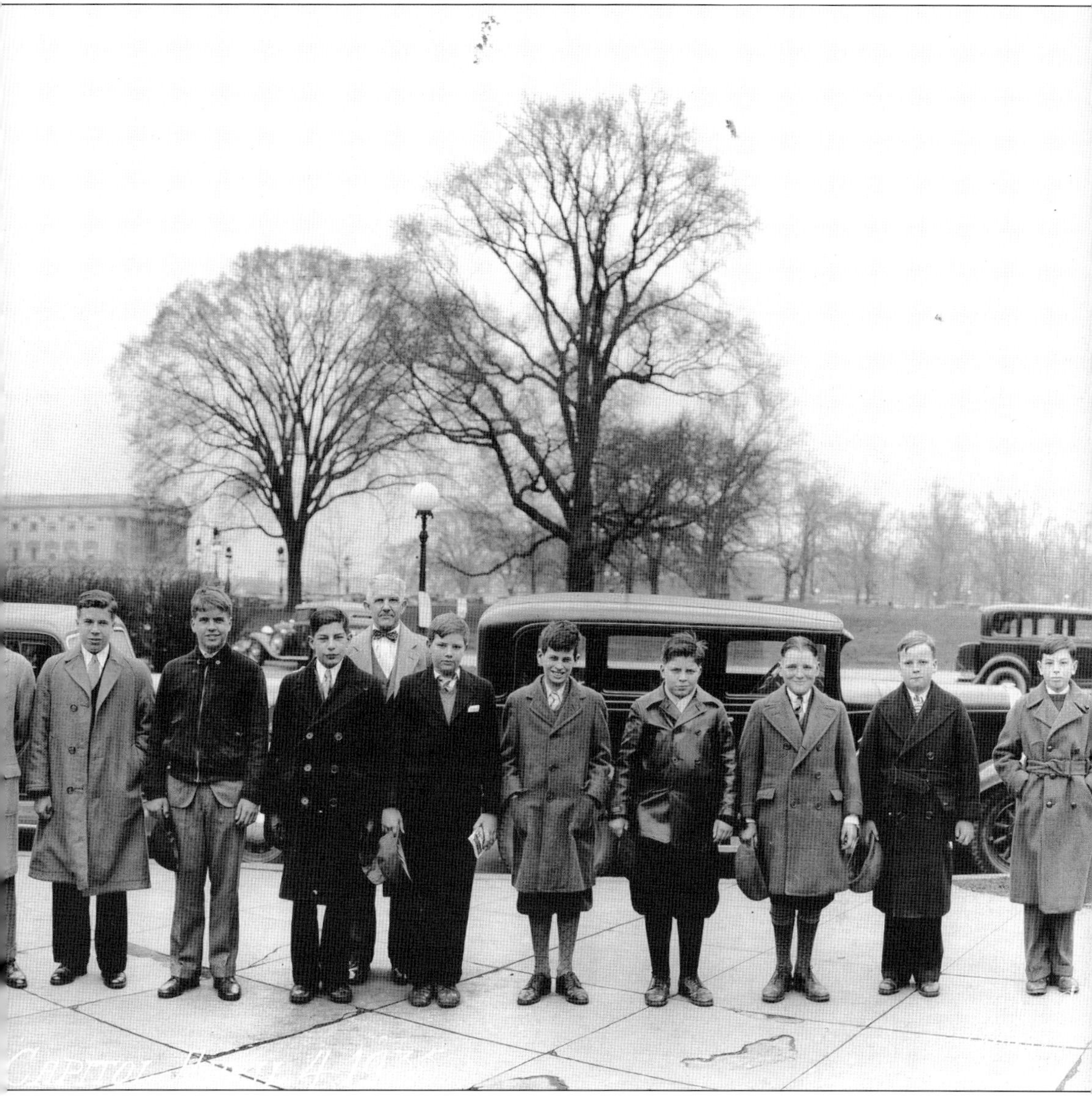

their study of the history of the American people in Quarta (seventh grade) and Upper Quarta (eighth grade). In 1935, when the photograph was taken, William Penn Charter was an all-boys school. (Courtesy of the William Penn Charter School.)

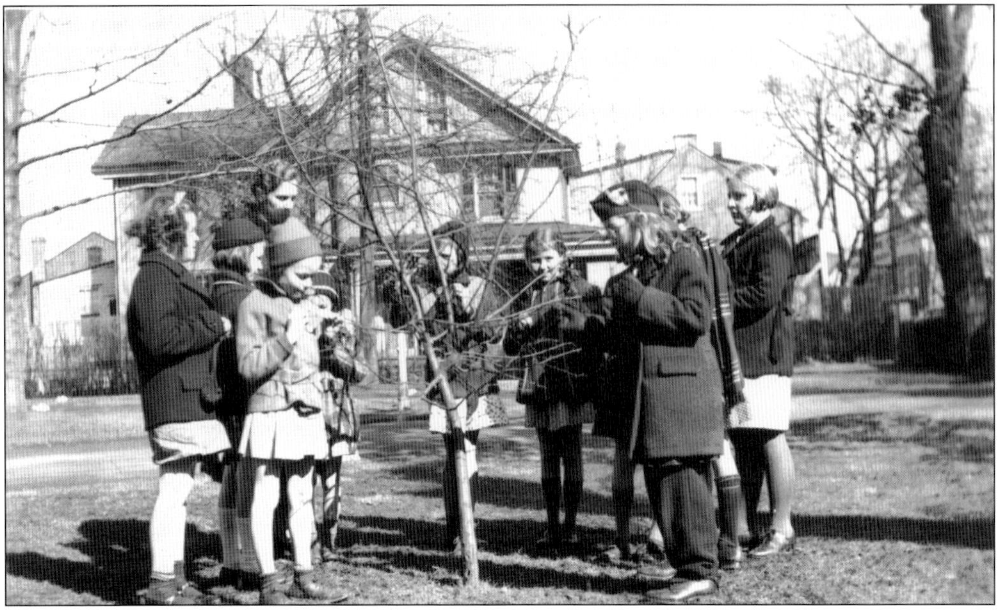

**Planting a Tree.** To teach children to be good stewards of the earth, many Friends schools engage in tree planting. At the beginning of the 20th century, William Wharton, a member of the Green Street Meeting's Property Committee, raised awareness of the importance of caring for trees through conversations with children playing outside during recess. Today Greene Street Friends School has a tree laboratory that grows saplings for the local community as a form of service. (Courtesy of Greene Street Friends School.)

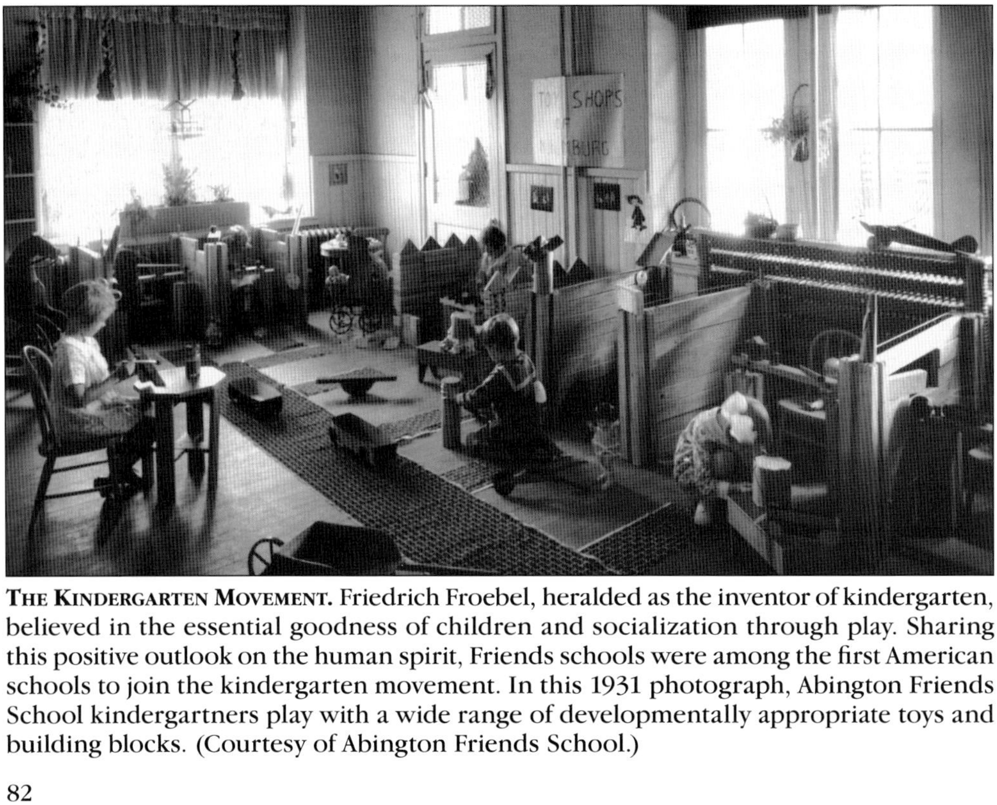


**The Kindergarten Movement.** Friedrich Froebel, heralded as the inventor of kindergarten, believed in the essential goodness of children and socialization through play. Sharing this positive outlook on the human spirit, Friends schools were among the first American schools to join the kindergarten movement. In this 1931 photograph, Abington Friends School kindergartners play with a wide range of developmentally appropriate toys and building blocks. (Courtesy of Abington Friends School.)

**Welcoming the Arts.** In earlier centuries, Quakers viewed the arts as potentially harmful for they lacked simplicity; Quakers preferred plain dress and disapproved of excessive displays. As a result, many Friends schools remained ambivalent about the arts through the early 20th century. At Greene Street Friends School, the first formal art class for elementary students (depicted in the photograph at right) was not offered until 1937. Classes that focused on crafts proved highly acceptable, since they involved creating something of practical use. The photograph below shows teacher Leah M. Perkins helping students to craft sculpture pieces at George School in 1943. Sometimes hybrid approaches such as "art and manual training" helped to bridge the gap from ambivalence to acceptance of the arts. Today Friends schools recognize the spirituality of creative expression and offer rich curricula in visual and performing arts. (Right, courtesy of Greene Street Friends School; below, courtesy of George School.)

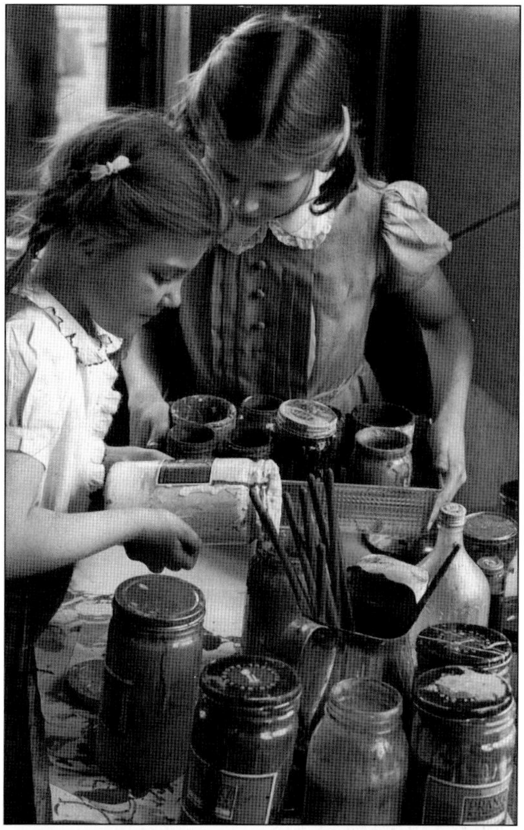

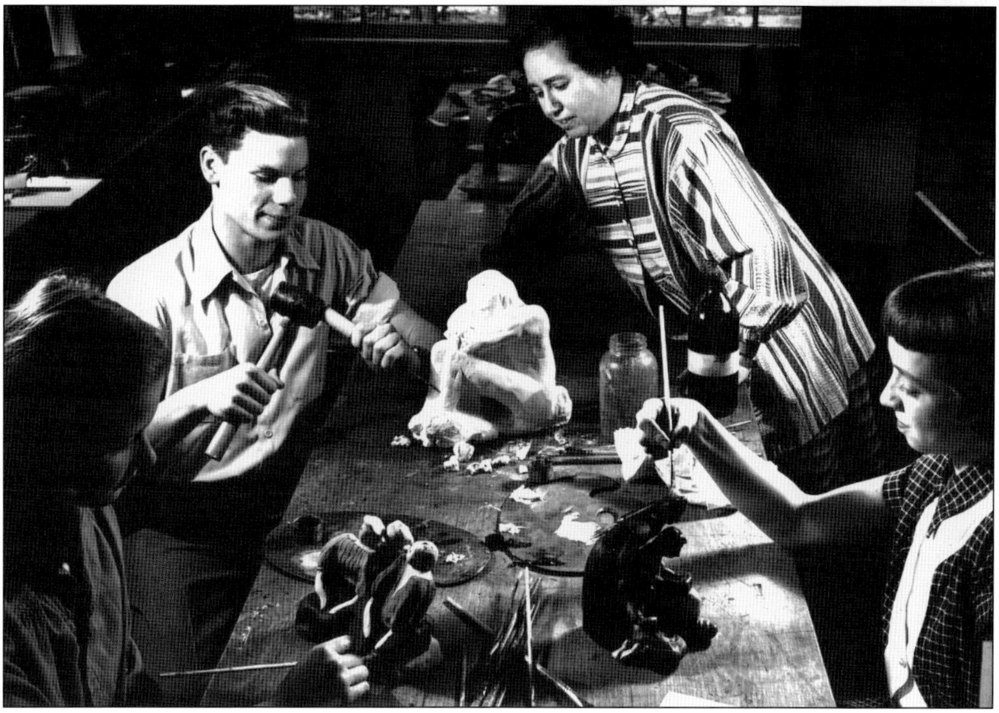

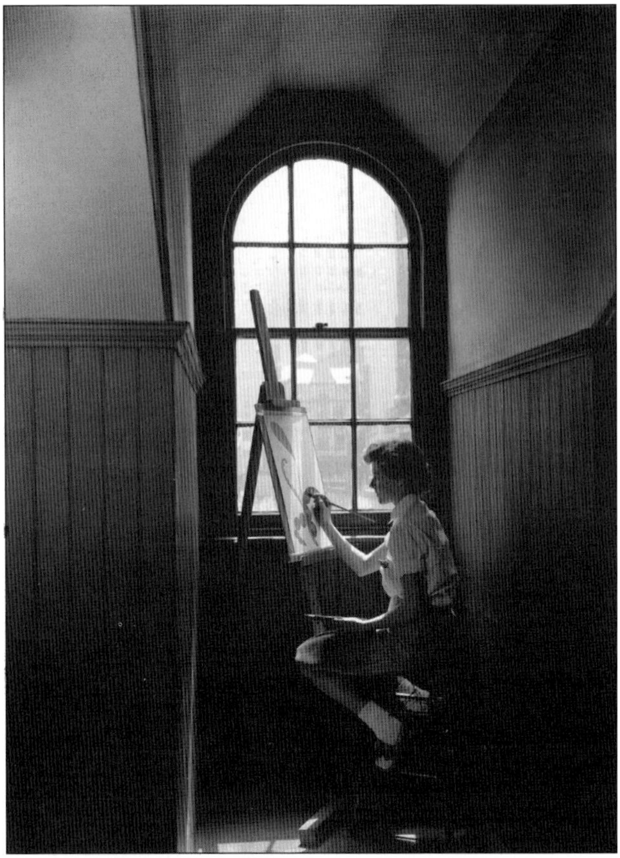

**QUIET NOOKS AND DESIGNATED SPACES.** To further improve experiential learning in arts and crafts, Friends schools such as Friends Select School sought out art spaces that provided exterior light. In the late-1930s image shown at left, Betty Olivit paints in a nook on the top floor of the main building. Art has been a part of the curriculum at Friends Select since the 1860s. Similarly in 1936, Westtown School created a dedicated space for its youngest students by building a three-room school using the foundation and stone walls of a barn on campus. In their new quarters, young students spent their days in an informal, homelike atmosphere that allowed for creative artistic exploration and use of tools. (Left, courtesy of Friends Select School; below, courtesy of Westtown School.)

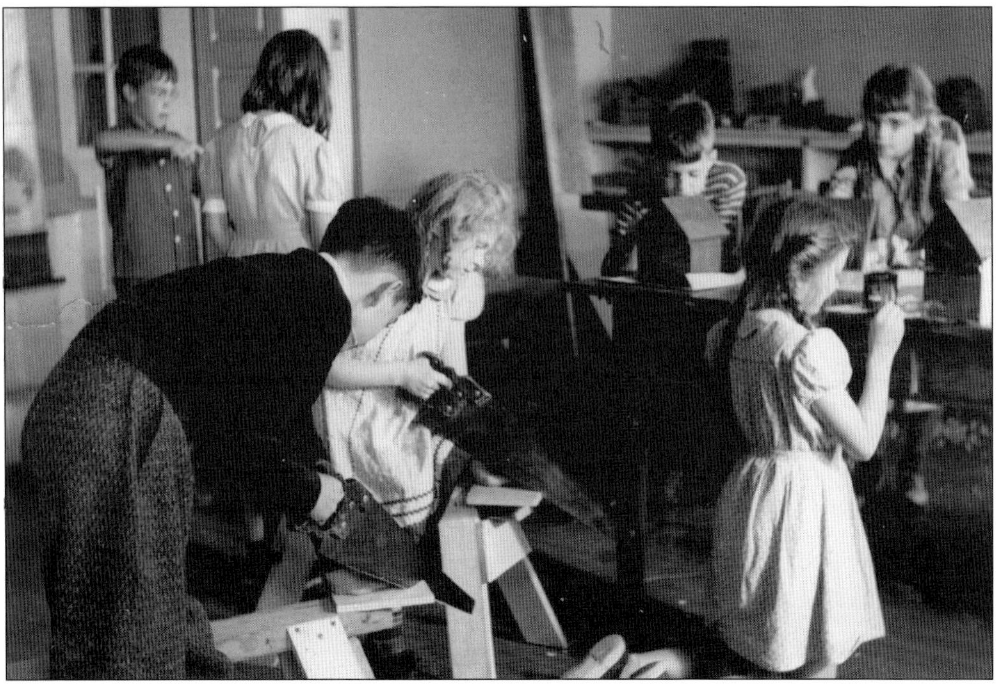

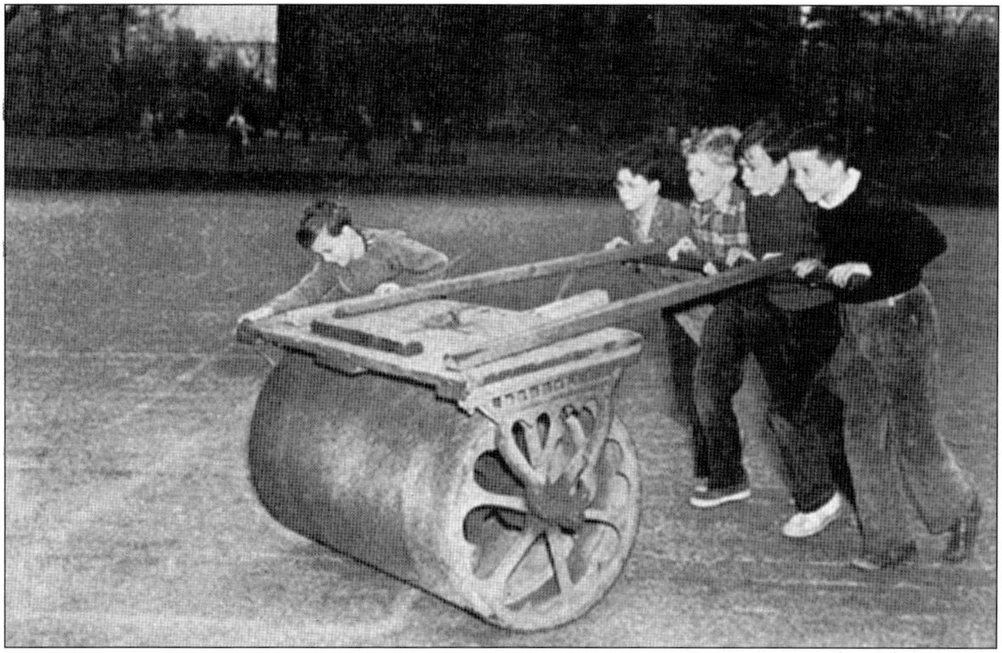

**The Mother of Invention.** Labor shortages during World War II led to various empowering hands-on learning experiences. In this photograph from 1945, lower school students at Germantown Friends School take a turn rolling the tennis court. (Courtesy of Germantown Friends School.)

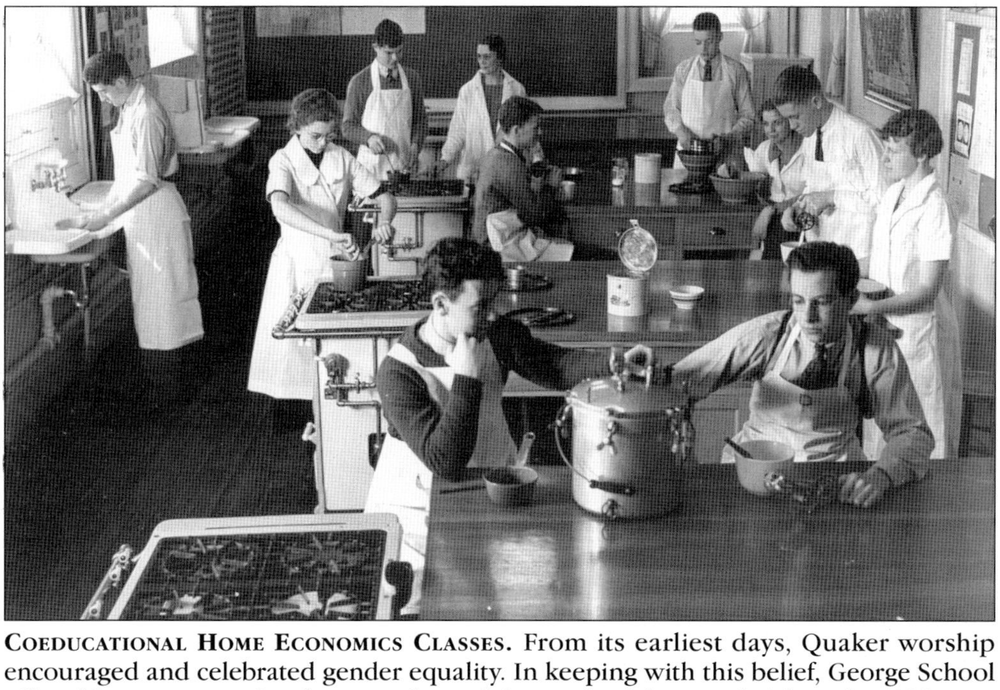

**Coeducational Home Economics Classes.** From its earliest days, Quaker worship encouraged and celebrated gender equality. In keeping with this belief, George School offered home economics classes and wood shop to both boys and girls in the 1930s, at a time when sex-segregated classes remained common, even at Friends schools. (Courtesy of George School.)

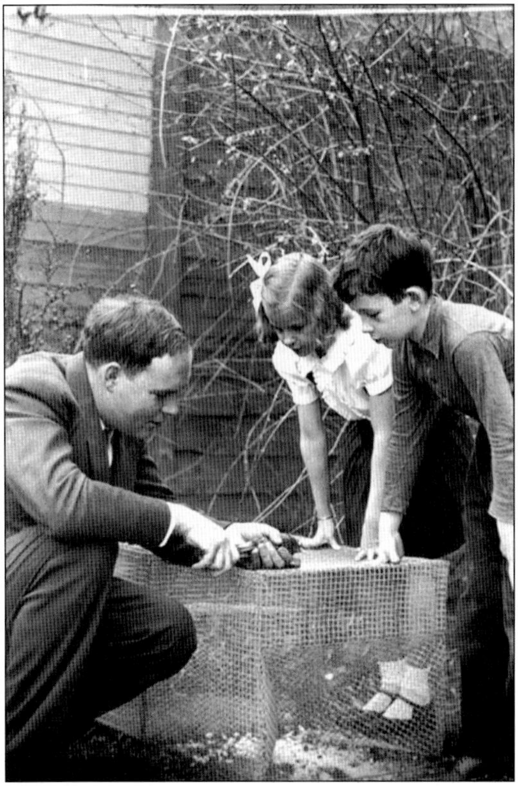

**Nature Club.** Some of the most exciting experiential learning in Friends schools occurs in science programs. At Germantown Friends School, Joe Cadbury's legendary science program included a nature club. In this 1940 photograph, he is teaching children to band birds for later identification. (Courtesy of Germantown Friends School.)

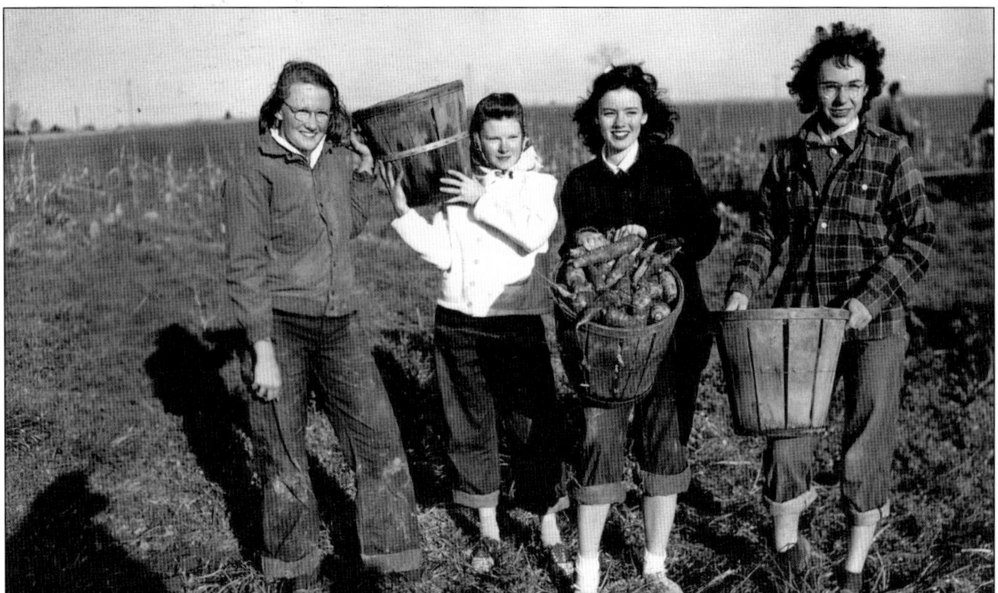

**Autumn Harvest.** During labor and food shortages, experiential learning often served a real and present need. On October 9, 1942, classes were suspended at Westtown School, and the combined efforts of students and faculty that day resulted in seven acres of corn husked and 1,700 bushels of apples collected. Beets and carrots were also harvested at two neighboring farms. (Courtesy of Westtown School.)

**Building Canoes.** In the mid-20th century, productive work with one's hands continued to be a celebrated aspect of the curricula in Friends schools. At George School, the wood shop offered girls and boys a chance to make their own canoe. Each student worked on a frame, crafted a canoe, and took home her own creation. (Courtesy of George School.)

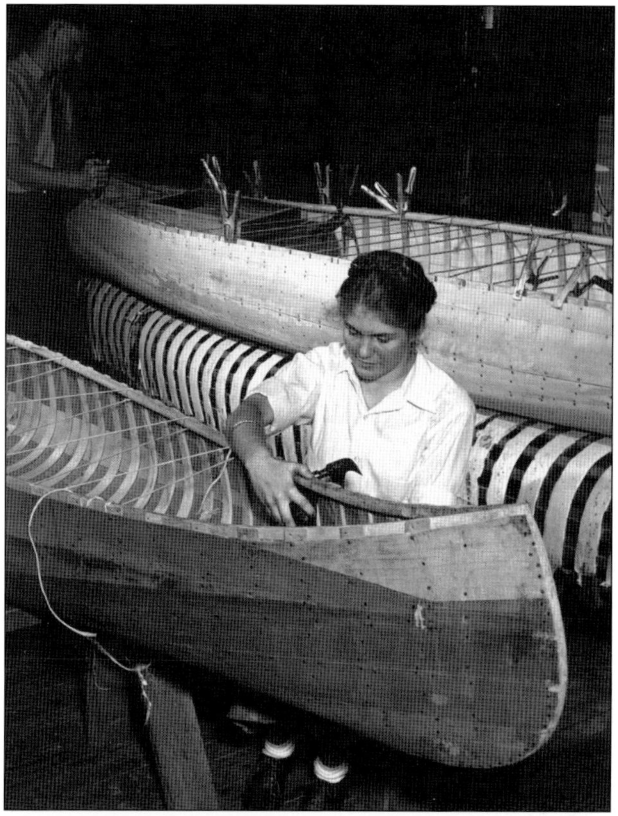

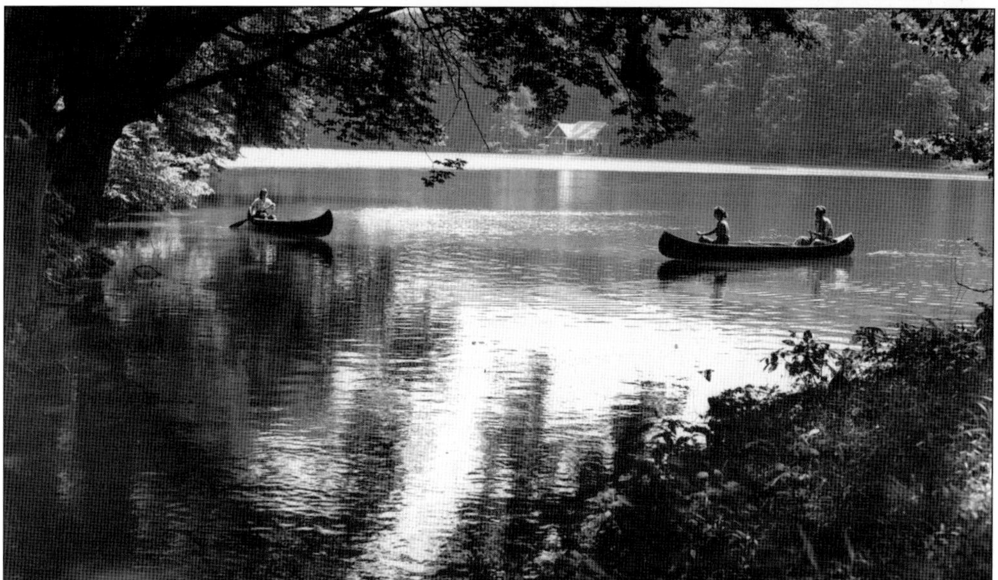

**Westtown Lake.** Long before *outdoor education* became a popular phrase, Friends schools encouraged students not only to exercise outdoors but also to experience the wonder of nature as a reflective, spiritual practice. This 1946 photograph shows students enjoying a peaceful moment on Westtown Lake, built in 1912. (Courtesy of Westtown School.)

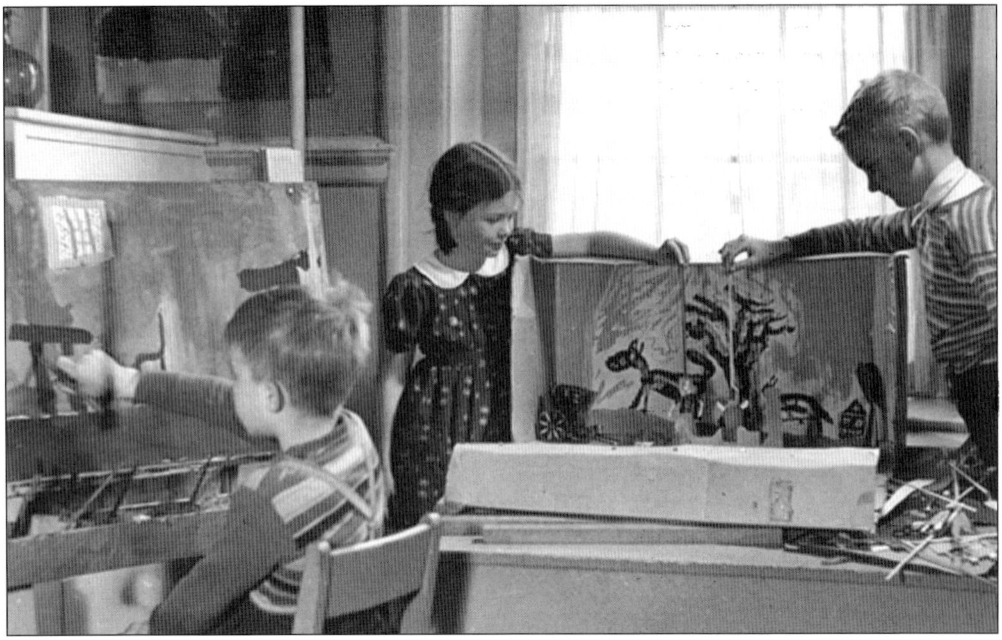

**Cooperative Storytelling.** Despite ambivalence toward the arts during earlier eras, by the 1950s, Philadelphia-area Friends schools incorporated hands-on creative arts projects into elementary school classrooms with enthusiasm and frequency. As shown here, kindergarten children at Germantown Friends School used dioramas as a form of cooperative storytelling during activity time. (Courtesy of Germantown Friends School.)

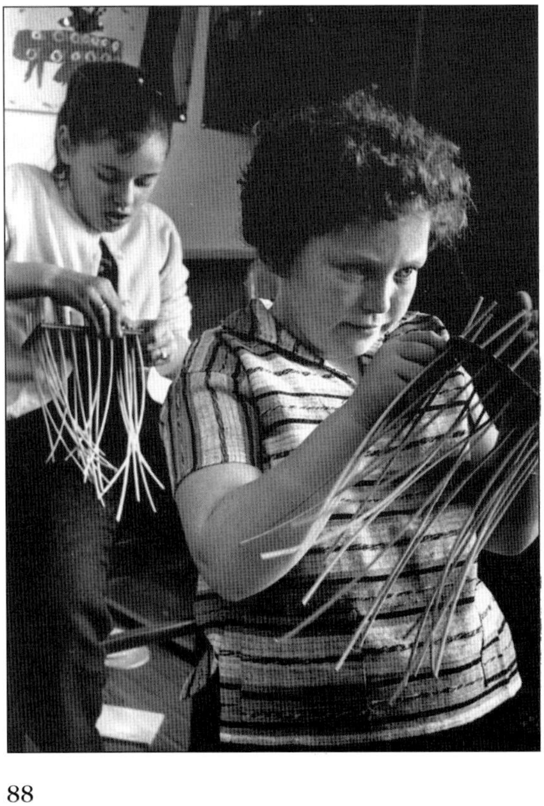

**Valuing Village Crafts.** For elementary school students, engaging in the ancient village craft of basket weaving improves creativity, concentration, and fine motor skills, while also demonstrating the importance of cultural enterprises. In the mid-20th century, basket weaving served as a meaningful hands-on activity that enhanced the social studies curriculum at Frankford Friends School. (Courtesy of Frankford Friends School.)

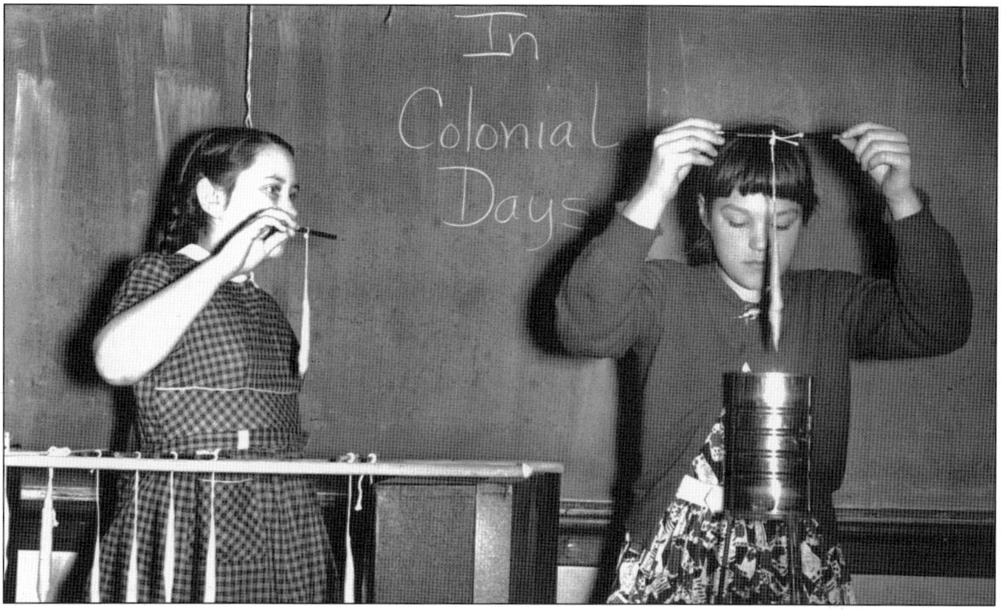


**Dipping Wax Candles.** In the mid-20th century, many Friends schools explored imaginative ways to enable students to experience aspects of life from an earlier era. To this end, students at Greene Street Friends School chewed on raw sugar cane, churned their own butter, and dipped candles (as shown here) as part of their experiential investigation of the Colonial period in American history. (Courtesy of Greene Street Friends School.)

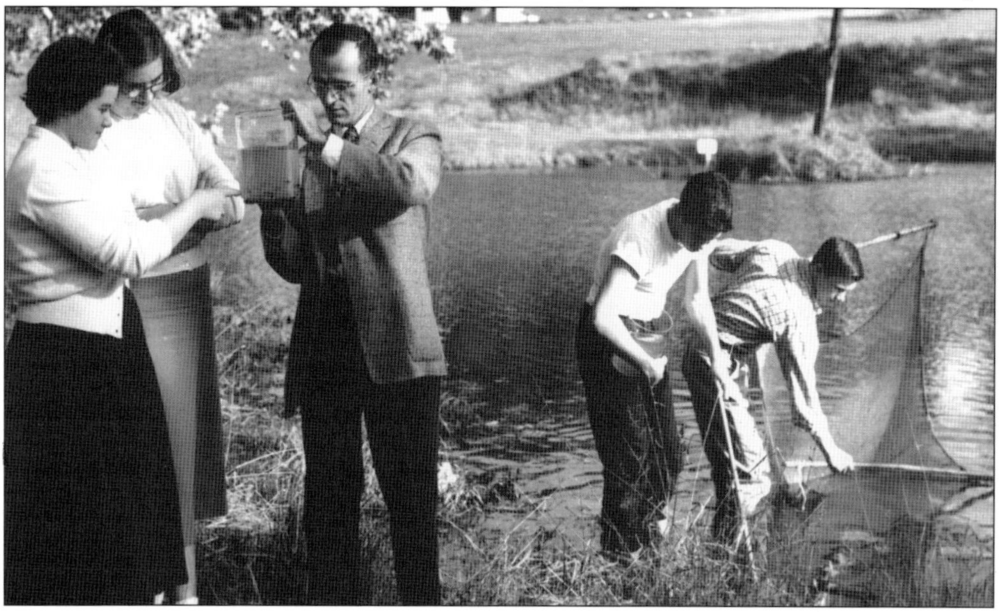

**Ecology by the Pond.** Friends school teachers often seek opportunities to educate outdoors. In this mid-20th-century image, William Craighead is meeting his class for an ecology lesson. They are collecting protozoa that later will be placed on slides and studied under a microscope. In addition to serving as a science laboratory, the George School pond offered bird-watching, boating, and fishing in warmer months, as well as skating in the winter. (Courtesy of George School.)

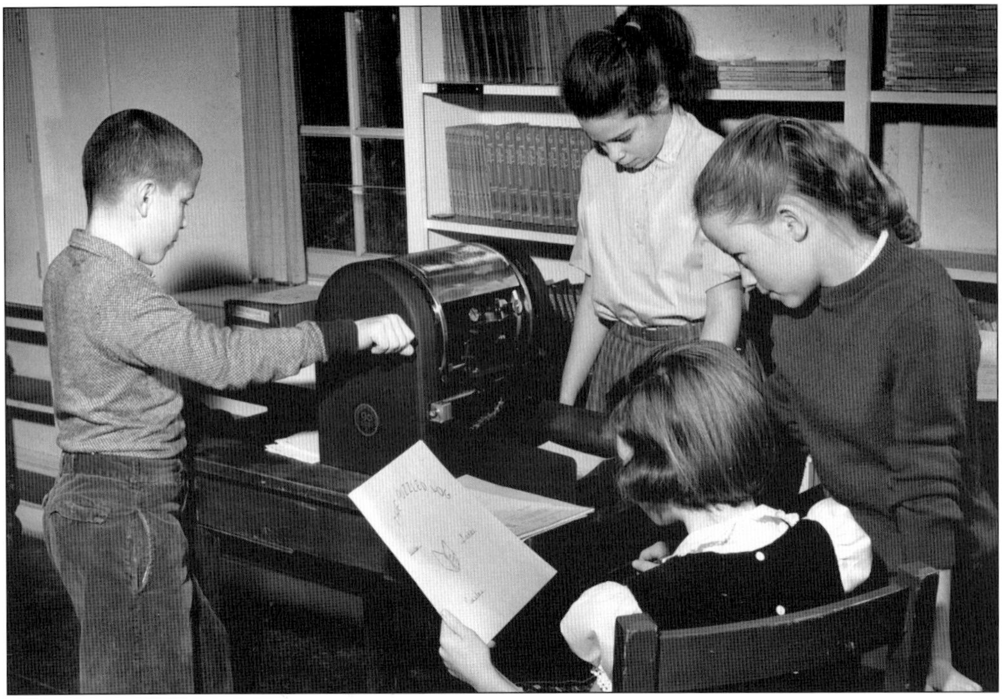

**Printing the *Log*.** At Friends schools, experiential learning involves not only kinesthetic activities but also collaborative efforts. As shown in this photograph from the late 1950s, lower school students at Westtown School edited and published their own magazine, the *Log*. To encourage a sense of agency and community, every student in third through sixth grades served on a student committee, such as the *Log*. (Courtesy of Westtown School.)

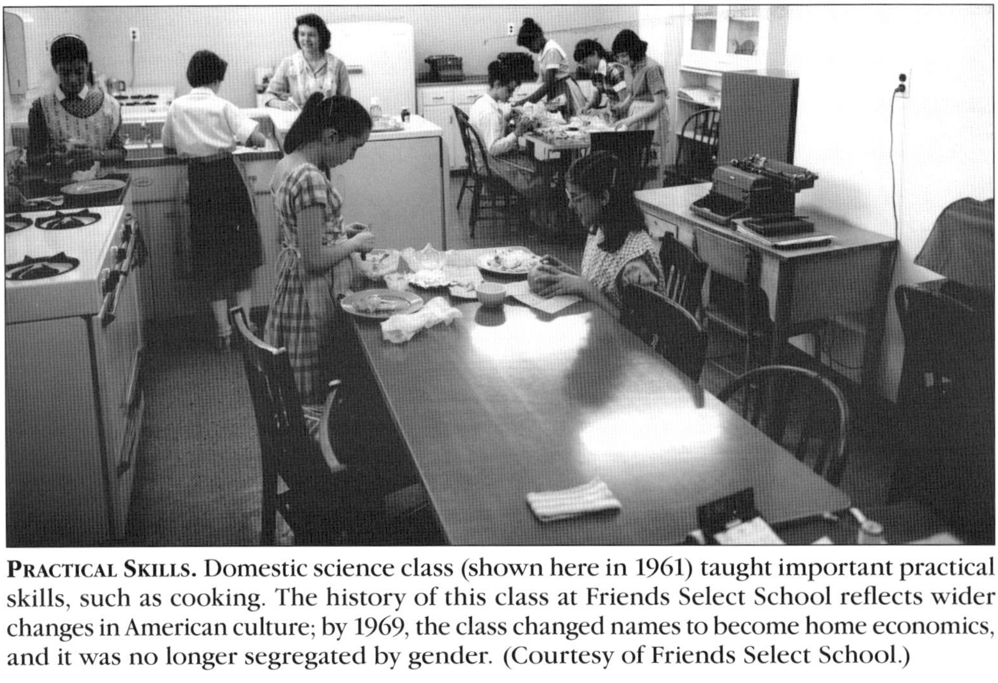

**Practical Skills.** Domestic science class (shown here in 1961) taught important practical skills, such as cooking. The history of this class at Friends Select School reflects wider changes in American culture; by 1969, the class changed names to become home economics, and it was no longer segregated by gender. (Courtesy of Friends Select School.)

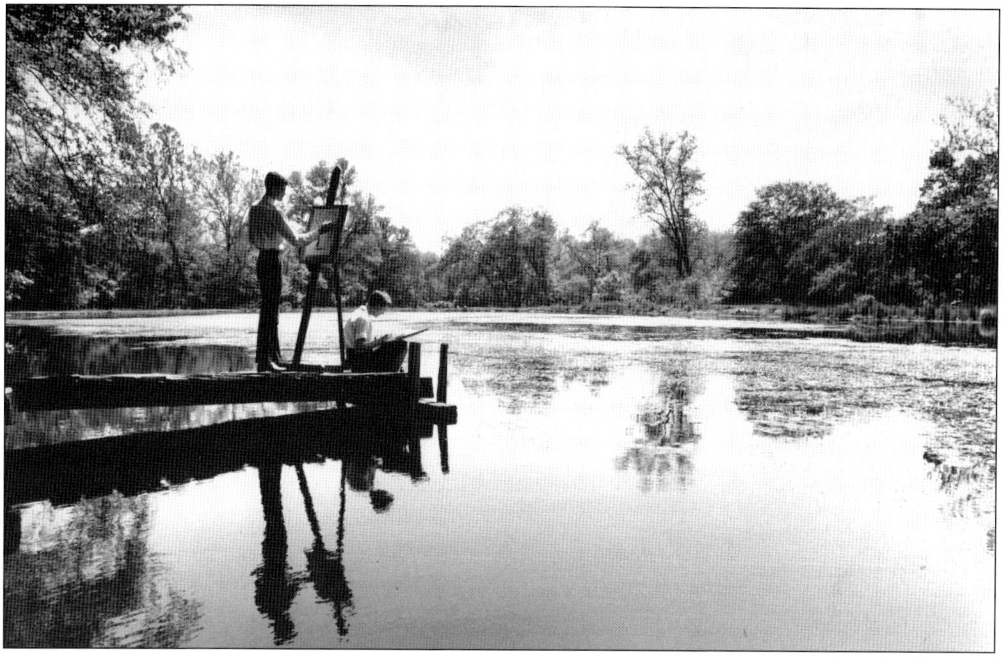

**Painting, Sculpting, Shaping.** As the pace of daily life quickened in the 20th century, Friends schools made an effort to encourage opportunities for silence, concentration, and reflection, and the arts provided a natural opportunity for these habits to develop. Painting provided a welcome opportunity for George School students to immerse themselves in the beauty of natural surroundings. As shown in the photograph above, the light reflecting by George School's pond invites quiet contemplation. In the photograph below, Abington Friends School teacher Winnifred Sudler provides patient guidance to her students as they experiment with clay and learn how to sculpt animals. (Above, courtesy of George School; below, courtesy of Abington Friends School.)

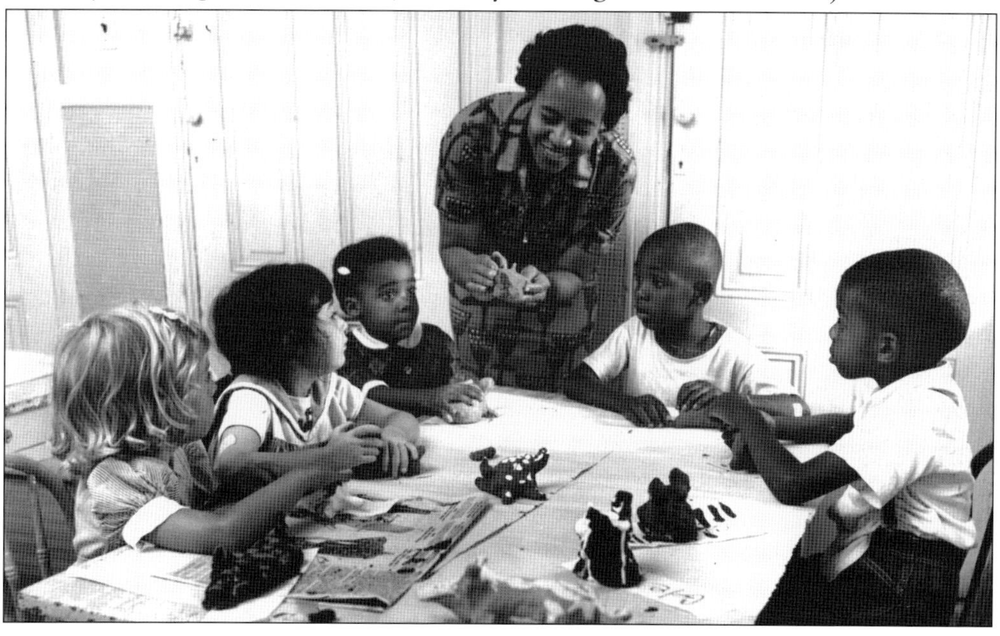

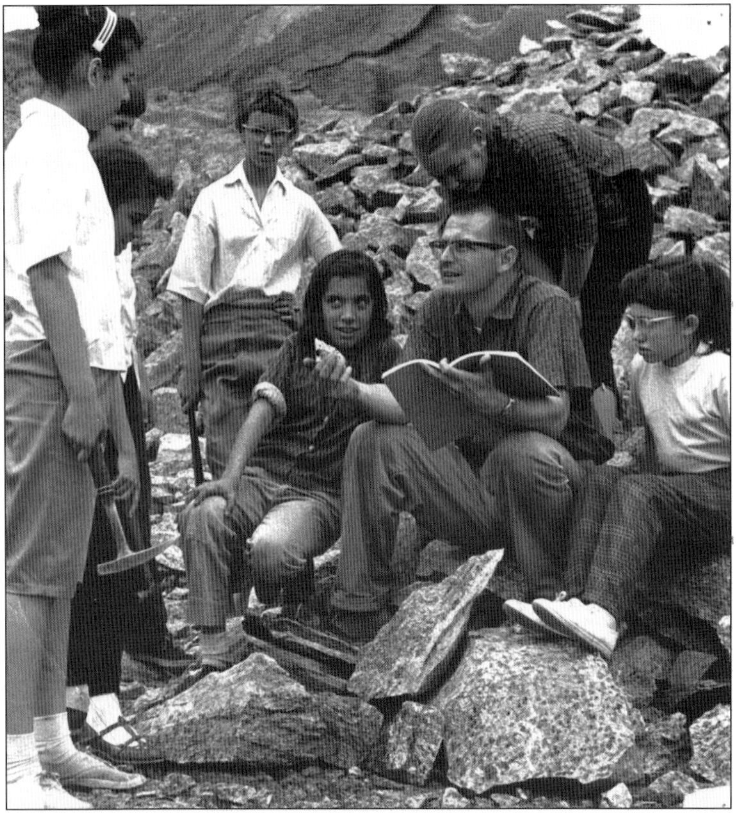

**The Wonders of Nature.** Through experiential learning, Friends schools guide their students' development of independent thought, critical inquiry, and observation. As John Dewey explained in his writings, developing these habits improves children's vibrant engagement with the world. This 1960s image from a course on the wonders of nature captures a glimpse of geological inquiry in action. (Courtesy of Greene Street Friends School.)

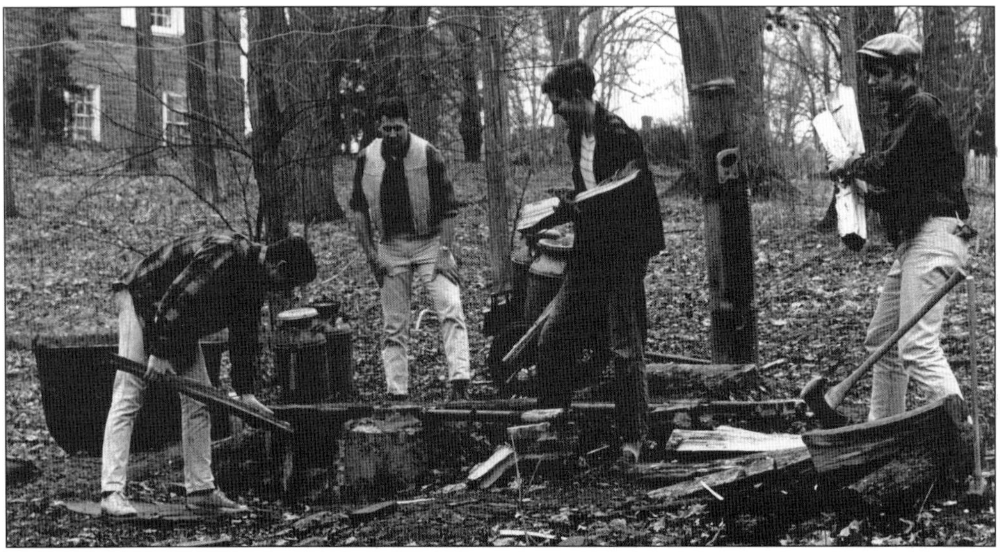

**Making Maple Syrup.** Approaches to experiential learning at Philadelphia-area Friends schools are vast and ambitious. On their tree-filled campus in 1966, Westtown School students and teacher Peter Lane (second from left) prepare to boil sap collected from maple trees. This activity, dating back to 1922, is just one way in which Friends school students grow in their understanding and care of natural resources—and pancakes. (Courtesy of Westtown School.)

**Dexterity and Fine Motor Skills.** Friends schools are known for developing hands-on approaches that meet each child at her level, recognizing the specific needs of the individual. In this image from 1969, kindergartner Cara Kaminski develops dexterity and fine motor skills, while exercising her creative instincts, at Frankford Friends School. (Courtesy of Frankford Friends School.)

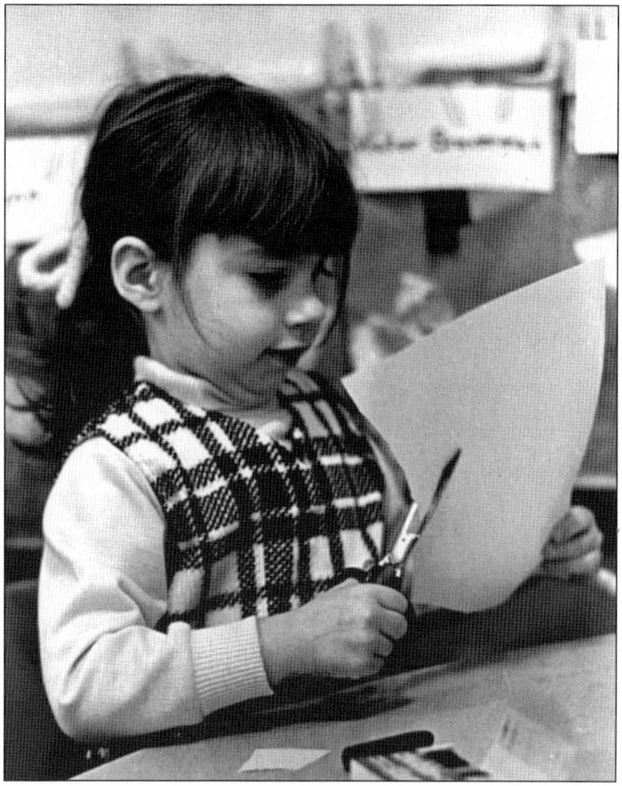

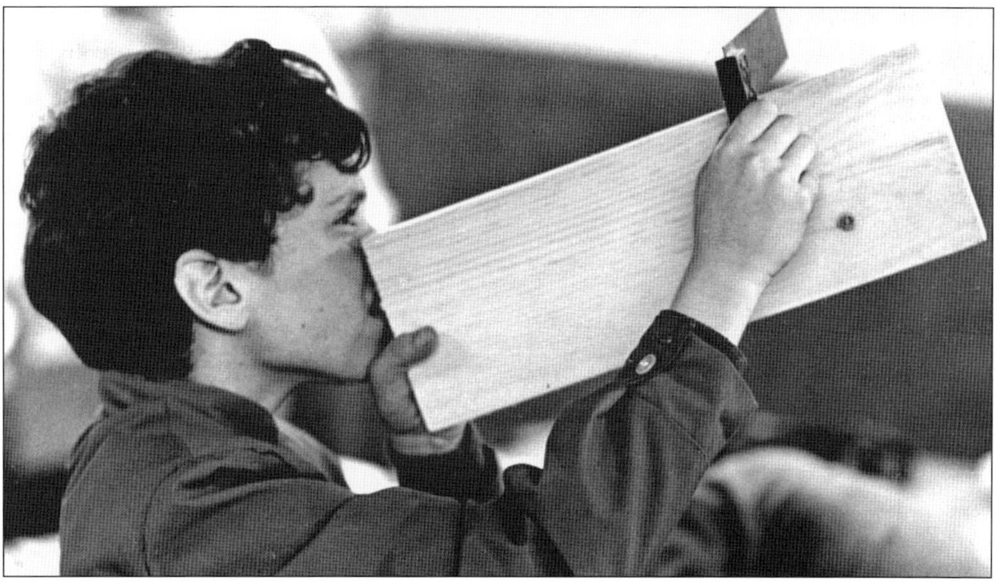

**Measure Twice and Cut Once.** Wood shop and mechanical drawing continued to be valued aspects of Friends education in the 1970s. In this image, Michael Kushner learns to "measure twice and cut once." The testing of his work to see if it was square, with mechanical precision, was the object of the lesson. To this day, similar classes capture the imaginations of young designers and engineers. (Courtesy of Frankford Friends School.)

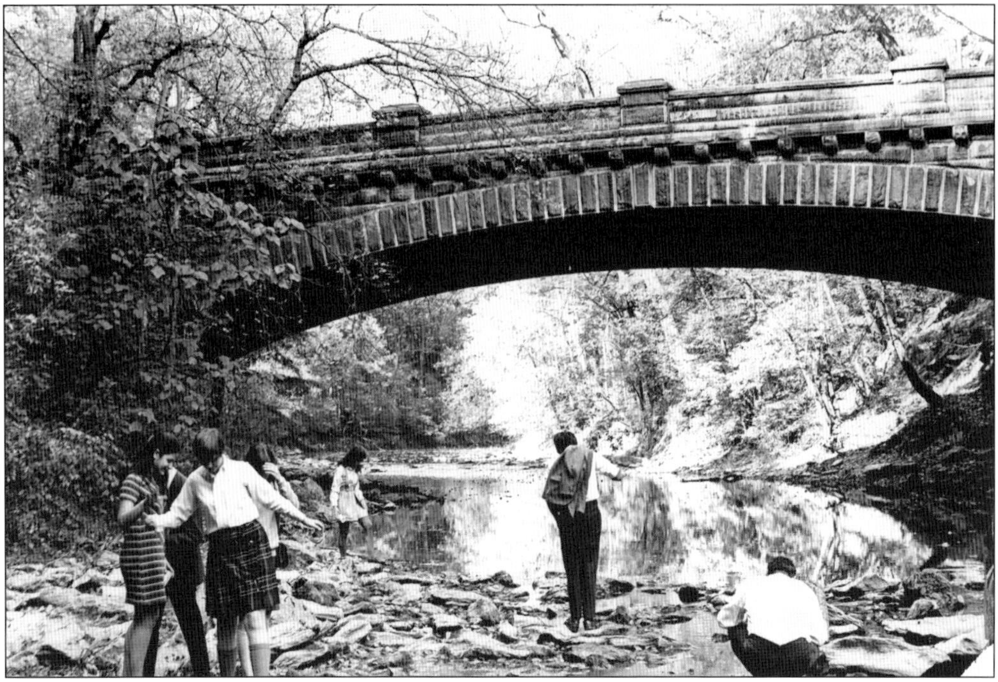

**Exploring the Wissahickon.** The Philadelphia region is blessed with many parks and outdoor camps, including Quaker camps. In the 1960s and 1970s, many Friends schools developed both day trips and overnight camping trips that invited children to become closer to nature, while building community with classmates. In this image, Friends Select School students explore the Wissahickon Creek. (Courtesy of Friends Select School.)

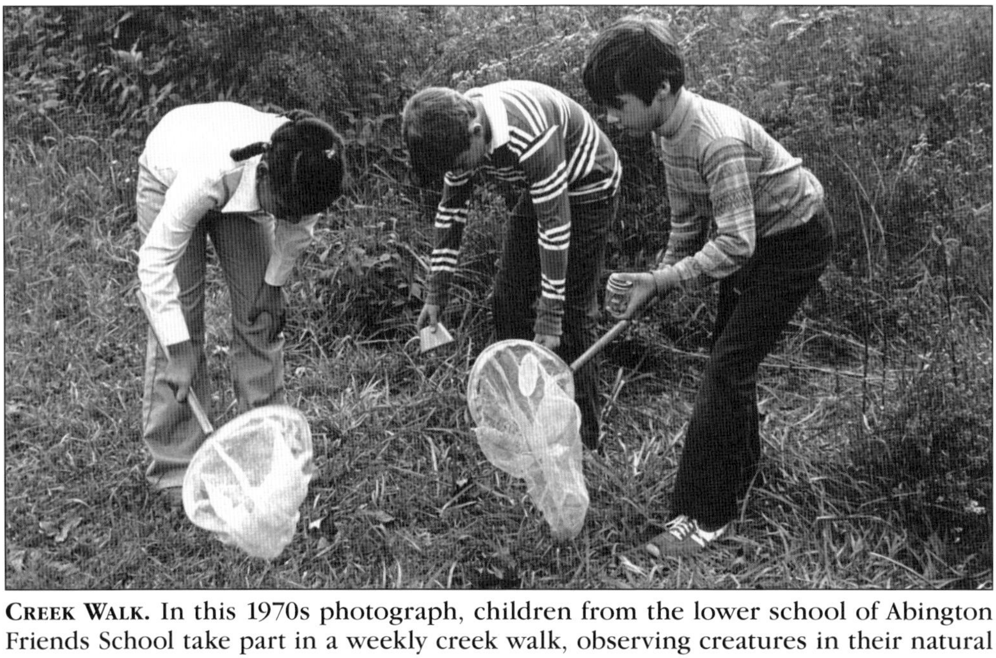

**Creek Walk.** In this 1970s photograph, children from the lower school of Abington Friends School take part in a weekly creek walk, observing creatures in their natural habitat. The land, creek, and trees on campus provide a superb location for teaching children to appreciate nature. (Courtesy of Abington Friends School.)

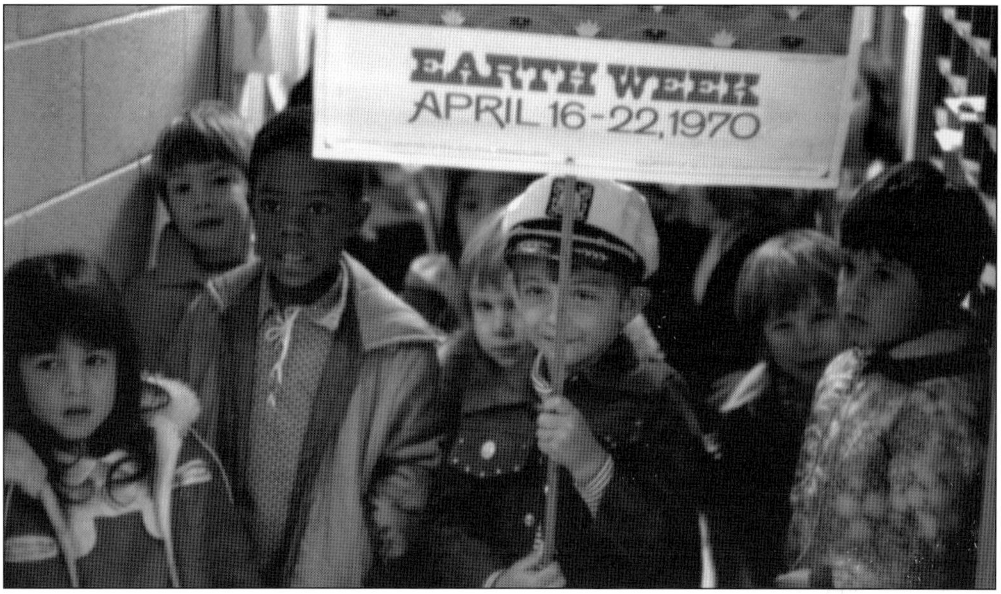


**EARTH DAY CELEBRATION.** Many Friends schools embraced Earth Day and Earth Week when they emerged on the national scene in 1970. Children at Friends schools are taught from an early age to practice stewardship and care for the earth and to appreciate the interrelatedness of all living things. (Courtesy of Abington Friends School.)

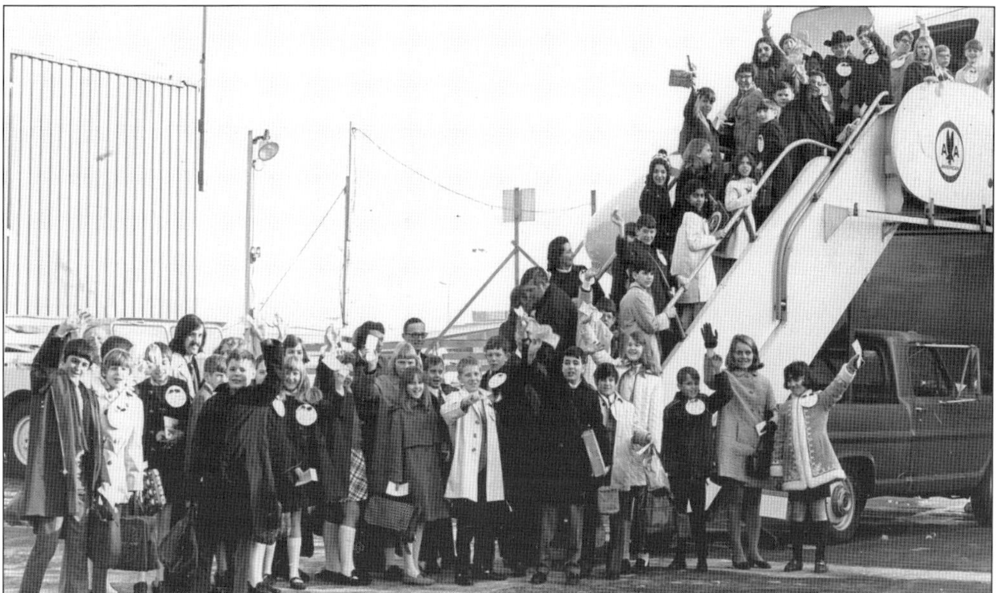

**MEXICAN EXCHANGE PROGRAM.** In the late 20th century, many Friends schools created foreign exchange programs as a way to raise cross-cultural awareness and encourage international friendships through first-hand experience. At Plymouth Meeting Friends School, teacher Dottie Leonard (second from right, on ground) developed this exchange, now in its 39th year, with the Williams School in Mexico, taking fifth-grade students to Mexico each February and welcoming their Mexican partners back to Plymouth Meeting each May. (Courtesy of Plymouth Meeting Friends School.)

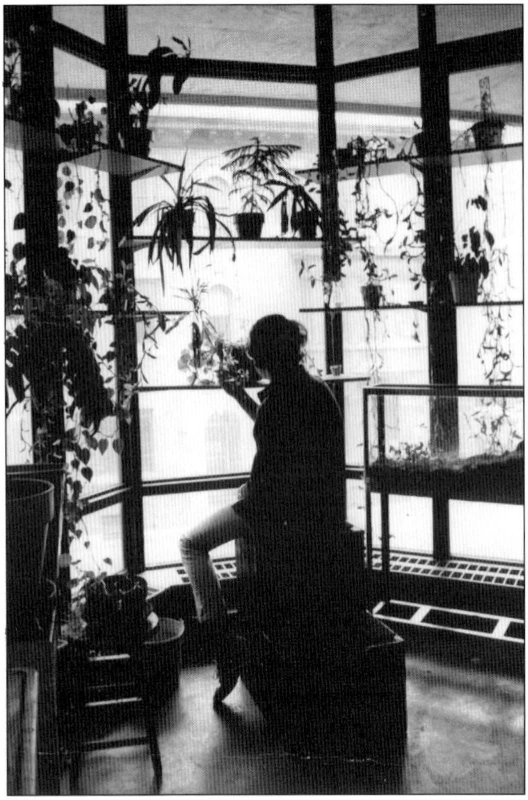

**Working with Greenhouse Plants.** To support experiential learning and stewardship of nature, some Philadelphia Friends schools designed or built new spaces for teaching ecology. At Friends Select School in the early 1970s, the new campus building included a greenhouse that made it possible for students to work directly with plants, observing and tending them throughout the year. (Courtesy of Friends Select School.)

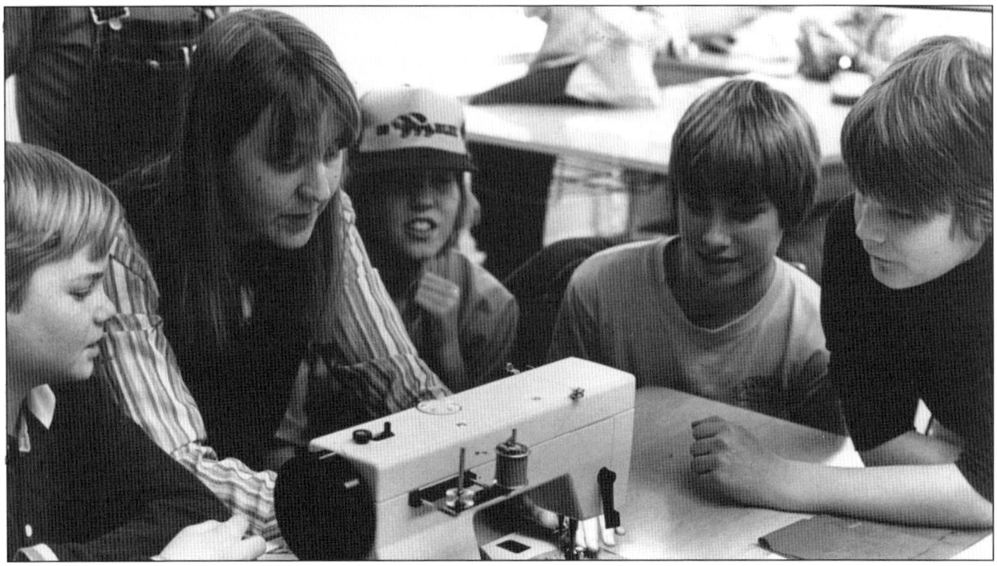

**Middle Schoolers Learn to Sew.** While technology changes, the emphasis on productive work with one's hands remains a constant thread in Quaker philosophy of education. "Newfangled machines" enhanced teaching of practical arts, such as sewing, at many Friends schools. In this photograph from the late 1970s, teacher Billye Price introduces her students to sewing skills in a coeducational home economics class. (Courtesy of Westtown School, photograph by Donald H. Byerly.)

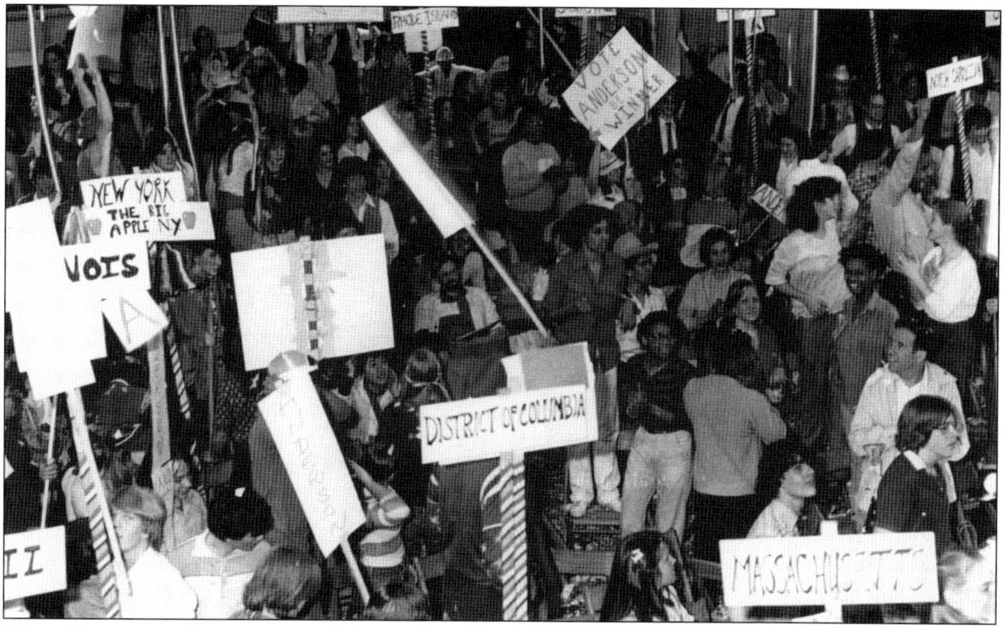


**Mock Political Convention.** At Friends schools, experiential learning occurs in all subject areas, including social studies, as demonstrated by this 1980 photograph. At Westtown School, the school's first mock political convention took place in 1948, and the tradition continued every four years thereafter. The experience provides students with a deeper understanding of the political process, as well as the issues that face the candidates and the electorate. (Courtesy of Westtown School.)

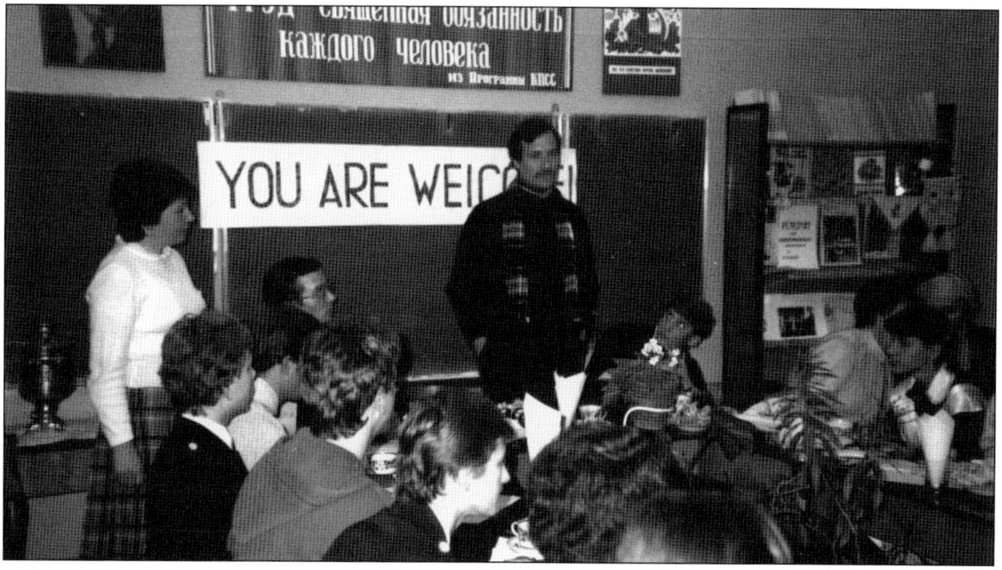


**Visiting the Soviet Union.** To deepen students' understanding of Russian history, Jacob Dresden, assistant head at the William Penn Charter School, took various groups of students to the Soviet Union throughout the 1980s. As shown in this 1985 photograph, students visited classes at school No. 23 in Pskov, approximately 150 miles from Leningrad, and learned the history of the town from their Russian peers. (Courtesy of the William Penn Charter School.)

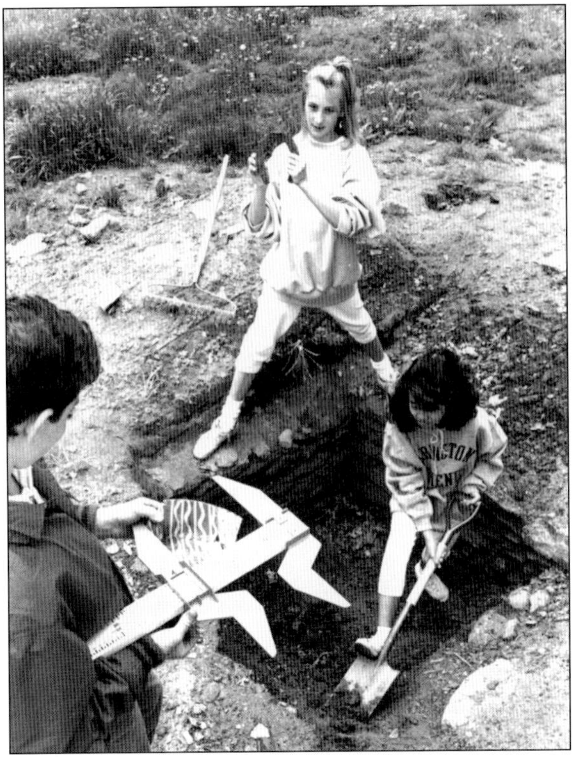

**UNEARTHING HISTORY.** Archaeological digs provide a compelling multidisciplinary approach to learning the process of collecting primary source information. After creating an accurate map, the Abington Friends middle schoolers shown here created a grid and selected a square to excavate. The students unearthed pipes, shoe buckles, Revolutionary War items, and a Victorian glass slipper, in a long-term project that began in 1985. (Courtesy of Abington Friends School.)

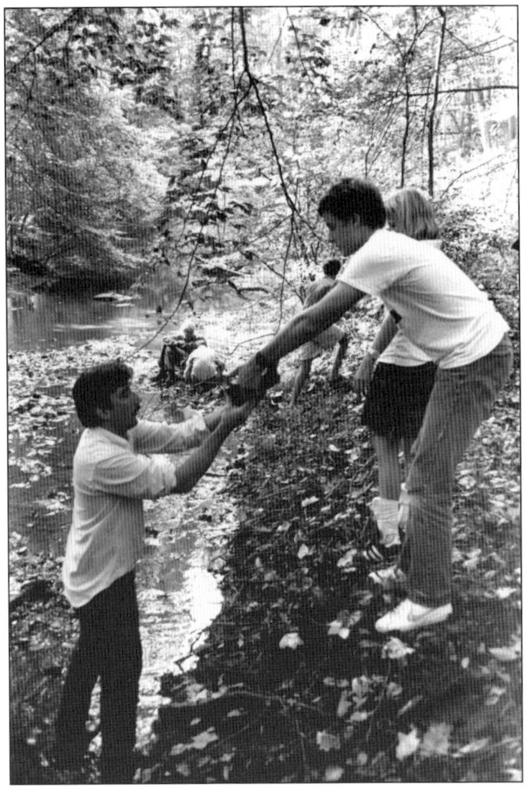

**COLLECTING FIELD SAMPLES.** Teacher Greg Davis hands a field sample to student David Crichton during an outing of the campus ecology class in 1987. Students studied the water, air, and soil of the Westtown School campus, using the resources around them as an outdoor classroom. To this day, similar learning experiences deepen students' commitment to stewardship of the earth at numerous Friends schools. (Courtesy of Westtown School, photograph by Bob Moss.)

# *Six*

# Peace and Social Justice

*We utterly deny all outward wars and strife, and fighting with outward weapons, for any end, or under any pretense whatsoever; this is our testimony to the whole world.*
—Declaration to King Charles II, 1660,
signed by 12 British Quakers including George Fox

For Friends, the belief that there is "that of God" in each person leads to a commitment to both peace and justice. The commitment to peace has been voiced since the earliest decades of Quakerism, when George Fox spoke against fighting in the English civil wars in the mid-1600s. In similar fashion, Quakers value the right sharing of world resources, believing that all people deserve to enjoy the earth's bounty and working to provide the basic needs of food, clothing, and shelter to all. For Philadelphia-area Friends schools in the 20th century, the commitment to peace emerged in many ways, such as teaching children to resolve conflicts through open, direct dialogue, providing teens with the information to decide if they wished to choose conscientious objection or alternative service during times of war, holding candlelight peace vigils, and reading historic works that highlight the courage and determination of peacemakers. Friends schools recognize the importance of working to create a more equitable, caring, and peaceful world, and service projects emerged as a central aspect of the curriculum. Finally, whether students are learning about peacemakers or engaging in service, the Quaker pedagogical approach is to raise questions, encouraging students to learn through research, reflection, and dialogue.

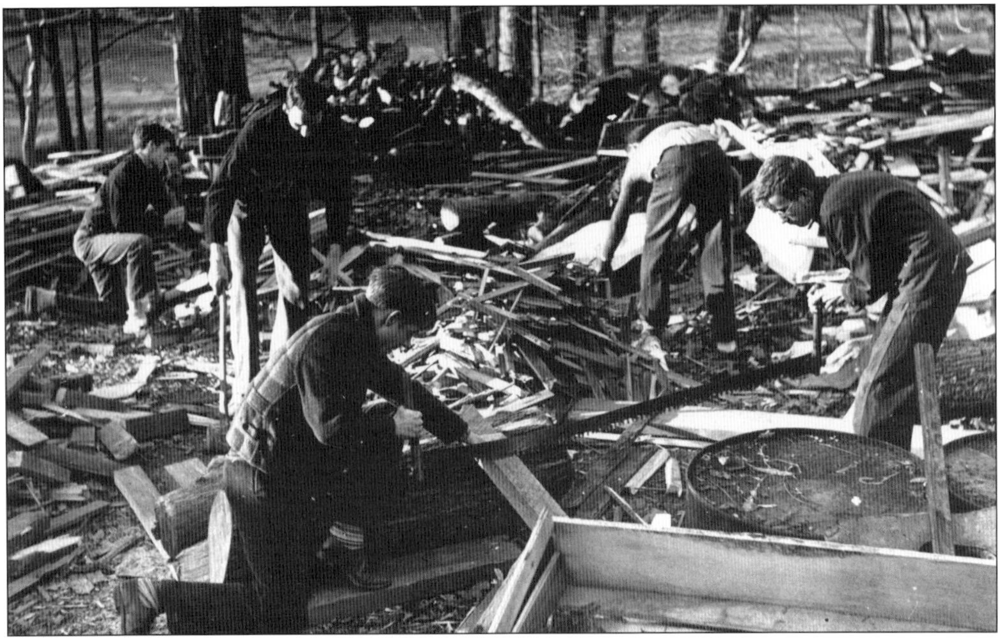

**Wood Delivery Service Project.** Throughout the 20th century, Philadelphia-area Friends schools regarded contributing to the surrounding community part of their mission. In this 1940s photograph, Westtown School students gather and prepare wood pieces on campus for delivery to families in the nearby West Chester area. The wood was to be used by local families to heat their homes during the winter months. (Courtesy of Westtown School.)

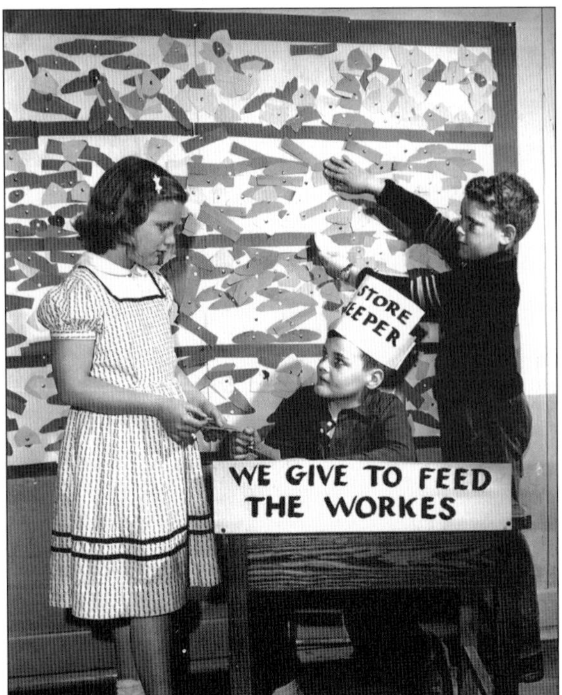


**Learning through Simulations.** In Friends schools, younger children are taught about the importance of right sharing of world resources and the idea that no person ought to suffer from a lack of essentials. In the 1940s, these lower school students from Friends' Central School engage in a hands-on relief work simulation that models the importance of generous giving. (Courtesy of Friends' Central School.)

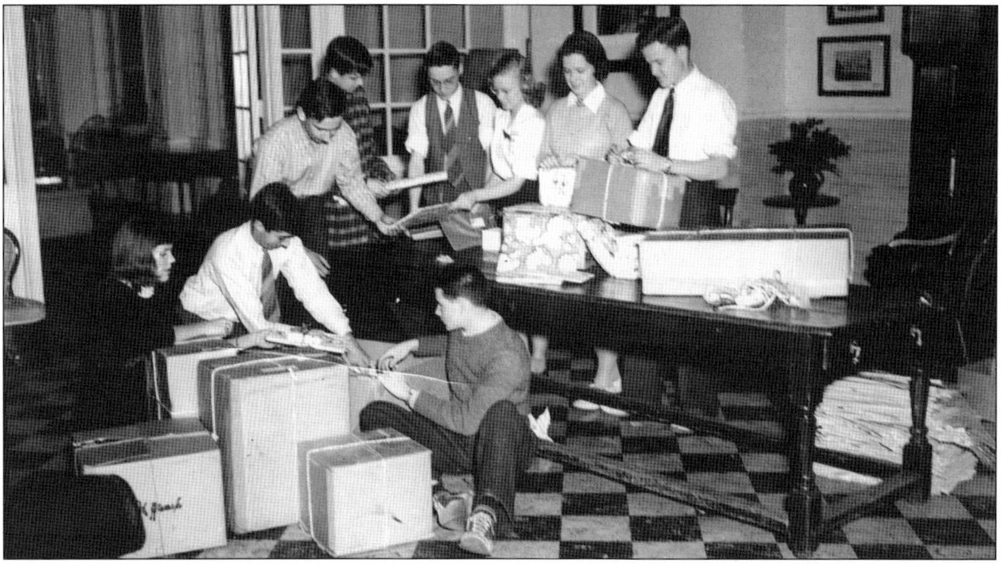

**RESPONDING TO INJUSTICE.** When the United States government imprisoned Japanese Americans in internment camps during World War II, many Quakers spoke out or took action in response to this injustice. Due to the camps' dire conditions, Westtown School students prepared Christmas packages for shipment to Japanese Americans. Furthermore, several Friends schools, including Westtown, found a way to enroll Japanese American teenagers during the war, offering these students both a respite from the camps and a quality education. (Courtesy of Westtown School.)

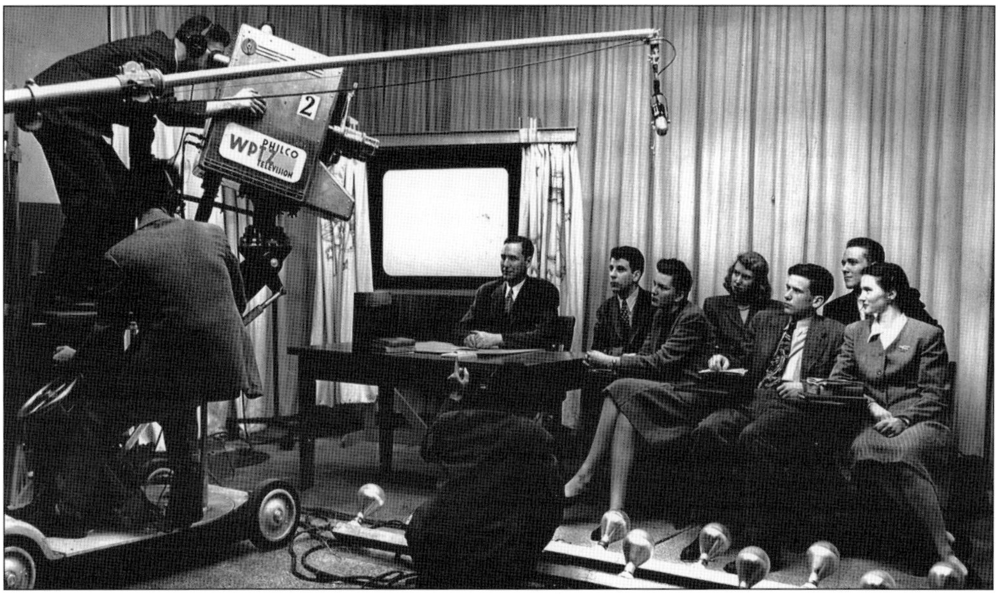


**DISCUSSION OF DEMOCRACY.** In 1947, Friends' Central School students participated in Philco Television's *Discussion of Democracy and Totalitarianism*. While television appearances were novel at that point, engaging in an open exchange of ideas was not. The importance of listening to and honoring all voices is a core value of Friends schools and often appears in classroom exchanges about the nature of democracy, social justice, and peacemaking. (Courtesy of Friends' Central School.)

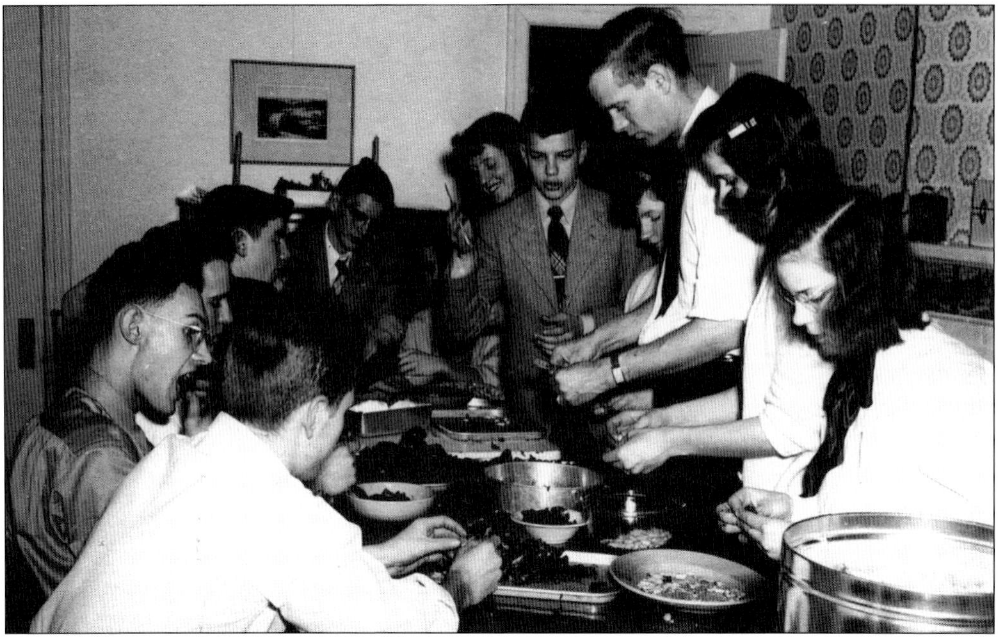

**Sister School in Holland.** Following World War II, many Friends schools lent support to those devastated by the effects of war. In January 1948, Westtown School students engaged in activities to support their sister school in Ommen, Holland. Many gifts were made, such as stuffed dates assembled by this group, fur-lined slippers, and stationery with the Ommen School letterhead made on the printing press at Westtown School. (Courtesy of Westtown School.)

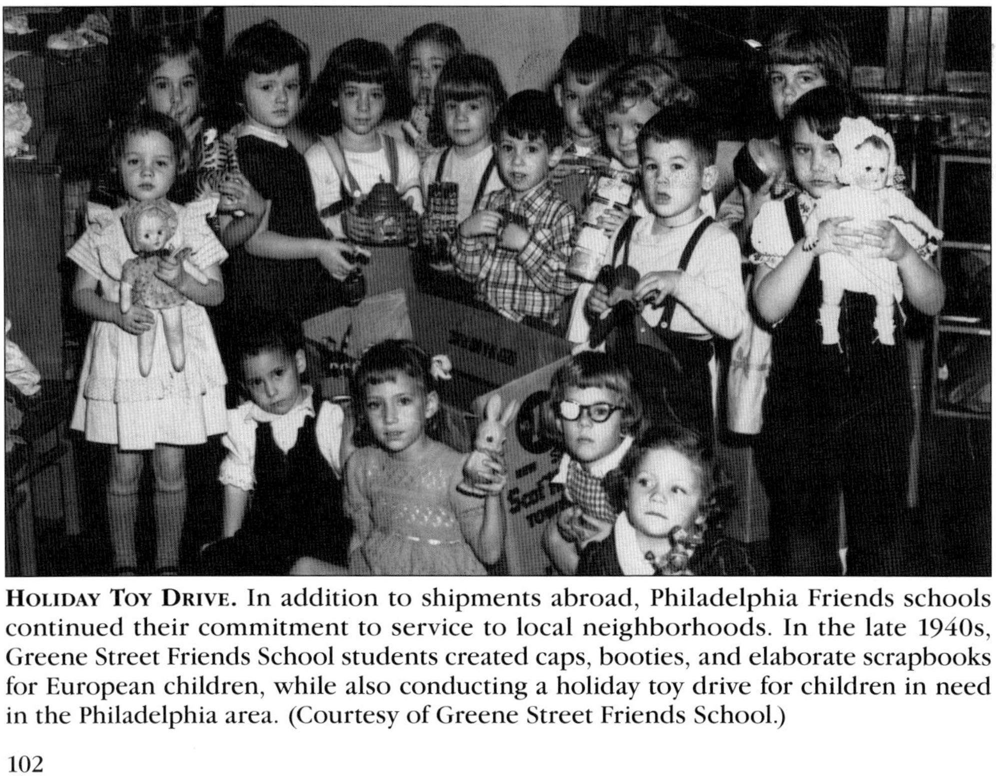

**Holiday Toy Drive.** In addition to shipments abroad, Philadelphia Friends schools continued their commitment to service to local neighborhoods. In the late 1940s, Greene Street Friends School students created caps, booties, and elaborate scrapbooks for European children, while also conducting a holiday toy drive for children in need in the Philadelphia area. (Courtesy of Greene Street Friends School.)

**COURAGE AND ACTION.** Since its founding in 1917, the American Friends Service Committee (AFSC), a Quaker organization, has played a remarkable role in promoting peace and social justice; in fact, the AFSC received the Nobel Peace Prize in 1947 for its work feeding German and Russian children immediately after World War II, at a time when it was still unpopular to reach out to these nations. The AFSC's courage and action became a powerful model for students at many Friends schools, including Germantown Friends School. In the photograph at right, kindergarten students wrapped and then presented gifts bound to Poland. The photograph below shows fifth graders participating in AFSC relief work. The students repaired 450 pairs of shoes and, with the assistance of the AFSC, sent them to Europeans in need. (Courtesy of Germantown Friends School.)

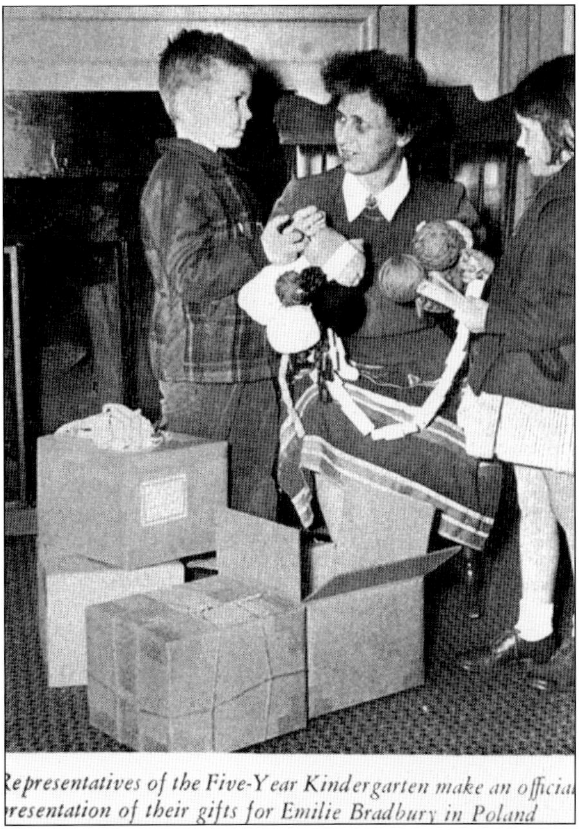


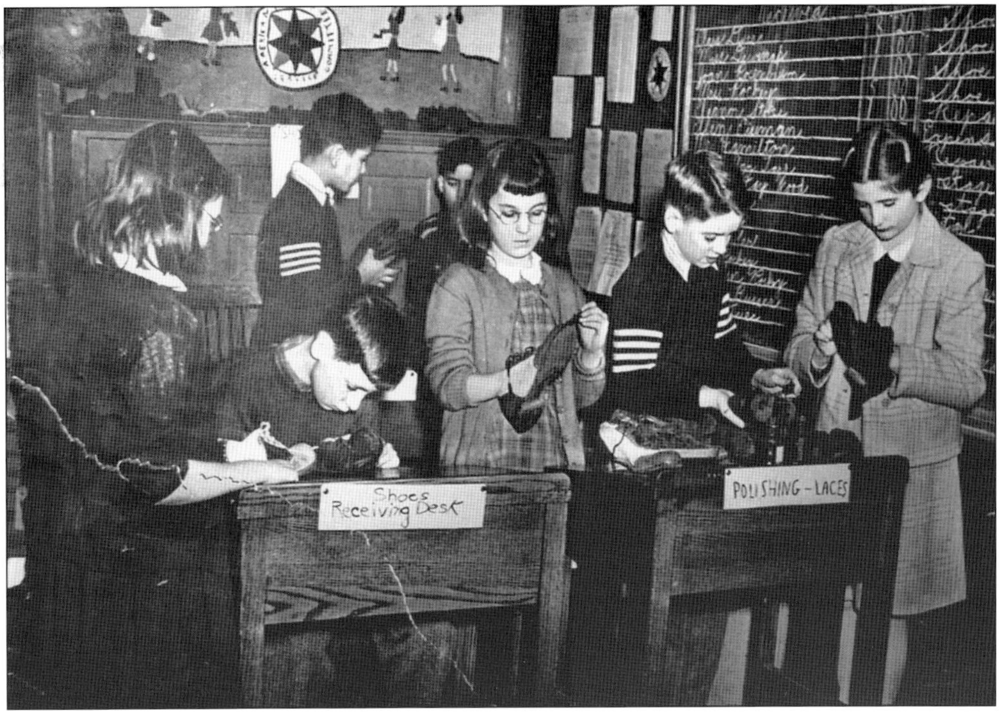

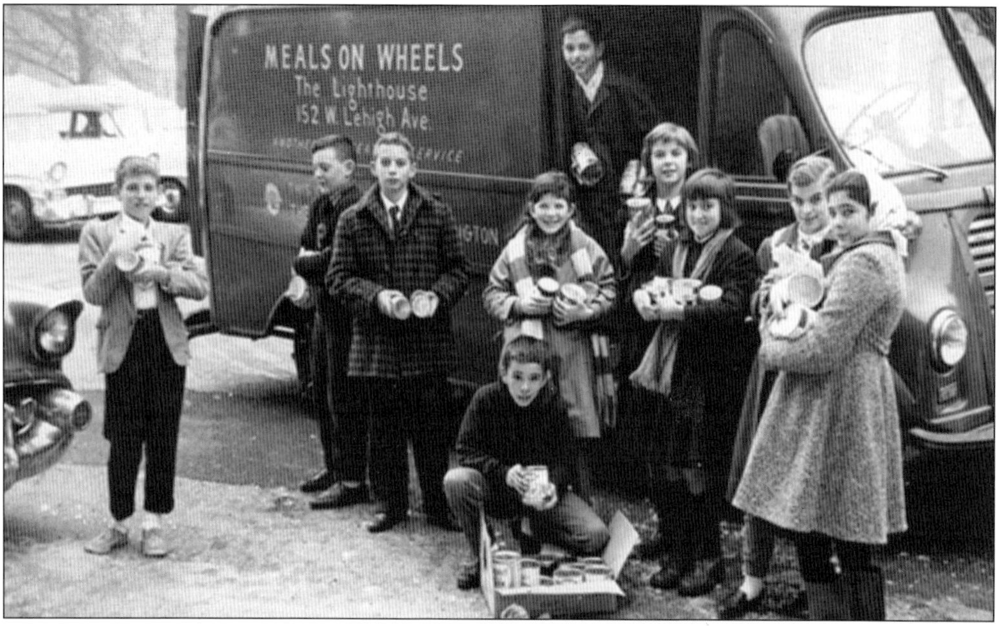


**MEALS ON WHEELS.** Philadelphia Friends schools have contributed to meals-on-wheels programs since their very beginnings. Borrowing a concept from Great Britain, the Lighthouse Community Center founded the first hand-delivered meal program in the United States in 1954. Quickly recognizing the value of this work, Germantown Friends School students donated canned goods to the nearby Lighthouse Community Center shortly after the program's founding. (Courtesy of Germantown Friends School.)

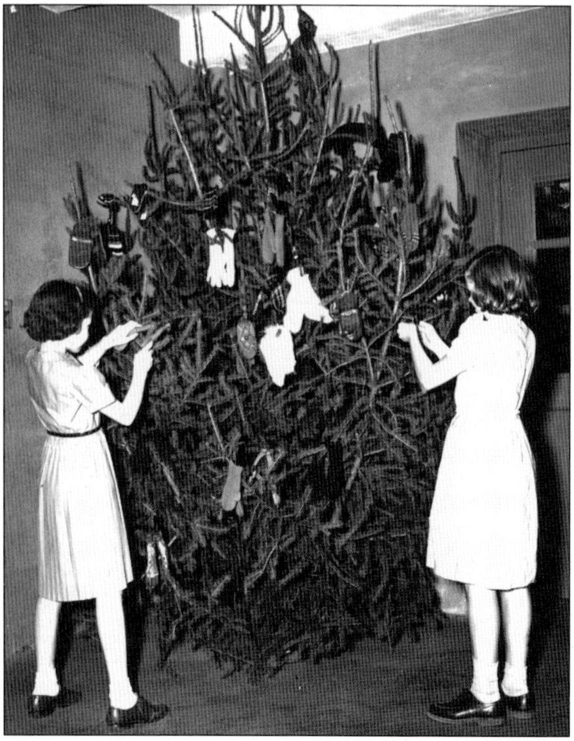

**THE MITTEN TREE.** Since winter creates added hardships for those in need, a popular Quaker school service activity is to collect much-needed items for distribution. In the 1950s, Abington Friends School students collected mittens to decorate an evergreen tree and then gave them to local service agencies. The mitten tree tradition continues to be popular among many Friends schools and Quaker meetings. (Courtesy of Abington Friends School.)

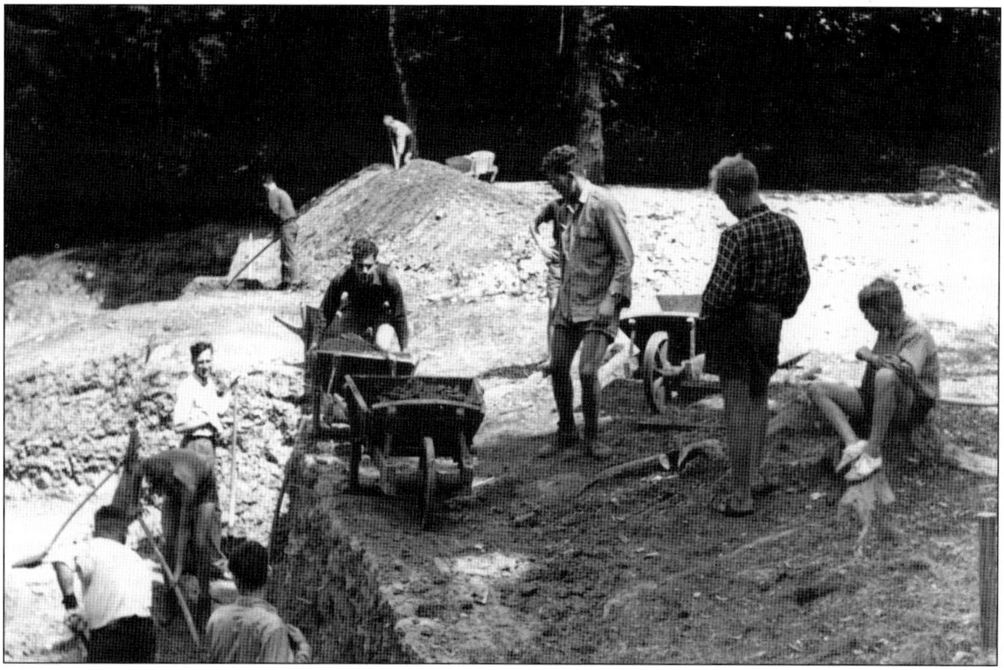

**Work Camps in Germany.** In response to the suffering created by World War II, Quaker-sponsored work camp programs provided a tangible way to contribute to world peace by offering aid and friendship to people in other countries. The German work camp movement lasted from 1949 until 1968; both Westtown and George Schools participated by sending groups of teenagers abroad to work alongside their peers. At Westtown School in 1952, a group raised the money to travel to Rotenburg to join students from one Dutch and two German schools in building a youth hostel. In similar fashion, George School students traveled to Wolfenbüttel and joined friends from affiliated schools in Düsseldorf and Berlin to participate in a camp near the former east-west border of Germany. (Above, courtesy of Westtown School; below, courtesy of George School.)

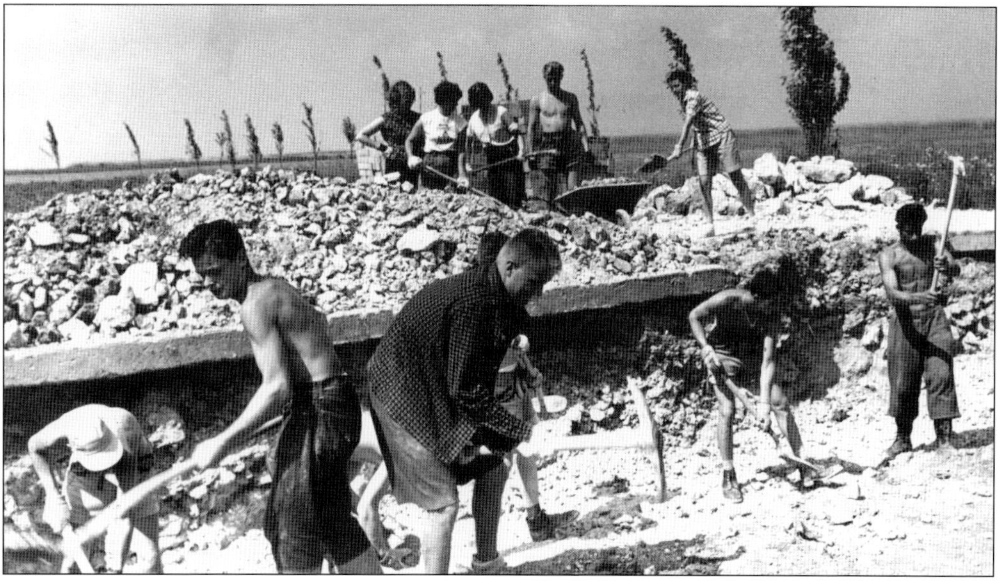

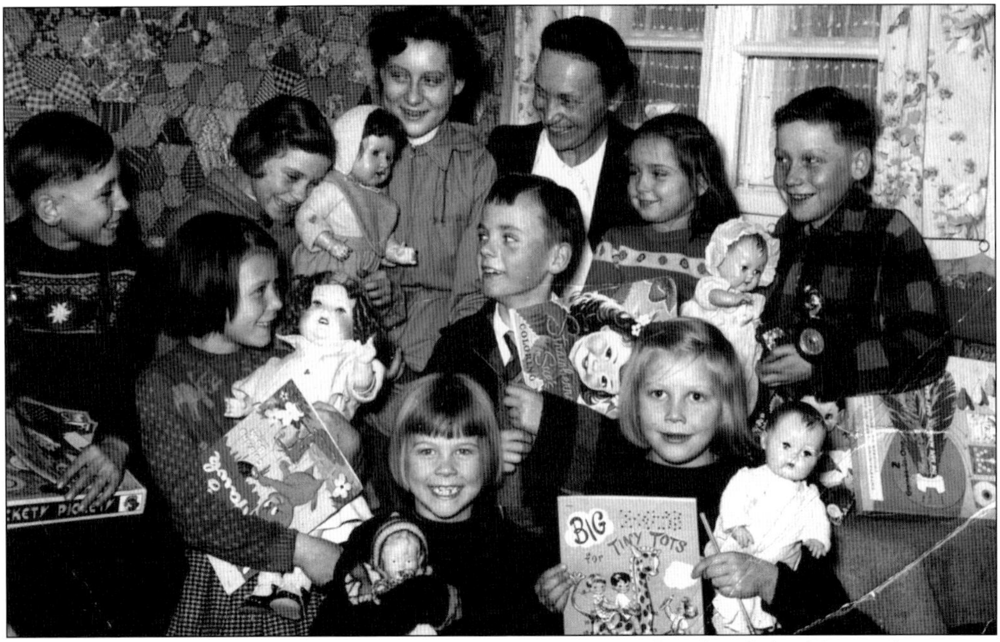


**Gifts to German Children.** By the late 1950s, many Friends schools had formed ongoing connections with their friends across the ocean. With the assistance of the AFSC, children from Plymouth Meeting Friends School sent gifts to their age-mates in Germany and then received photographs with handwritten thank-you messages, such as this one. (Courtesy of Plymouth Meeting Friends School.)

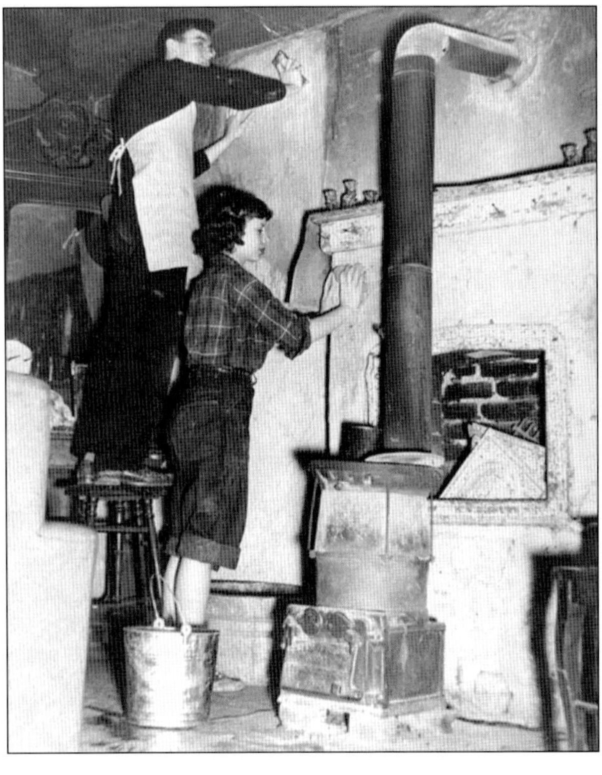

**Community Involvement.** As they had in earlier decades, Philadelphia-area Friends schools continued to embrace both local and global outreach efforts; work camps that involved construction or repair of dwellings were thriving not only abroad but also at home. In this 1950s image, Germantown Friends School students roll up their sleeves to clean and refurbish a house in the Mantua section of Philadelphia. (Courtesy of Germantown Friends School.)

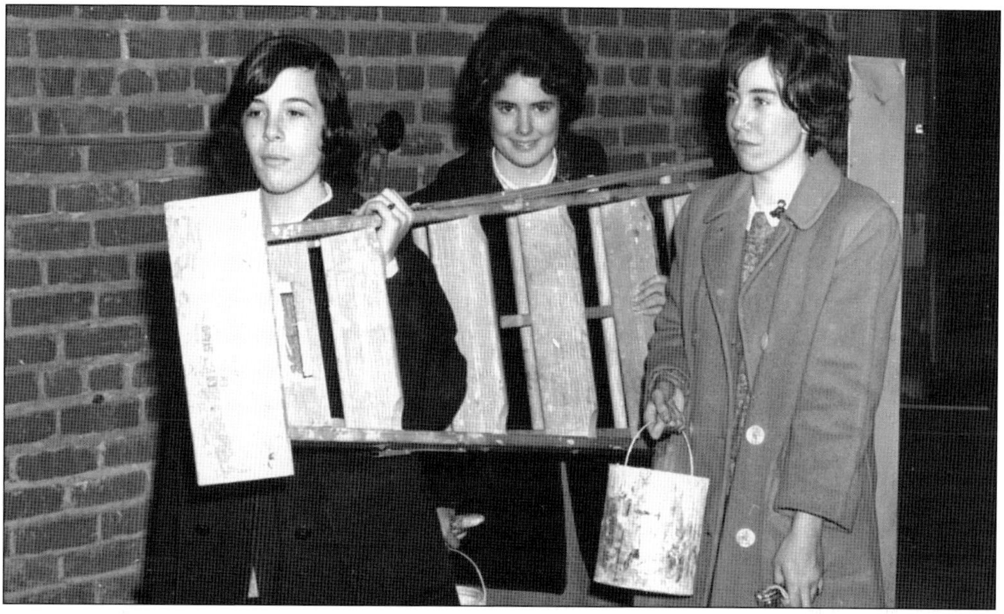

**WEEKEND WORK CAMP.** In the 1960s, the Civil Rights movement heightened awareness of the socioeconomic inequities caused by racial injustice. As a consequence, the desire to act locally to address injustice created renewed energy for community involvement programs. Abington Friends School organized weekend work crews to paint and clean dilapidated houses in the area. Pictured here are Cornelia Miller, Kathy Adams, and Olivia Buck. (Courtesy of Abington Friends School.)

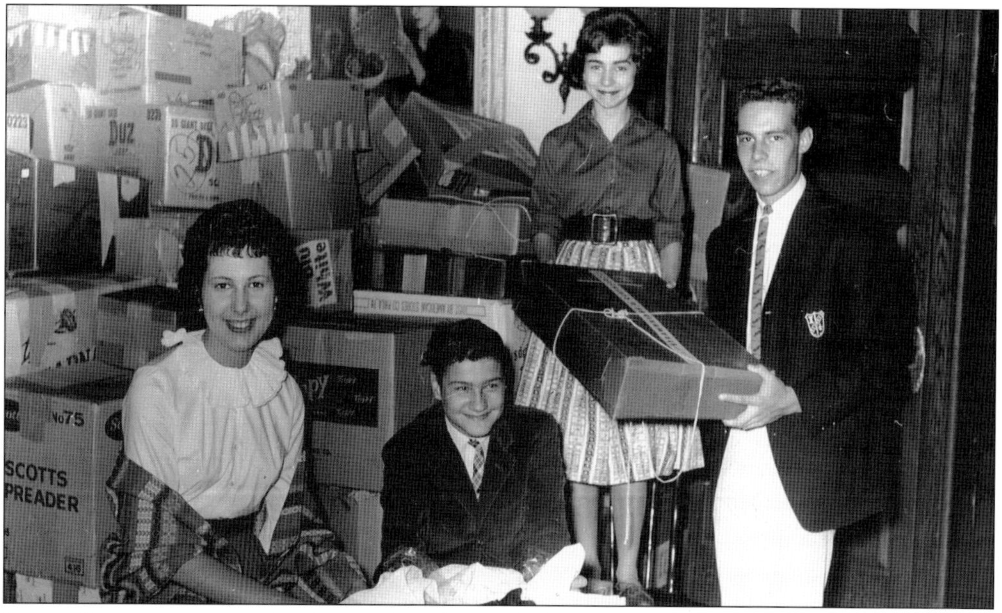


**JOY IN SERVICE.** As seen in the smiling faces of these students, Friends schools embrace service as a joyful activity. This emphasis echoes George Fox's 17th-century call to "walk cheerfully over the earth, answering that of God in everyone." The Friends' Central School service committee enjoyed collecting gifts for a local orphanage in the 1960s. (Courtesy of Friends' Central School.)

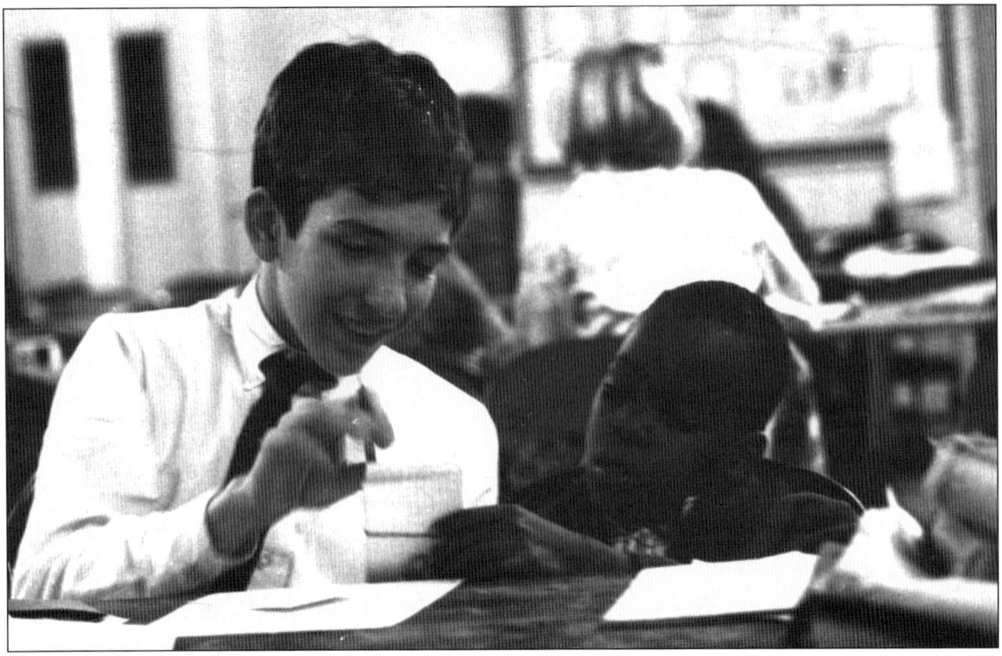

**Trenton Tutoring Project.** With time and experience, Friends schools recognized the importance of developing closer long-standing connections with specific individuals, organizations, and communities. George School's relationship with the Trenton Tutoring Project began in the 1960s. In this photograph, Jonathan March (left) tutors a younger student from Trenton. (Courtesy of George School.)

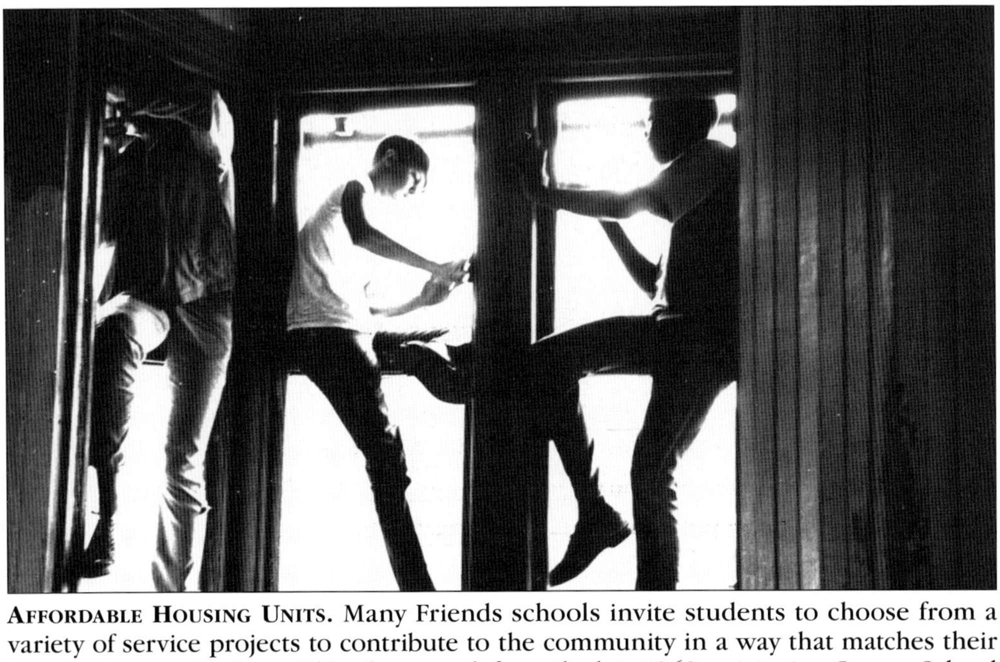

**Affordable Housing Units.** Many Friends schools invite students to choose from a variety of service projects to contribute to the community in a way that matches their own interests and talents. This photograph from the late 1960s, picturing George School students constructing affordable housing units in Philadelphia, illustrates Friends schools' contributions to communities through direct action. (Courtesy of George School.)

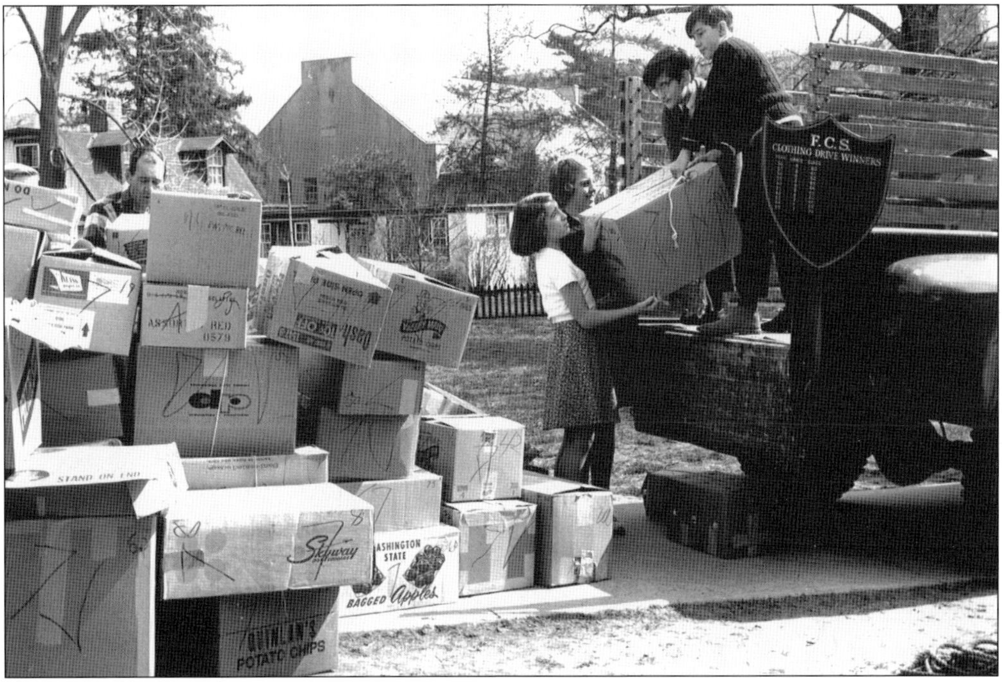


**Sharing Resources.** This scene, with students packing and moving boxes as part of a clothing drive, reveals a regular occurrence at Friends schools. Throughout the 20th century and into the present era, many schools organize collection drives for items, such as clothes, toiletries, and canned goods, as a way of sharing resources and benefiting those in need locally and throughout the world. (Courtesy of Friends' Central School.)

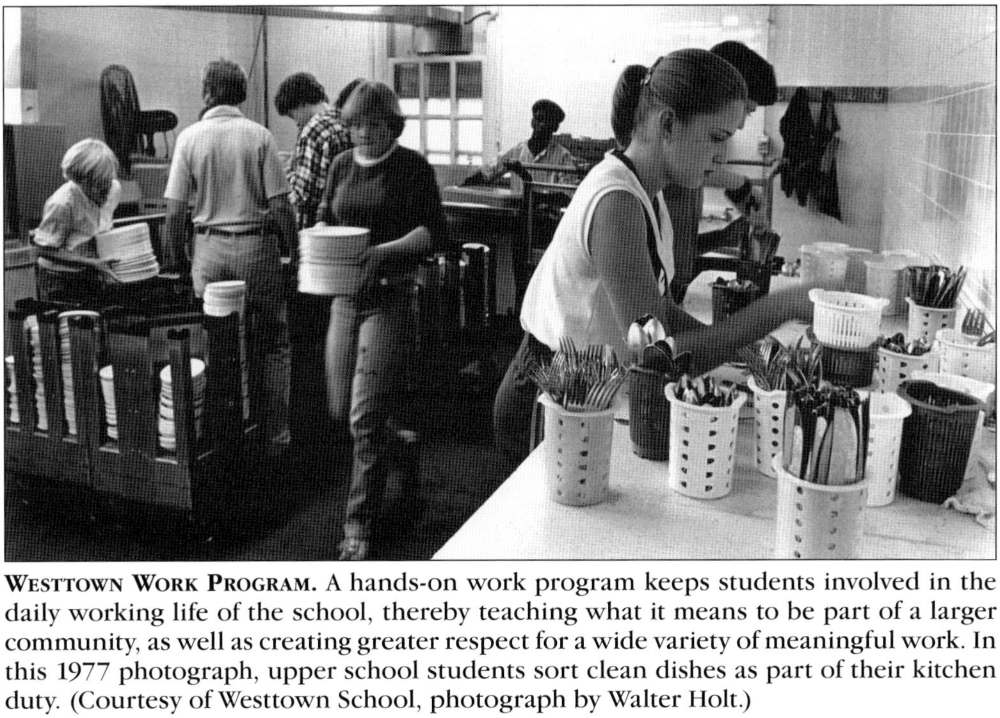

**Westtown Work Program.** A hands-on work program keeps students involved in the daily working life of the school, thereby teaching what it means to be part of a larger community, as well as creating greater respect for a wide variety of meaningful work. In this 1977 photograph, upper school students sort clean dishes as part of their kitchen duty. (Courtesy of Westtown School, photograph by Walter Holt.)

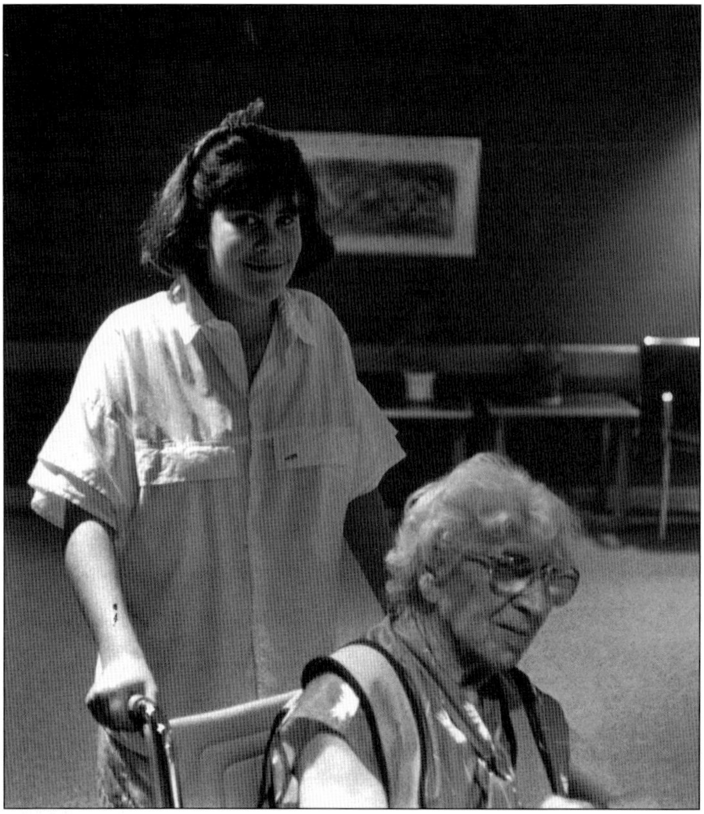

**Service Learning Emerges.** By the latter part of the 20th century, many Friends schools articulated their commitment to service learning, service that includes components of learning, relationship building, and reflection. Given the reflective nature of worship and pedagogy in Friends schools, this approach is a natural fit. In this photograph from the 1980s, Friends Select School student Deborah Switzenbaum assists an elder at a local nursing home. (Courtesy of Friends Select School.)

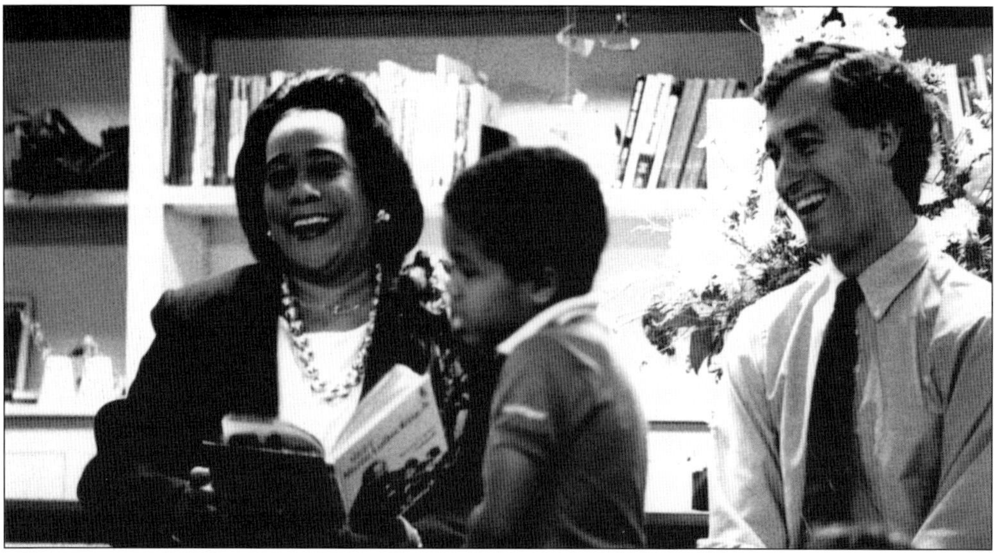

**Peace Speaker Coretta Scott King.** Friends schools frequently invite speakers to lead inspiring dialogue about current world issues. During a two-day visit to Westtown School in 1989, Coretta Scott King spoke of nonviolence as a way of life and the patience, love, and courage it takes to find nonviolent solutions to difficult problems. In this photograph, she is pictured with lower school principal Peter Vermilye and a student. (Courtesy of Westtown School.)

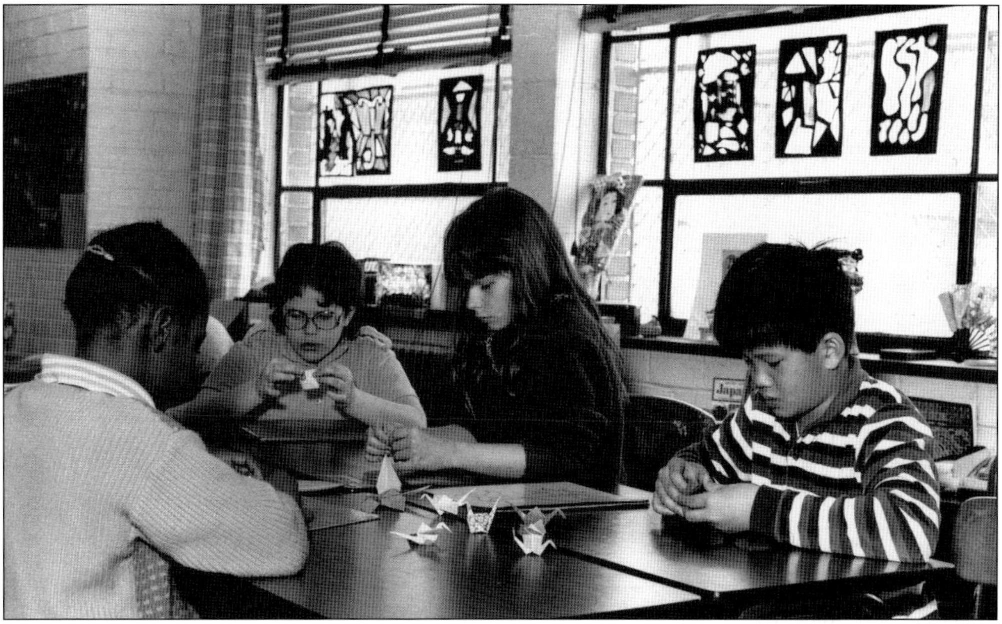

**Making Paper Cranes.** Friends schools also teach about peace through literature and the arts. Students from many Friends schools learn the story of Sadako, a Japanese girl who acquired a fatal illness caused by the atomic bombing of Hiroshima. These fifth graders fold paper cranes to demonstrate their wish for world peace, replicating Sadako's act of creating origami cranes to maintain her sense of hope. (Courtesy of Frankford Friends School.)

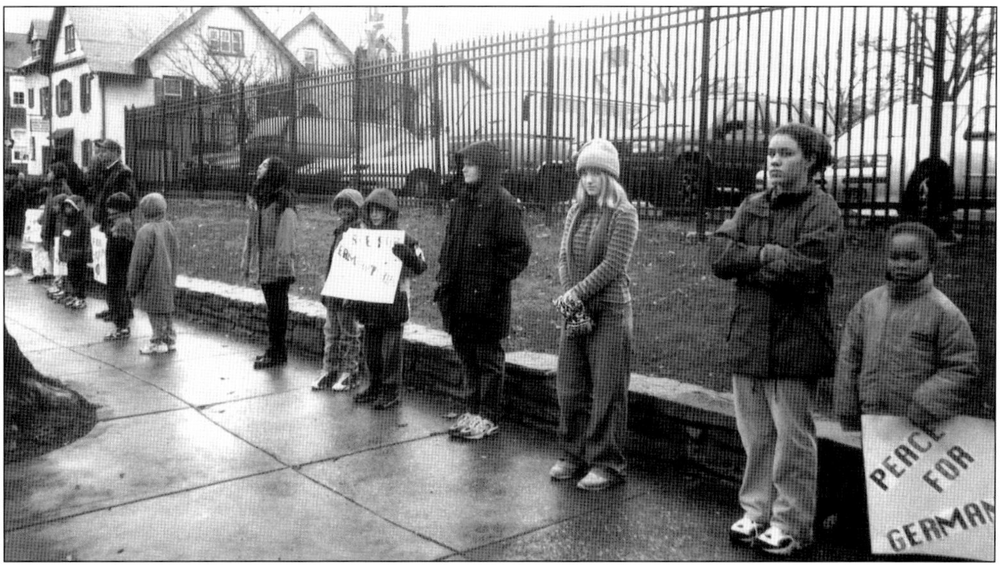

**Silent Peace Vigil.** Quakers hold silent vigils to promote the hope for peace and unity. To mark the 50th anniversary of the AFSC and British Foreign Service Council winning the Nobel Peace Prize, the entire student body at Germantown Friends School formed a human chain around the border of the campus. Three neighboring schools, including Greene Street Friends School, held simultaneous vigils on their campuses. (Courtesy of Germantown Friends School.)

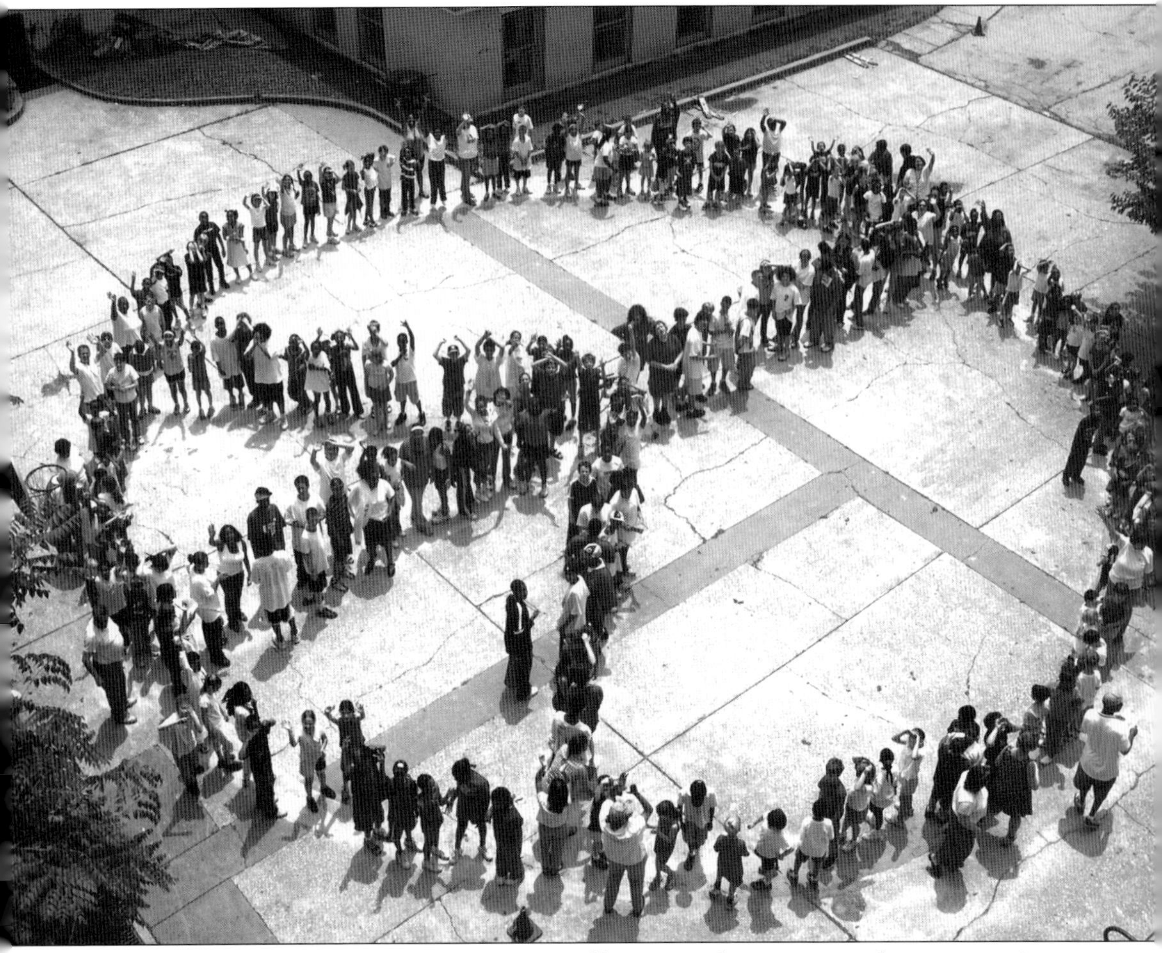

**All-School Peace Sign.** Paul Lacey writes, "Affirming and maintaining the peace testimony has been a starting point in Quaker education." In Friends schools, classroom engagement in peace and social justice takes many forms, including reading about the lives of noteworthy peacemakers such as Lucretia Mott and Bayard Rustin; hearing elders share their reasons for choosing conscientious objection or alternative service during times of war; learning specific approaches for solving conflicts when they arise on the playground; discussing the causes and costs of war using critical-thinking skills; and learning to play cooperative games that encourage team building. Consequently, students have found meaningful ways to express their own desire for peace and social justice, ranging from writing letters to politicians, to sharing matters of conscience during meeting for worship, to choosing service as a way of life. As seen in this all-school photograph from Greene Street Friends School, peace education holds a place of central importance in Friends schools. (Courtesy of Greene Street Friends School, photograph by Edward Marshall.)

# *Seven*

# The Experiment Continues

*The contributions of the Friends Council on Education have been very significant in keeping alive the difficult work Friends do in helping to create a better world. Education is the foundation and the Council is instrumental as a support of that foundation.*

—Susan Hopkins, Quaker educator

The educational experiment that began in 17th-century America, rooted in the faith and practice of the Religious Society of Friends, carries on today. By 1931, there were 34 Friends schools in the United States. The year 1931 is significant in Friends education as the year when the vision of a national consultative organization uniting Friends schools under one integrated network of educational service was realized in the founding of the Friends Council on Education. Today 81 Friends schools and 4 newly formed Friends schools network through the Friends Council on Education. Nearly half of the Friends Council's member schools within the United States are located in the Greater Philadelphia area. These schools live William Penn's vision for a moral education rooted in love, compassion, and respect, growing responsible citizens for an engaged democracy.

This chapter illustrates the Friends Council's work in nurturing the Quaker life of schools, strengthening the national network of Friends schools, and assisting in establishing new Friends schools. The Friends Council on Education provides professional development for trustees, administrators, and faculty to further the goals of Quaker education. The first multiday conference for new teachers took place in 1949. The first peer network gathering took place in 1945 for school secretaries. Today the Friends Council on Education supports 17 peer networks and provides national and regional workshops on best governance practices, Quaker pedagogy, and leadership development for Friends schools.

The Friends Council sustains the essential Quaker nature of these religiously, ethnically, and socioeconomically diverse Friends school communities, unified through Quaker processes for worship, learning, decision making, and service. Current Friends Council initiatives focus on lifting up diversity work in Friends schools, strengthening Friends school governance, and amplifying the national voice of Friends education.

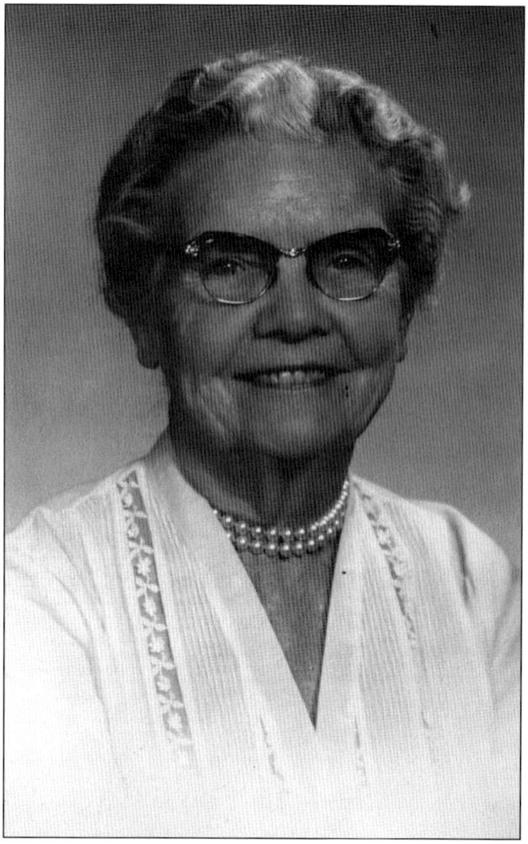

**Friends Council Founders.** Three Philadelphia Quakers, Hadassah and Morris Leeds (shown above and below) and Howard Brinton, dreamed of a national consultative organization to unite diverse Friends schools under one integrating canopy of educational mission and service. They invited 90 Quaker school trustees and principals to a meeting at Friends' Central School in December 1930, where the vibrant vision of a national council for Friends education was founded by representatives from 3 Yearly Meetings, Friends General Conference, 12 secondary schools, 13 elementary schools, and 3 Quaker colleges. The aims of the Friends Council on Education were to develop a feeling of friendliness and mutual understanding among Friends institutions and impress upon the schools and colleges the importance of reverence for the truth and respect for the divine element in each person, students and teachers alike. (Courtesy of Friends Historical Library, Swarthmore College.)

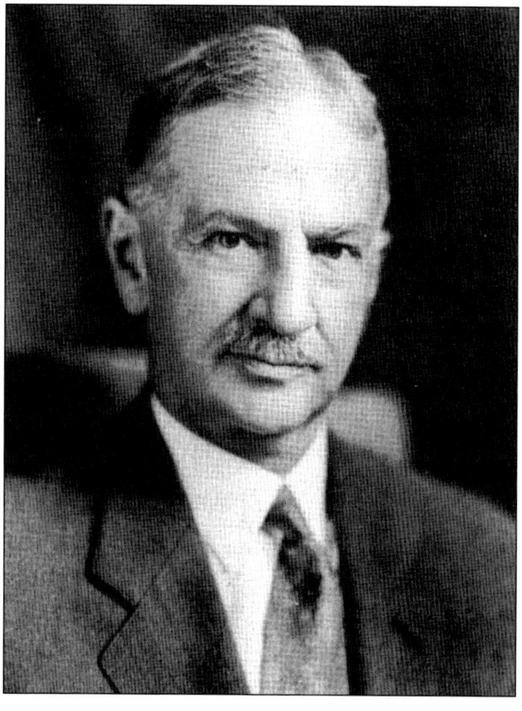

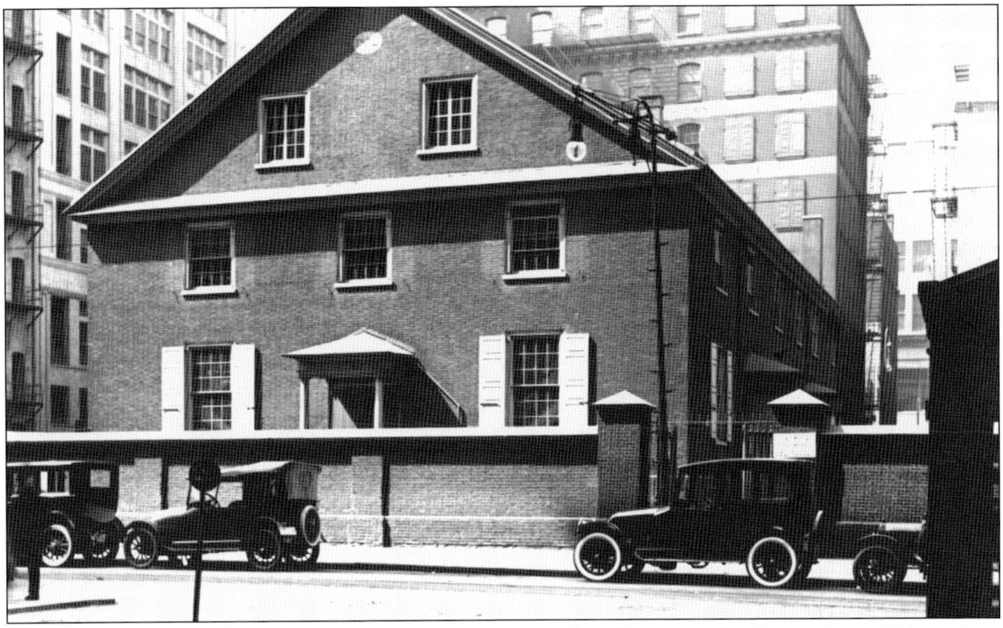

**ORIGINAL OFFICE, *c.* 1923.** Original office space for the Friends Council on Education was in the former Twelfth Street Meetinghouse, Philadelphia. To make way for new construction in the city, the meetinghouse was relocated in the early 1970s, towed on a trailer up Interstate 95, and became the George School Meetinghouse, Newtown. (Courtesy of the Library Company, Philadelphia.)

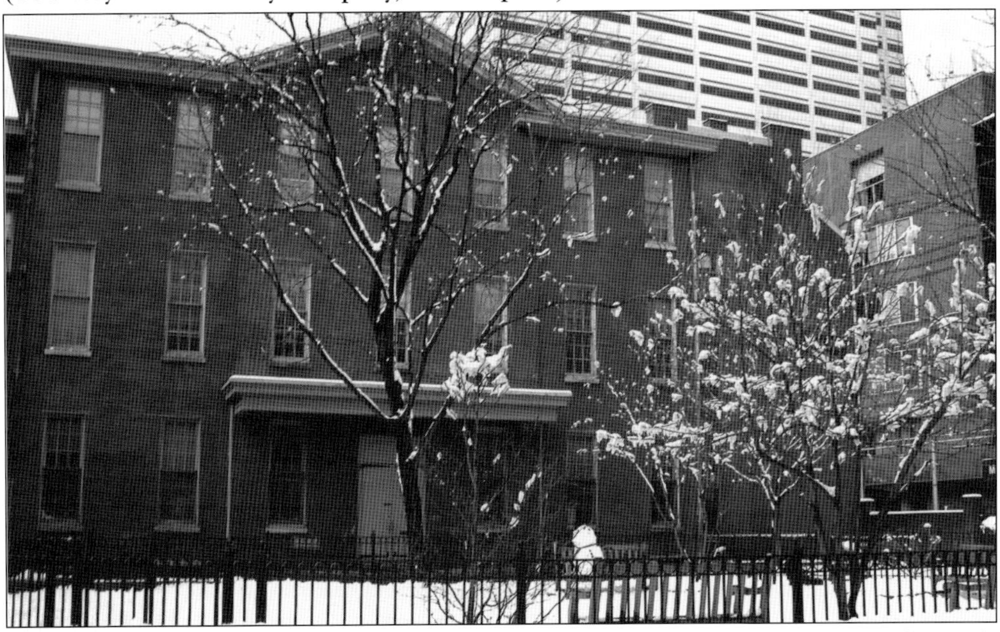

**AT THE CENTER.** The offices of the Friends Council on Education have been part of Friends Center in Center City Philadelphia since 1971. Friends Center is a gathering place for diverse Quaker and like-minded community groups responding to local, national, and international issues. (Courtesy of the Friends Council on Education, photograph by April Diop.)

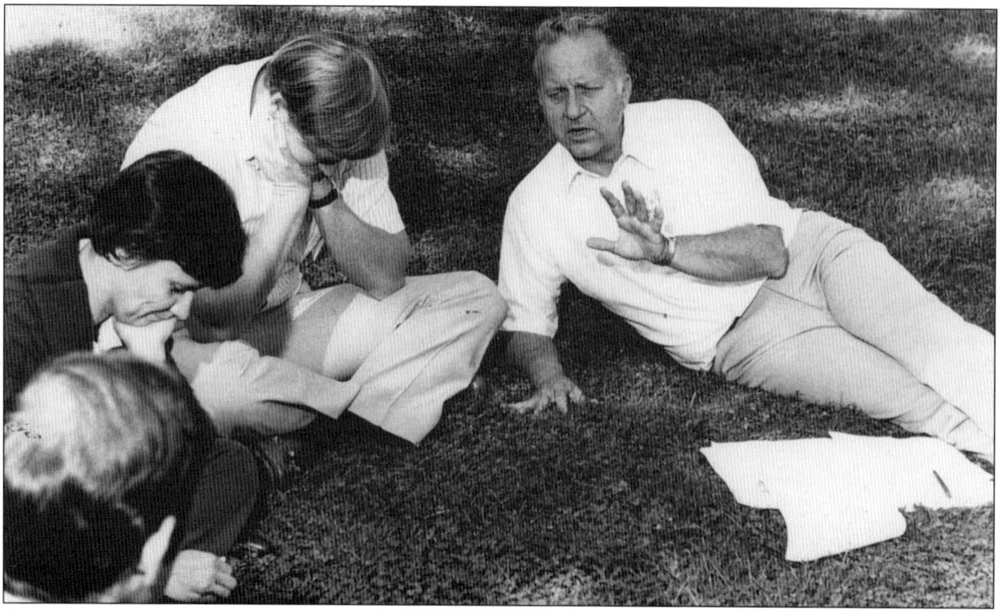

**Inspiring Professional Development.** At the root of Friends pedagogy is direct experiential learning through worship, shared decision making, and active exploration, analysis, and reflection. David Mallery, shown here in 1978, joined the Friends Council on Education staff in 1963, offering enrichment programs for teachers and providing "brief inoculations of inspiration with plenty of space for dialogue and inordinate doses of encouragement." (Courtesy of the Friends Council on Education.)

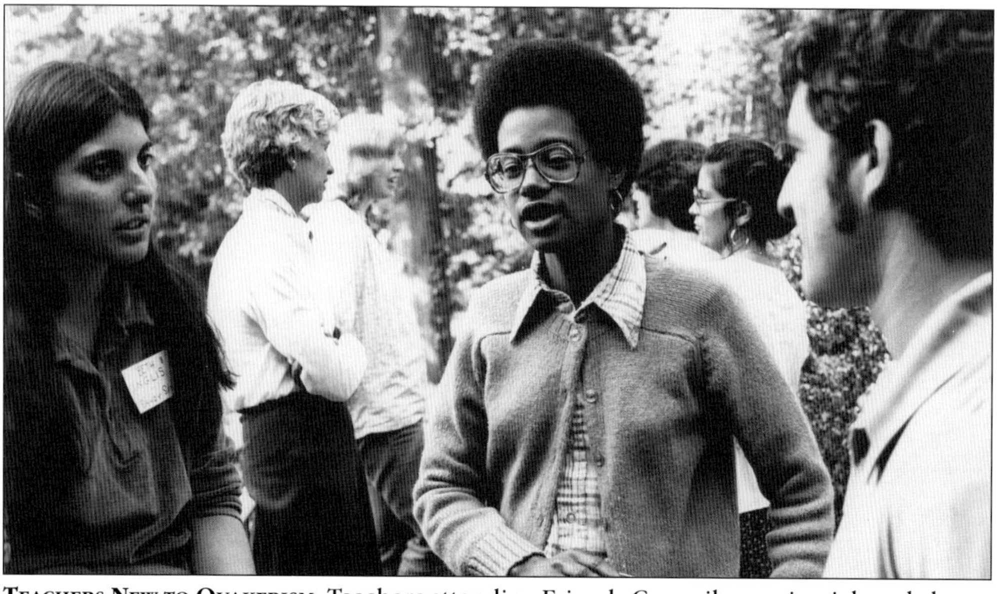

**Teachers New to Quakerism.** Teachers attending Friends Council experiential workshops, like those shown here at a 1978 conference, learn as much from one another as from program facilitators and connect with educators across the national network of Friends schools. Many Friends schools send each new faculty member to the Friends Council's most sought-after workshop, Educators New to Quakerism. (Courtesy of the Friends Council on Education.)

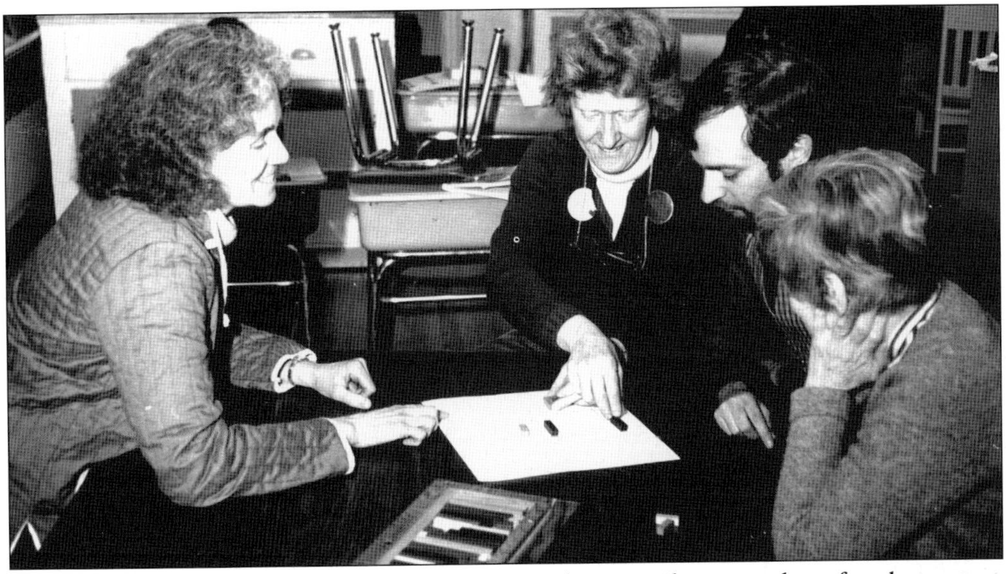

**Supporting Quaker Pedagogy.** Joining the Friends Council as consultant for elementary Friends schools in 1978, Holly Locke worked with teachers on experiential values-based curricula and Quaker pedagogy. Here she works with teachers at Greene Street Friends School. Providing experiential professional development and publications to deepen spiritual engagement and exploration in Friends school communities is central to the Friends Council's work. (Courtesy of the Friends Council on Education.)

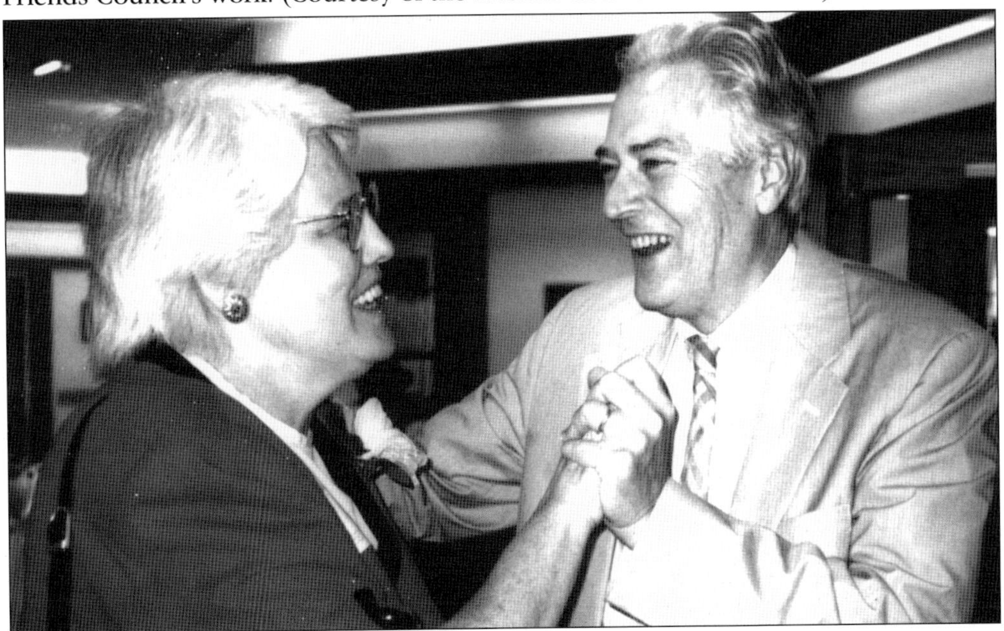

**Inspired Leadership.** Upon her retirement in 2000, Friends Council executive director Kay Edstene shares a dance with interim director Earl Harrison (former head of Sidwell Friends School). Edstene said, "The best of Friends education is when schools continue to struggle to be better than they are. Quakers don't have answers, only questions. We need to continuously try to define ourselves and move toward revelation." (Courtesy of the Friends Council on Education.)

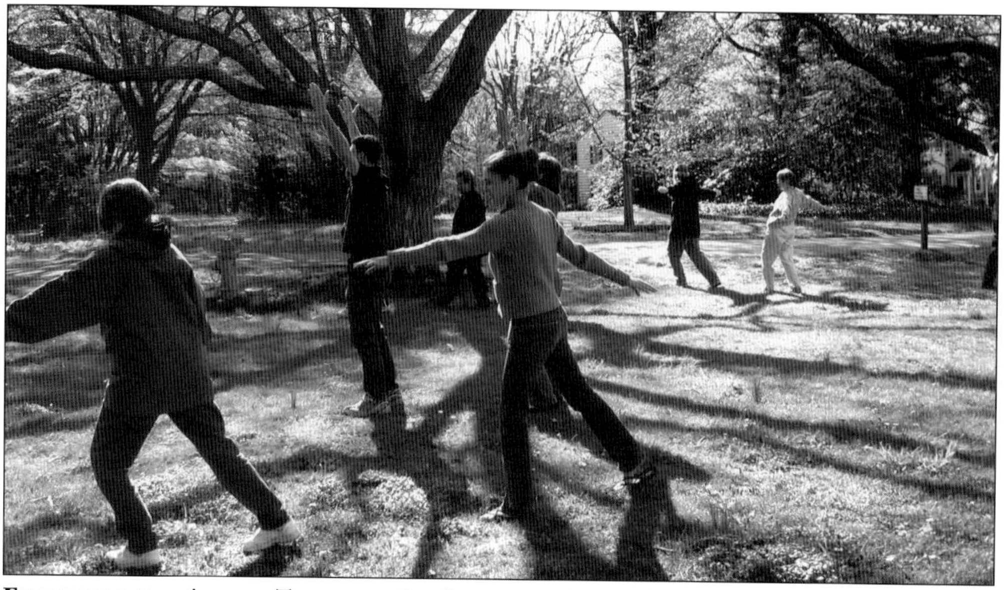

**Examining the Art of Teaching.** In these two 2005 photographs, teachers explore movement improvisation at Friends Council on Education SPARC retreats (Spirited Practice and Renewed Courage) for teachers in Friends schools. Launched in 2003, the SPARC program is a collaborative community that uses reflective tools for self-directed professional development. Based on the principles of teacher formation from Parker Palmer's Courage to Teach work, the ripple effects of this spiritual leadership program are gaining strength in Friends schools. Some 70 Friends school educators have now experienced the program, with many schools sending multiple faculty members to participate. Schools report experiencing a "spiritual boost" as SPARCers emerge as confident spiritual leaders in many aspects of school process and programs. (Courtesy of Javier Ergueta.)

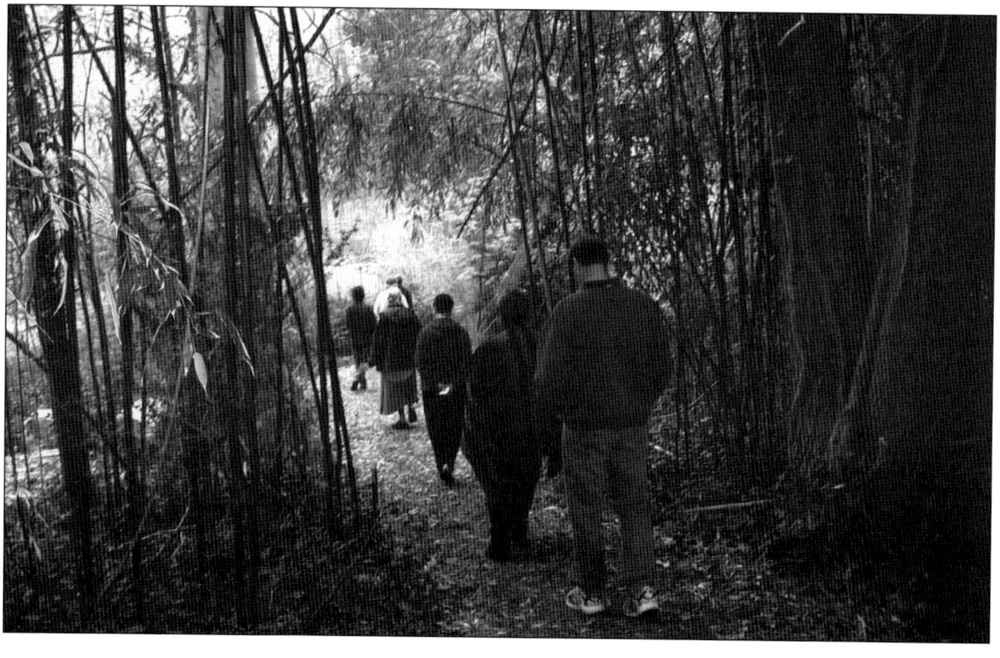

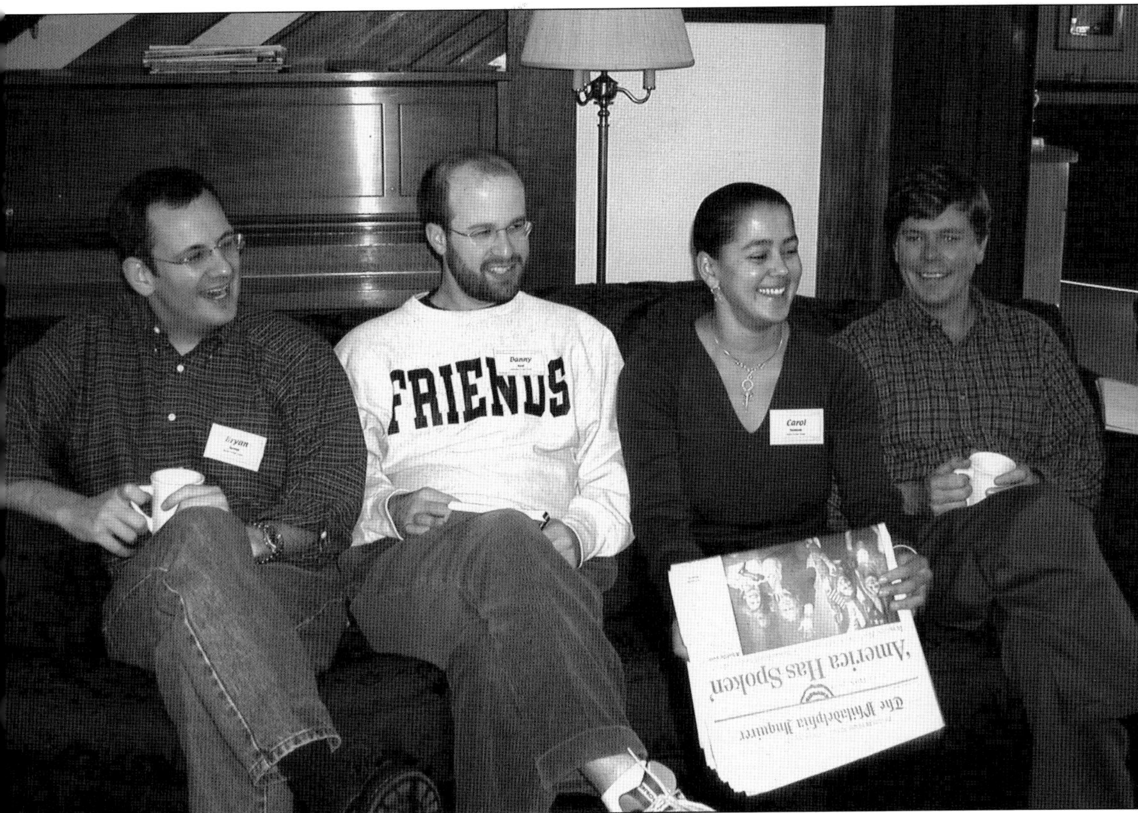


**Growing Leaders for Tomorrow.** Developed out of a strategic initiative in 2003, the Friends Council's Institute for Engaging Leadership in Friends Schools engages rising leaders in developing their capacity and skills for the distinctive practice of leading and sustaining the Quaker ethos of a Friends school. Aspiring Friends school leaders generate action research projects that serve all of Friends education, develop professional partnerships with heads of Friends schools, use Quaker process to renew their vitality and sense of purpose as leaders in Friends education, strengthen their leadership styles, and actively prepare for the unique role of Friends school headship and primary leadership roles. In the first five years of the program, of the 29 graduates, 5 have been named heads of Friends schools and more than 80 percent have moved to positions of increased leadership responsibility in schools across the country. Pictured above at a 2004 retreat are, from left to right, Bryan Garman, Danny Karpf, Carol Swainson, and Ted Lutkus. (Courtesy of the Friends Council on Education.)

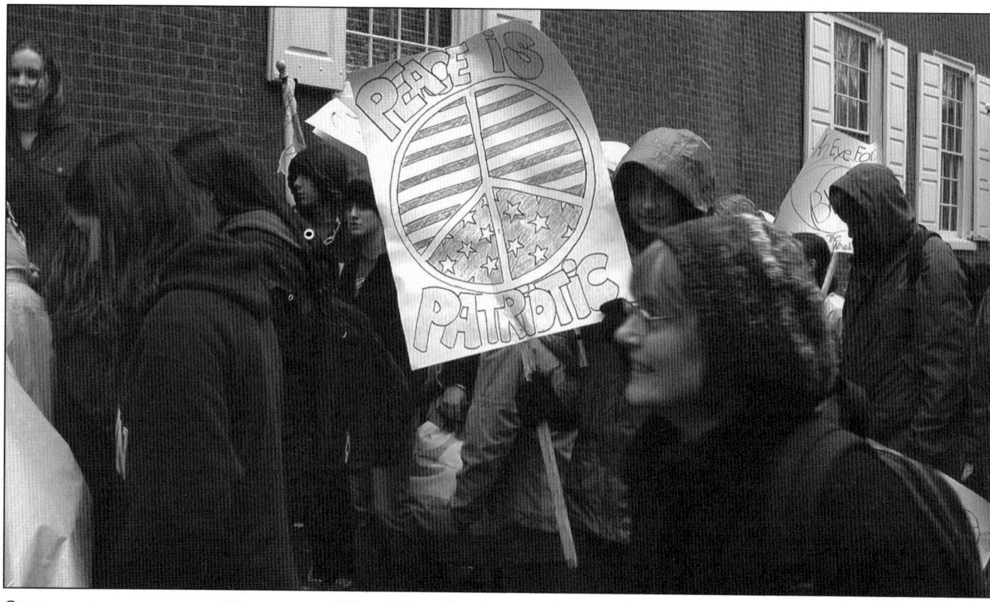


**STRENGTHENING THE NETWORK.** The Friends Council on Education strengthens the network of support across Friends schools. In April 2004, 300 students and faculty from 25 Friends schools and a dozen Philadelphia-area Quaker meetings came together for a day of workshops, activism, and community building during the second Friends Schools Day of Peace, held at Arch Street Meeting House, Friends Center, and Friends Select School. (Courtesy of the Friends Council on Education.)

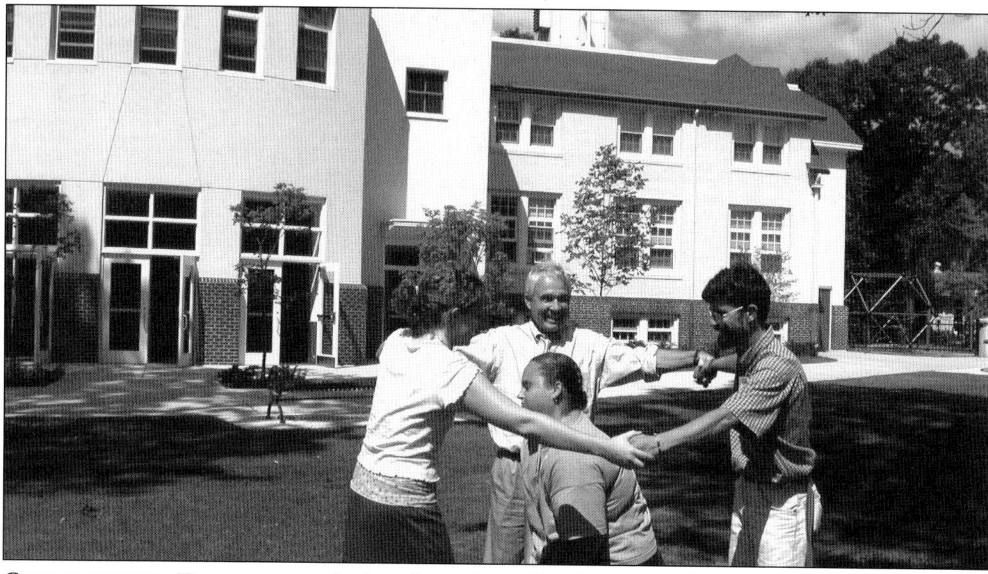

**COLLABORATIVE ENGAGEMENT.** Arthur Larrabee, Quaker consultant and general secretary of the Philadelphia Yearly Meeting, joins teachers from the Meeting School in Rindge, New Hampshire, in collaborative play at Lincoln School, Providence, Rhode Island. Some 200 faculty members from four New England Friends schools came together in the fall of 2005 for a program on Quaker pedagogy and Friends decision making, provided by the Friends Council on Education and made possible through funding from the Obadiah Brown Benevolent Fund. (Courtesy of the Friends Council on Education.)

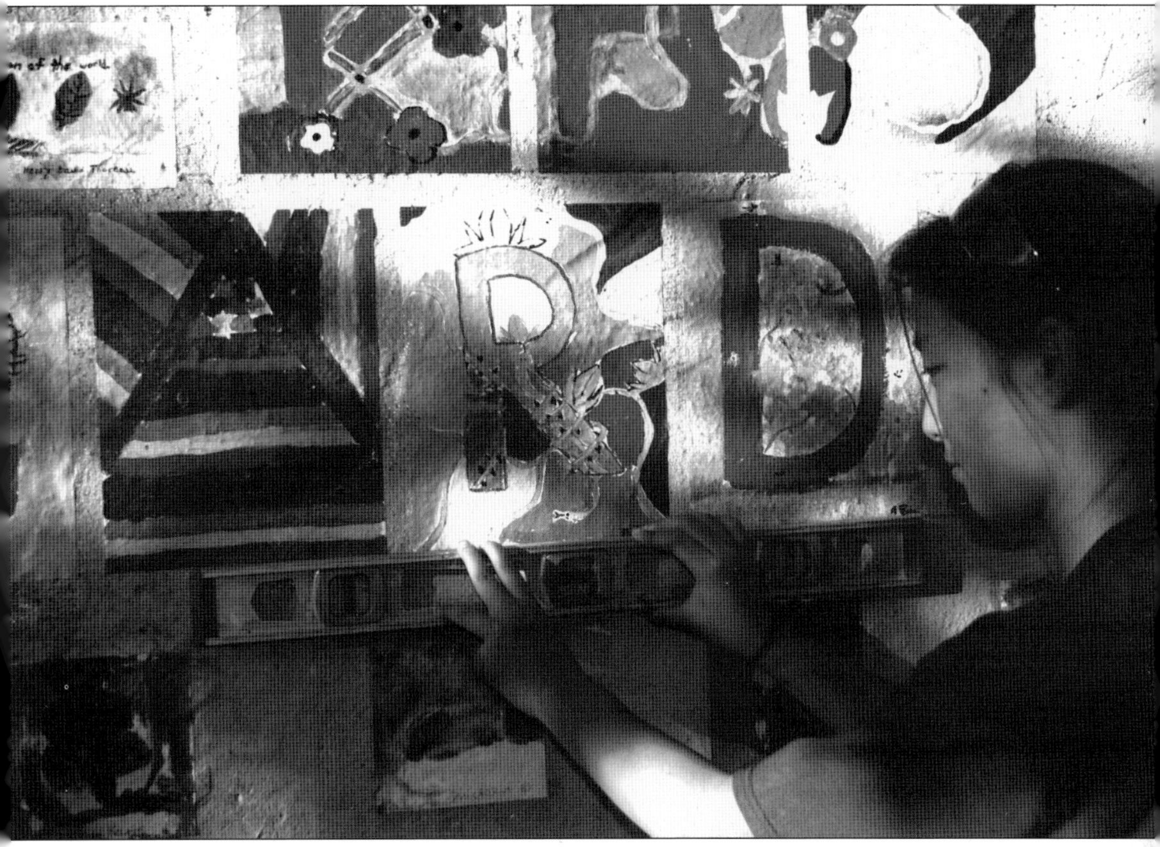

**Experiential Projects.** A student at Frankford Friends School helps to install a mosaic sign in the school's community garden, a 2007 project that was funded through a grant from the Friends Council on Education. Launched in 1968, the Friends Council's grants program each year funds experiential, student-centered projects that are grounded in the Quaker testimonies. (Courtesy of Frankford Friends School, photograph by Rufus Standefer.)

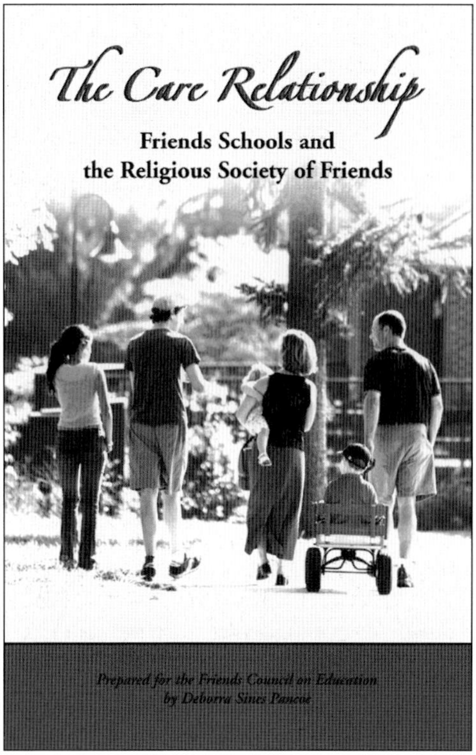


**MUTUAL CARE.** Arising from a research study conducted as part of the Institute for Engaging Leadership in Friends Schools by Plymouth Monthly Meeting member Deborra Sines Pancoe with members of Friends school and meeting communities, this 2006 booklet articulates guiding principles and positive practices for school-meeting "care relationships." The Friends Council on Education supports Friends schools and meetings in developing effective and meaningful communities of practice. (Courtesy of the Friends Council on Education.)

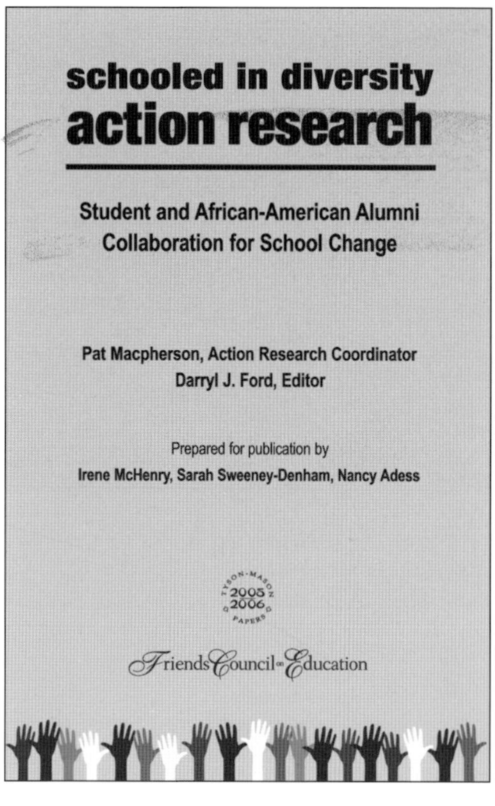


**RESEARCH ON RACIAL CHANGE.** In its publication *Schooled in Diversity Action Research,* the Friends Council on Education published landmark documentation and analysis of multicultural change as recounted through alumni interviews from two Friends schools in the first 50 years since desegregation. In addition, guidelines to engage in action research around racial change in other school communities support teachers and administrators in ongoing exploration. (Courtesy of the Friends Council on Education, graphic by April Diop.)

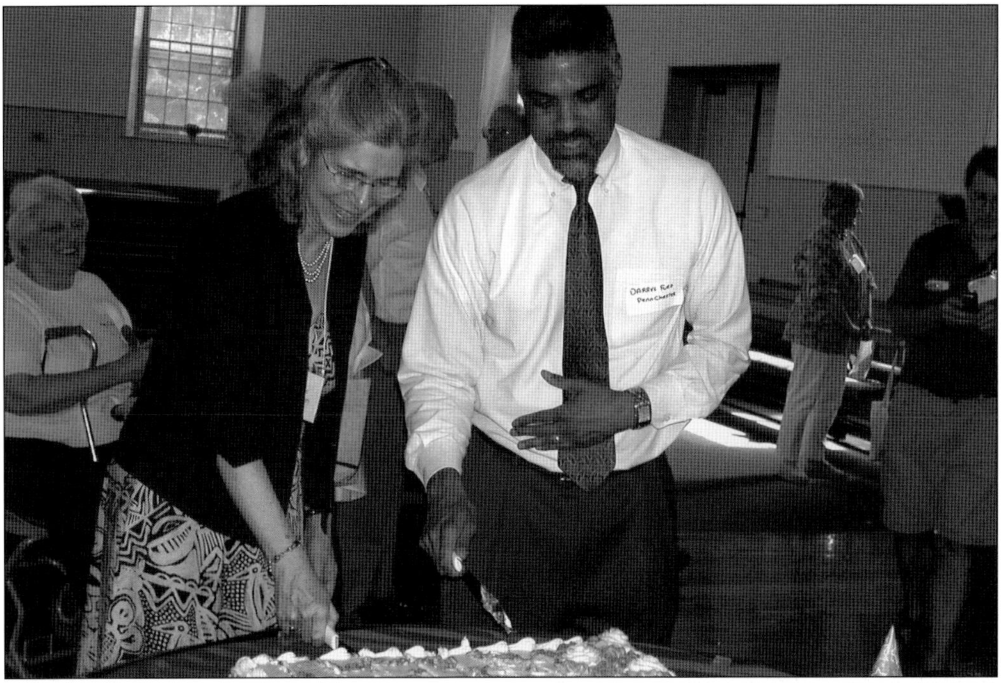

**Anniversary Celebration.** Irene McHenry, executive director, and Darryl J. Ford, clerk of the Friends Council Board of Directors (head of the William Penn Charter School), lead the celebration of the Friends Council on Education's 75th anniversary in June 2006 at George School, Newtown. More than 250 people participated in the four-day conference for Friends educators from around the country and throughout the world. (Courtesy of the Friends Council on Education.)

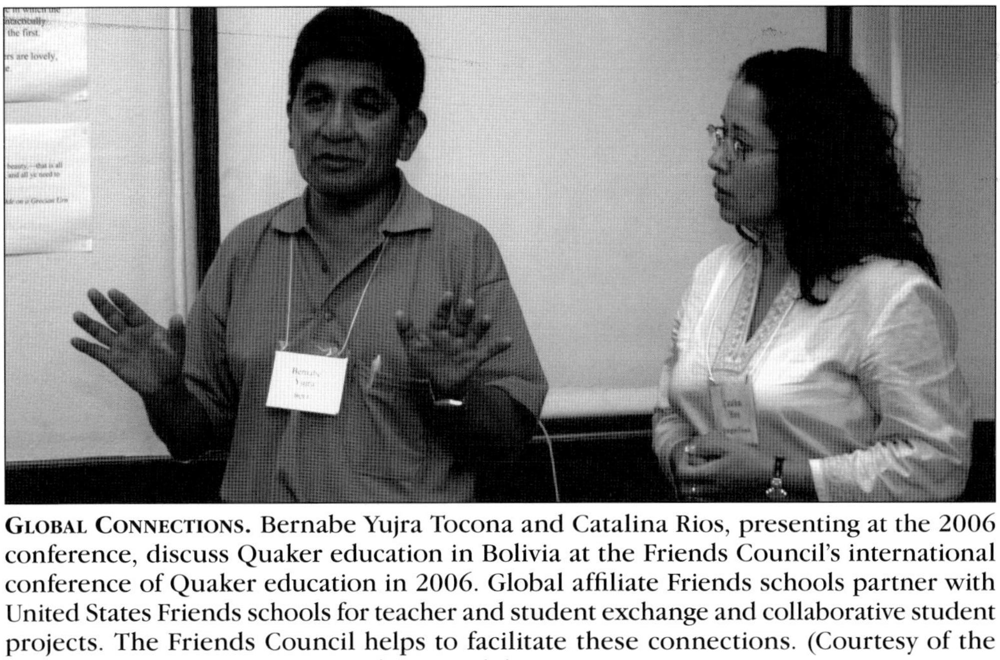

**Global Connections.** Bernabe Yujra Tocona and Catalina Rios, presenting at the 2006 conference, discuss Quaker education in Bolivia at the Friends Council's international conference of Quaker education in 2006. Global affiliate Friends schools partner with United States Friends schools for teacher and student exchange and collaborative student projects. The Friends Council helps to facilitate these connections. (Courtesy of the Friends Council on Education, photograph by Anna Mays.)

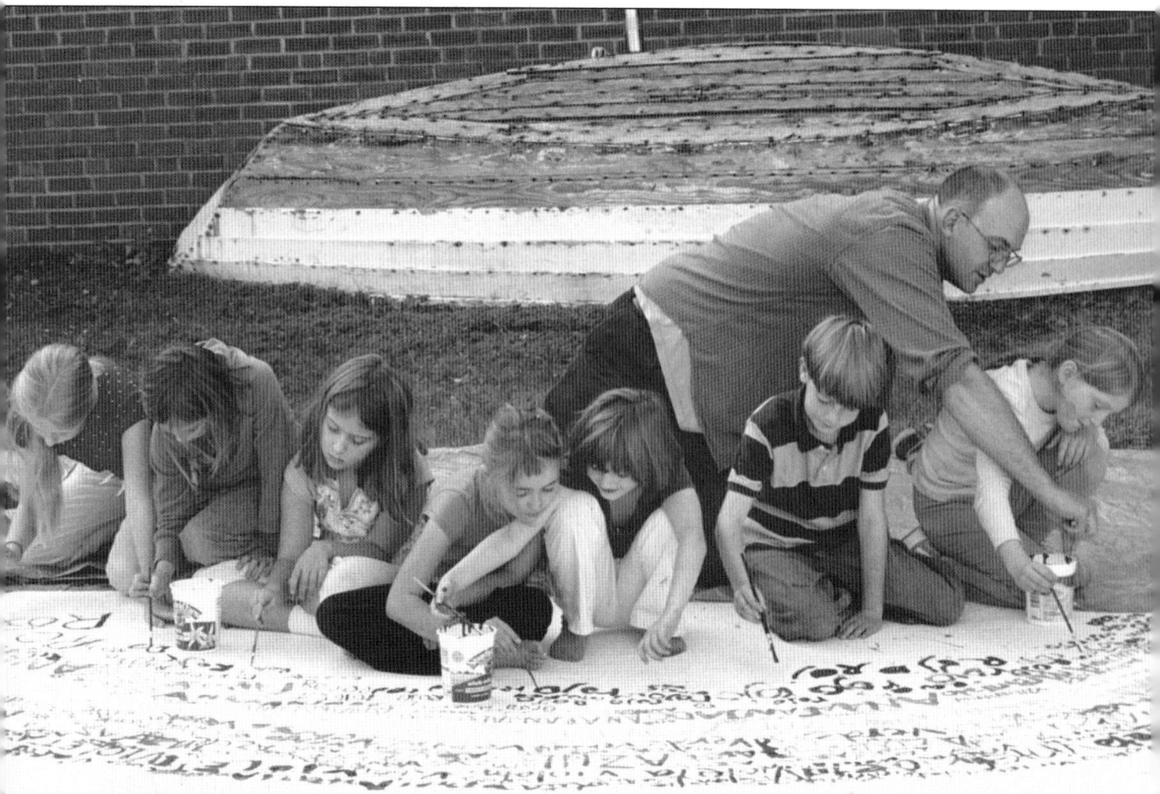

**Supporting New Friends Schools.** Students at Friends School of Portland collaborate on a painting of a rainbow. The school, one of the newest in the Friends Council on Education's prospective member pool, is located on Mackworth Island off the coast of Maine. The Friends Council supports newly forming Friends schools through publications, consultations, and programs. Both the number of students in Friends schools and the number of Friends schools continues to grow. (Courtesy of Friends School of Portland.)

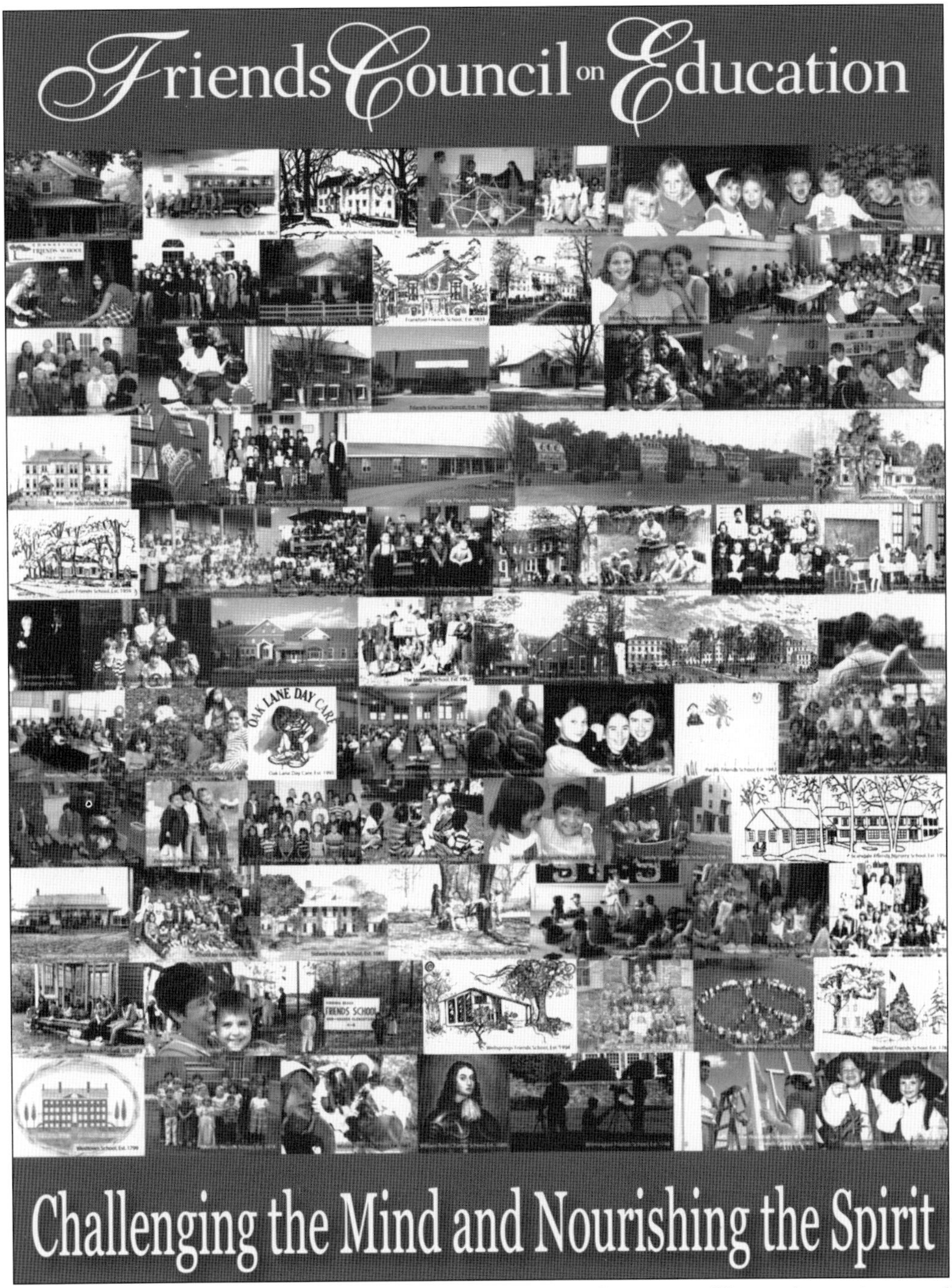


**GEOGRAPHICAL DIVERSITY.** The Friends Council on Education affirms the variety and diversity of its more than 80 independently operated member schools across the country. (Courtesy of the Friends Council on Education.)

# BIBLIOGRAPHY

Brinton, Howard. *Quaker Education in Theory and Practice.* Wallingford, PA: Pendle Hill Publications, 1965.

Hays, Kim. *Practicing Virtues: Moral Traditions at Quaker and Military Boarding Schools.* Berkeley: University of California Press, 1994.

Heath, Douglas. *The Peculiar Mission of Friends Schools.* Wallingford, PA: Pendle Hill Publications, 1956.

———. *Schools of Hope.* San Francisco: Jossey-Bass Publishers, 1994.

hooks, bell. *Teaching to Transgress.* New York: Routledge, 1994.

Jones, R. Bruce. *Greene Street Friends School: 1855–1955.* 1955.

Lacey, Paul. *Growing into Goodness: Essays on Quaker Education.* Wallingford, PA: Pendle Hill Publications, 1998.

McHenry, Irene, Jane Fremon, Nancy Starmer, and J. Harry Hammond. *Readings on Quaker Pedagogy.* Philadelphia: Friends Council on Education, 2004.

Palmer, Parker. *Meeting for Learning.* Philadelphia: Friends Council on Education, 2000.

Philadelphia Yearly Meeting. *Mission Statements of the Friends Schools of Philadelphia Yearly Meeting of the Religious Society of Friends.* Philadelphia: Philadelphia Yearly Meeting, 2001.

Smith, Robert Lawrence. *A Quaker Book of Wisdom.* New York: Eagle Brook, 1998.

www.friendscouncil.org

# About the Friends Council on Education

More than 300 years ago, the core of Quaker education in America took root in Philadelphia. The founding of the Friends Council on Education in 1931 sprang from the vision of Philadelphia Quakers. The Friends Council on Education now serves more than 80 Friends schools in the United States as well as a network of affiliate member schools and educational organizations throughout the world.

Friends schools serve a diverse general public with a mission to develop the human capacity for love and goodwill, analysis and reflection, and respect for and responsibility toward others. Today those values are learned and lived by nearly 21,000 students, 4,500 teachers, and 1,200 trustees in Friends schools across the country. These Friends school communities form a vibrant collaborative network through the Friends Council on Education, which maintains the Quaker identity and ethos of the schools and their relationship with the Religious Society of Friends.